PRAISE FOR *GOD IN 3D*

"Christians find the Trinity a challenge: it is a doctrine they have to defend, a topic that seems difficult to understand and something about which all that could be said seems to have been said. At the heart of this fresh, thought-provoking, and yet profoundly biblical book is a challenge for us to rethink how we understand the Trinity and an encouragement to see Father, Son, and Holy Spirit in a new and richer light."

—J. JOHN, SPEAKER AND WRITER

"Colin Green attempts to recover the Hebraic roots of the doctrine of the Trinity. The Hebrew Bible tells us of God's name and his glory which dwell in his temple. These mediate God's presence to his people. So, when the early followers of Jesus began to ask how God was present in him, they had to hand established Jewish ways of thought to make sense of what they had experienced in Jesus and in the subsequent transforming arrival of the Holy Spirit into their lives.... Semitic ways of speaking about Jesus and the Spirit continued in the Syriac tradition and among the Desert Fathers and Mothers. They form a significant complement to the Greek and Latin patristic tradition and are important as the church grows in non-Western cultures more akin to that of the Hebrew Bible and Syriac Christianity. Colin Green has performed an important service in returning the church to its Semitic roots at a time when Christianity is becoming mainly a non-Western faith."

—MICHAEL NAZIR-ALI, ANGLICAN BISHOP

God in 3D

God in 3D

Finding the Trinity in the Bible and the Church Fathers

COLIN GREEN

WIPF & STOCK · Eugene, Oregon

GOD IN 3D
Finding the Trinity in the Bible and the Church Fathers

Copyright © 2019 Colin Green. All rights reserved. Except for brief quotations in critical publications or reviews, no part of this book may be reproduced in any manner without prior written permission from the publisher. Write: Permissions, Wipf and Stock Publishers, 199 W. 8th Ave., Suite 3, Eugene, OR 97401.

All scripture quotations, unless otherwise indicated, are from The ESV® Bible (The Holy Bible, English Standard Version®) copyright © 2001 by Crossway, a publishing ministry of Good News Publishers. Used by permission. All rights reserved.

Scripture quotations from the Holy Bible, New International Version®. NIV®, published by Zondervan for the International Bible Society. Copyright © 1973, 1978, 1984 by International Bible Society. Used by permission of Zondervan. All rights reserved.

Scripture quotations from the New American Standard Bible (NASB), © Copyright 1960, 1962, 1963, 1968, 1971, 1972, 1973, 1975, 1977, 1995, by the Lockman Foundation. Used by permission.

Excerpts from THE NEW JERUSALEM BIBLE, copyright © 1985 by Darton, Longman & Todd, Ltd. And Doubleday, a division of Random House, Inc. Reprinted by Permission.

Scripture quotations from the New Revised Standard Version Bible, and the New Revised Standard Version Apocryphal/Deuterocanonical Books, copyright 1989 by the Division of Christian Education of the national Council of Churches of Christ in the United States of America, and are used by permission. All rights reserved.

Other Scripture quotations are from translations in the public domain.
All quotations are under fair use.
Illustrations copyright © 2019, Steve Oakley.

Wipf & Stock
An Imprint of Wipf and Stock Publishers
199 W. 8th Ave., Suite 3
Eugene, OR 97401

www.wipfandstock.com

PAPERBACK ISBN: 978-1-5326-8121-9
HARDCOVER ISBN: 978-1-5326-8122-6
EBOOK ISBN: 978-1-5326-8123-3

Manufactured in the U.S.A.   12/10/19

Dedicated to Mel for all her prayers and loving patience

Contents

Abbreviations — xi

Chapter 1: People Like You Can Understand the Trinity — 1

Chapter 2: The 3D Launch of the Church — 52

Chapter 3: A Time-Traveler's Guide to the Name, the Glory, and the Temple — 72

Chapter 4: 3D Letters to Christians — 86

Chapter 5: The Gospels in 3D — 99

Chapter 6: Links in the 3D Chain — 136

Chapter 7: 3D Discipleship — 155

Chapter 8: Church Creeds and Beyond — 184

Epilogue: Academic Case for the Thesis — 217

Bibliography — 255

Abbreviations

Hebrew Bible / Old Testament (where referenced):

Gen: Genesis
Exod: Exodus
Lev: Leviticus
Num: Numbers
Deut: Deuteronomy
1–2 Sam: 1–2 Samuel
1–2 Kgs: 1–2 Kings
1–2 Chr: 1–2 Chronicles
Ezra: Ezra
Neh: Nehemiah
Ps/Pss: Psalm/Psalms
Isa: Isaiah
Jer: Jeremiah
Ezek: Ezekiel
Joel: Joel
Zech Zechariah
Mal: Malachi

New Testament (where referenced):

Matt: Matthew
Mark: Mark
Luke: Luke
John: John
Acts: Acts
Rom: Romans
1–2 Cor: 1–2 Corinthians
Gal: Galatians
Eph: Ephesians
Phil: Philippians
Col: Colossians
1–2 Tim: 1–2 Timothy
1Heb: Hebrews
Jas: James
1–2 Pet: 1–2 Peter
1-2-3 John: 1-2-3 John
Rev: Revelation

For the ease of the non-specialist, other ancient texts, including apocryphal and deutero-canonical works have not been abbreviated in this work.

Chapter 1

People Like You Can Understand the Trinity

1. WHY THIS BOOK WAS WRITTEN

This is the untold story of the church's belief in the Trinity. It is a journey back in time, to the land of Israel in the days of Jesus and his disciples, to see how believers understood the Trinity in ways now barely remembered. And it is a journey further back in time to the era of King Solomon's temple, a thousand years before Christ, to uncover the origins of their beliefs.

We will rediscover the Israelites' ancient wisdom about the God who was present in their temple. And, in doing so, we can come to recognize the Trinity in just the way the Bible represents it. This is a journey to discover how the first Christians were primed by the temple stories of the Old Testament, and prepared by Jesus, to understand the three-in-one God—the Father, the Son, and the Holy Spirit.

The Christian God

Christians believe in a God who wants to have a mutual relationship with them, one of understanding. And not only with them, but a relationship with the whole church and all the people he longs to gather to it. In response, all around the world, Christians desire to live in God's presence. It is common for Christians to say that there is nothing they enjoy more than the times in which they sense God's presence. They sometimes even sense God's Spirit somehow inside themselves, with them.

An individual Christian may speak of himself or herself as a "temple of the Holy Spirit," and pray to be "filled with the Holy Spirit." A church community may think of itself as a temple of the Holy Spirit where Christ dwells.

Why mention this now? Because a Christian—or anyone—who knows these things is already holding a key that will unlock a door to understanding the Trinity.

But to listen to some Christian preachers and writers, you would think the Trinity was something impossibly difficult for anyone to understand. Some teachers say it may seem irrational, but then they don't make it rational for you. Some teachers say it will always be a mystery, but they don't mean the kind that will be revealed. Anyway, we do not find anything in the Bible that takes that pessimistic view. There is no reason for people to be put off who want to understand.

You don't need to have had any special training. This book is for the trained or untrained reader alike, for anyone who wants to understand the Trinity, and for anyone who may have doubts about believing in it.

If you listen to some people, you could think the Trinity is not in the Bible at all. To put right any misunderstanding, this book is for those who want their answers from the Bible first. If you have looked for the Trinity in the Bible yourself, but struggled to prove it is there, this is for you. Why? Because what if it is hidden in plain sight? What if we were just following the wrong set of clues? What if it is all in your hands already?

This is not like many a book on the Trinity that takes a Bible verse here, a verse there, and claims that this should satisfy us. This book won't present the Bible evidence that way. What many people are asking for is just to be shown in the Bible exactly where they can see the Trinity. They want more than the creeds to be explained, although that is a good thing to do. They want to be able to put their finger on a page in the Bible, and say, "That's the Trinity, there!" That's what this book is about. Can we explain the Trinity using only Scripture language and concepts? Can we explain how it works? Can we explain the relationships in our three-in-one God? Yes, we can, on all fronts.[1]

There are not many things in life where we settle for saying, "it's a mystery." In other things, we prefer to have an answer. In science, even if at first something is not understood, what scientists do is observe it. They watch. When we watch something enough, we may start to understand it. That is

---

1. Implicit throughout this book is that Scripture is a foundation of orthodox belief and doctrine.

how it is with the Trinity: we must simply observe this God in the pages of the Bible. We will do this in its stories of Solomon's temple especially. And after observing, we start to understand the object of our study—that is how understanding comes. It pays off because really it is God showing himself.

We see many examples of this scientific way of observing and understanding things in our world. For instance, the bumblebee. No one understood how its little wings could lift its bulky body off the ground. But with modern cameras, how its wings flap has been observed. Now we understand how bumblebees fly. With observing came understanding.

And the Old Testament gives us every help to observe the Trinity. In particular the temple of Solomon gives us a perfect place to get our minds around it. We will observe the Trinity, and understanding it comes from that. So don't be discouraged if you have ever heard anyone say that the Trinity is a mystery that cannot be understood. We will observe the Trinity, and we can go from there. This will not be done using the sort of intellectual language that sometimes goes over people's heads or leaves people behind. Instead, we will look at the Trinity in the language of Bible times, which we all can try to grasp.

Understanding the Trinity is an important way of finding solutions to questions and longings that Christians have, to know God better. And others have questions too that we can try to answer.

With Boldness

In an era where the Trinity is treated with unbelief and skepticism by groups such as Jehovah's Witnesses and by Islam, we should be confident in sharing why it deserves its central place in Christian belief. Jesus came to reveal God to the world, not to hide God away. You can help people to understand the Trinity. I know that Christians sometimes feel stumped if they are asked to explain the Trinity, especially by people who have had contact with Islam or Jehovah's Witnesses. They may raise skeptical questions about the Trinity. We can learn how to respond with confidence, by telling the Bible's story. It is hoped that the Christian reader will benefit from this book in a strengthening of faith, in talking about the three-in-one God, and will find here an answer to offer to anyone who enquires about why Christians believe in the Trinity. An easier answer to share.

The Famous Word

There are a few things to clear up before we get going, starting with the word "Trinity" and why it isn't in the Bible. Some worry about that. Christians came up with the word a few generations after the New Testament books were written. This word was coined in light of how the Bible talks about the Father, the Son, and the Holy Spirit. "Trinity" is shorthand for speaking of all three of them as one. It's such a handy word that, once coined, you can hardly not want to use it. There are lots of useful words inside and outside the Bible, and this is one, so that's not a problem.

In this book, you'll also come cross other phrases that mean exactly the same as "Trinity," such as "three-in-one God" and "triune God." Be confident reading these terms. That's all they mean—three-in-one.

Housekeeping

I quote various English translations of the Bible in this book. Sometimes, when speaking of God, they put the word "name" with a capital letter—Name—and sometimes they don't. It has been left as it is in Bible quotes. When using my own words, I use capitals—the "Name" where it means God's Name. The same goes for God's Glory. Sometimes to emphasize words in Bible passages, I put them in *italics like this*. I don't say so every time as it would become irritating for the reader to see again and again.

Those who wish to read the academic case first are invited to turn to the Epilogue prior to reading this first chapter.

Three Dimensions

By speaking of the 3D God, I don't mean in the way that St. Paul speaks of three dimensions when he speaks of "the height, breadth and length of the love of God."

I mean 3D in a different way. It is to help us see a solution to a problem. The problem is that religion in some churches has become a kind of bland one-dimensional Church-ianity or God-ianity—there may be talk of church or God in it, but not much is said about Christ and the Holy Spirit. In some churches, it is as if Jesus and the Spirit only come out at certain times of year, such as Easter and Pentecost! If that is all there is, spirituality can be in short supply. But there is a good supply in the fullness of Christianity. The extra dimensions brought by Christ and the Holy Spirit transform our picture of God—into 3D. Christianity, not God-ianity.

This is why we want to know about the phenomenon of the Trinity, and the treasure of a truly biblical way of understanding it. It is an open door to discover and enjoy Christian belief and spirituality with new confidence.

The Very Short Version

Here is a very short version of how to find the Trinity in the Bible. An obvious place to look for God is in the place where God lives. In the Bible, this is in his temple, his sanctuary, his dwelling place. It is a temple for only one God. The Bible speaks of a few temples—houses of God—from heaven's sanctuary to stone temples, and even inside Christians as "temples of the Holy Spirit." A living temple made up of Christians, living stones, the church community—they are called a temple because God dwells in them. The New Testament reveals that such a temple of living stones is a good place to look for God as a Trinity. This is because it is a place where all three persons of the Trinity can be found dwelling:

- The Holy Spirit dwells in Christians as his temple—they are called "temples of the Holy Spirit"—and he fills them
- Jesus dwells in those Christians as his temple too
- "Our Father in heaven" dwells in his linked heavenly temple

There's the Trinity—the three-in-one God—in a temple of living stones, his people. In this temple, the Father, the Son, and the Spirit are dwelling as its God. But what actually makes this a "three-in-one" God, a Trinity? Well, to start with, God's temple is their temple. They live in it as their rightful dwelling place. There, they count together as one God. Father, Son, and Spirit in one temple can only be one God.

Why not more than one God, some might ask? Why are they not three Gods? The answer is that there can't rightfully be three Gods in a temple made for one God. And God's temple is made for one God. The Bible is clear about that, as we shall see. So, these three have to be living there united as one for it to be rightfully theirs. There is no other explanation for why the three of them can be dwelling in a temple that was made for only one God. Only God can rightfully do what they are doing. The only way this works is to say that these three are united as one God, three-in-one.

So, stuff that is common knowledge to Christians about being "temples of the Holy Spirit" can help us to understand of the Trinity. When we grasp the idea that Christians are temples of the Holy Spirit—and we grasp that they are temples of the Father, Son, and Spirit—then we know enough to make this statement: Christians are temples of the three-in-one God. The church community is the temple of the Trinity.

Anywhere in the Bible where you read that God's Holy Spirit and Christ are dwelling inside Christians, that's clear sight of the Trinity. That is a picture of God's Spirit and Christ, as one, in a living temple.

That's the really short version of how to find the Trinity in the New Testament. It's the God who dwells in the living temple. We'll look at lots of Bible verses where you see it. If that feels a bit rushed, shortly at a slower pace we'll go through the evidence.

So, if the right place to find the Trinity in the New Testament is in God's house—a temple of living stones—then the obvious place to go and look for the Trinity in the Old Testament is in God's house there—a temple of actual stones. This is where it gets *really* interesting.

In the Old Testament, the Trinity is found in the temple built in Israel by King Solomon. Built of great elegant stones. A fine dwelling for God. We find three things about the Trinity here that look a bit familiar now, but the words are changed, because the Old Testament has a Trinity of *God, his Name, and his Glory*:

- God's Glory dwells in the temple, and fills it
- God's "Name" dwells in the temple, in the midst of his people
- And God dwells in the heavenly sanctuary (temple)

It's a very familiar looking Trinity. Let's make it simpler to see. Look at these two rows, how they have a matching pattern, where what's on top matches with what's underneath:

| God the Father | the Son | the Spirit filling | a living temple |
| God | the Name | the Glory filling | a stone temple |

There are two temples, the New Testament living temple and the Old Testament stone temple. And who is in these temples? On the top row, we find the Father, the Son, and the Spirit. On the bottom row, we find God, his Name, and his Glory.

Look how Jesus, the Son (on the top row), matches with the Name (bottom row). Think of those two words together: Jesus, Name. Christians are very familiar with talking about Jesus as "the Name high over all." Many Christians, seeing this, may start to realize that they already have some knowledge in this area.

And see how the Holy Spirit (top row) matches with the Glory (bottom row). There is no surprise in this match. Christians are familiar with a story of how the Holy Spirit came like fire, and how it is like when the Glory came like fire in older times. Two temples: a temple for the Holy Spirit to fill, a temple for the Glory to fill.

What are we to make of all these matches? Both rows are to do with a temple where God's presence dwells. One is where the Trinity is found in the New Testament. And one is where the Trinity is found in the Old Testament, in its stone temple. It's three persons as one God, the way the Bible teaches it. That is, Father, Son, and Spirit dwelling in a living temple. And the Trinity of God, his Name, and his Glory dwelling in the Old Testament temple.

"The Name" is a mysterious figure. Calling him simply "the Name" has a little bit in common with how television characters can be called simply "the Joker" or "the Doctor" in television shows such as Batman and Doctor Who.

We will look at the Scriptures where this Trinity is found, especially in the book of 2 Chronicles, chapters 5–7, the story of God's presence arriving in the stone temple of King Solomon. Here we discover God's magnificent powerful spiritual presence. Along the way, it will teach us how the church community is a magnificent spiritually powerful temple of *living* stones.

This is how we will observe the Trinity in the pages of the Bible. We are going to go at a slower pace, because this will be like a detective case, or a treasure trail. We need to pick up the clues. It is time to begin.

2. WHERE TO FIND THE TRINITY IN THE NEW TESTAMENT

This first chapter sets out the basics of this book in a nutshell—all the basics you need to understand the three-in-one God, in the way the Bible reveals it.

To recap, it is to do with Christians being temples of the Holy Spirit. That is an idea familiar to Christians all over the world. This is one of the first things I learned when I became a Christian at the age of nineteen: the Holy Spirit lives permanently inside everyone who is born of the Spirit, a Christian. My body is a temple. It is a temple for God's own spiritual presence to be at home in. This is a sweet presence that sometimes gently nudges Christians in the right direction in situations when we might not know the right direction. This is a voice that teaches Christians what kind of people God wants them to be, even if sometimes the Holy Spirit's suggestions are not what we had in mind for ourselves. This is a presence with a touch that reminds Christians that they have met God and he has come to live in their own hearts. It is a presence that makes Christians realize they want honest living, even if they never desired it before—a clean temple for the Holy Spirit to live in.

But how many of us have discovered that Christians are temples of the *whole* Trinity: Father, Son, and Holy Spirit? The church is a people who should be able to say, "Jesus stands among us," and to say "Christians are filled with the Holy Spirit." It is a temple of the Trinity.

If we haven't discovered that yet, then we have been missing out on the easiest way to understand the three-in-one God. But the time of missing out is over, if we take this journey of discovery together. If you already know that you have become a temple of the Holy Spirit, may this journey make your experience all the richer as you read this book. If you have not become a temple of the Holy Spirit, I hope you will find here some answers to questions you might have about what Christians believe about the Trinity.

So, Christians are temples of the whole Trinity, the three-in-one God. But we need to take a step back. How do we get to that conclusion? Without just assuming it, what is the evidence?

It was never possible for me to understand the Bible's Trinity until I had learned what a temple is meant to be. Jesus understood it, and he expected his followers to understand it too. They have provided us with what we need to understand it.

What Are Temples About?

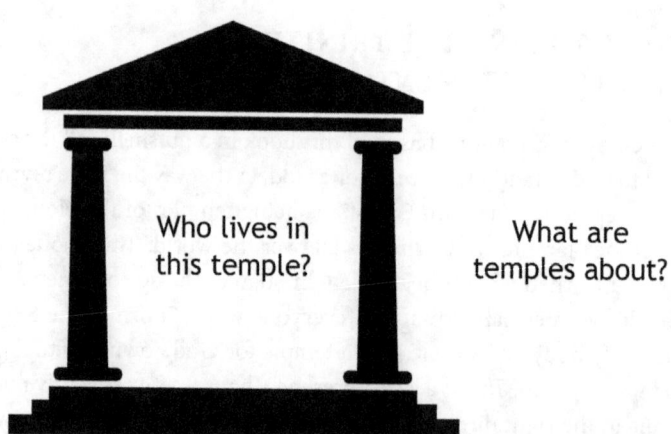

In the first place, a temple is a god's dwelling place on earth. That's the idea anyway. Ancient peoples lived in a world where gods had temples, even if false gods sometimes. God-houses—such gods were worshiped there— were their temples. The Jerusalem temple even had furniture like a house so that people would not forget that it was God's house.[2]

---

2. Leithart, *House for My Name*, 83.

Ancient peoples had a really simple way of showing that they recognized a god—by dedicating a temple to it. They would build a temple, and their god would live in it. At least, that was their idea. The Bible has this idea in its pages: a home for God.

Here's the bottom line: the thing to know about any temple is to which god it belongs. Since the idea of any temple is that it is *the house of a god*— here on planet earth—then you needed to know which god was meant to live there. This mattered. After all, there were many temples, with many so-called gods of other religions. In the Bible, the God of Israel had his temple in Jerusalem. The Bible says that in other places, temples were built for pagan idols. Some of these ancient places exist to this day, most in ruins. Back in their era, people needed to know one temple from another.

So the Jerusalem temple was the dwelling place of Israel's God: the home of their God and no other god, just the one true God. This was very straightforward, and black and white, to them. It was Israel's most sacred and holy religious site.

Mixing up temples and gods was a bad idea in Israel. You went to your temple to worship *your* God. In a pagan temple, this meant having this or that so-called god—a handmade idol of wood or stone—inside. People could be very sensitive about their temple and their god. Some would say you couldn't put one wooden god in the temple of a different god—not without risking offense to someone else's religion anyway. Other religions would want to fill their temples with all kinds of gods. The ancient Israelites had a "one God only" loyalty to their temple, the Jerusalem temple. It was the house of their God alone. Their God was not a handmade idol. Israel's God would be in his temple as a spiritual presence, and with no pagan idol sharing the place.

So it was meant to stay that way. It was expected that God should keep possession of his own house, his temple. To be sure, no one else but Israel's God lived in the sanctuary at the heart of the Jerusalem temple complex. The priests didn't live in the sanctuary, they just worked there. They had places to stay nearby in the temple courts, and the king had his palace in the courts too.

King Solomon's temple was the most prestigious temple in Jerusalem's history, centuries before Christ. For Israelites, it was the center of the world. It was where heaven met earth. It was the place where God's presence was sensed more than in any other place. This very idea meant that Israel's God was committed to blessing his people by dwelling with them in the land, in the temple. It stood for a few centuries, ending in destruction in war. In later times—including the days of Jesus' apostles—speaking of the story of Solomon's temple meant harking back to a golden age for Israel, and its memory kept hopes alive for a glorious future for their nation. A second temple had been built on these hopes, but they weren't living in any golden age.

To get an idea of how important their temple was, we can turn to the influential Christian St. Paul, in his own words found in the Bible. In one of his letters, he spoke of his dread of someone or something wicked having the worst attitude imaginable to the Jerusalem temple, an enemy he called "the Lawless One":

> who opposes and exalts himself above every so-called god or object of worship,
>
> so that he takes his seat in the temple of God,
>
> proclaiming himself to be God. (2 Thess 2:4 ESV)

This had not actually happened in Paul's day. But it was something Paul feared would happen, that people would not respect that God's house is God's alone. Paul hated the idea of an enemy helping himself to the Jerusalem temple, stealing the true God's rightful place in it. After all, the only rightful dweller of the Jerusalem temple is Israel's God; having a wrongful dweller of the true God's temple would be a scandal, a blasphemy.

How Important Was the Temple?

If there is one Bible verse that tells how strongly the ancient Israelites felt about the Jerusalem temple, this is it. It's a cry of anguish from when King Solomon's temple, especially its inner "sanctuary," was destroyed by Israel's enemies:

> They set your sanctuary on fire;
> they profaned the dwelling place of your Name,
> bringing it down to the ground. (Ps 74:7 NIV)

This precious sanctuary was sacred to them. It was not for being "profaned," which means misusing a holy place to the point of making it unholy.

That verse tells of a disaster that befell the Israelites hundreds of years before Jesus Christ came. Israel's enemies destroyed the city of Jerusalem and its temple. In the days of Jesus' disciples, people were still living in the shadow of that disaster. We see a bit of that in the dramatic tone of the book of Revelation, which says that "the Beast" was speaking against God, "blaspheming his name and his dwelling" (Rev 13:6). And although centuries had passed, and a replacement temple had been built for God's Name, Israel had never seen a return of their glory days of old when Solomon's temple was at its shining best.

There are no paintings from the time of Solomon that tell us exactly what his temple looked like. But we can get some impression of the sight. On a trip to Egypt, I visited some ancient temples (and took plenty of photographs). I got a great sense of the awe that would have struck anyone who visited them. These are ancient pagan temples that are still standing to this day. An awesome sight, they reveal a lot. I found a typical sight—when one steps inside the temple, one is in a courtyard. The walls have fine carved pillars. Inside, there is a small building in front of you. Go inside and you see a passage to a special room in front of you. It is like a nest of boxes, one inside another.

And the innermost room was that Egyptian temple's most holy place. In it, they would have had their wooden idol. It represented their pagan god. Its priests would have been its servants and they would have worked there. Everything was top quality to look at, beautiful buildings, beautiful pictures painted on walls and ceilings. The priests would have been dressed in beautiful clothes.

But what about Jerusalem's magnificent temple? Solomon's temple has long since been destroyed, and so has the one that replaced it. But in their day, they would have been majestic sights. Israel's priests served there. God's spiritual presence was there. But there was no idol to see. Instead there was simply God's spiritual presence.

By thinking about the temple, we can get a biblical definition of God. This is it: the rightful dweller of the true temple of the Bible is God. In Old Testament days, that true temple was Solomon's temple in Jerusalem, and its rightful dweller was Israel's God. As they would see it, if all was well, a visit to the true temple would mean a visit to the true God.

It is discovering these things about the temple that gets us ready to go into the Bible with open eyes for the right kind of clues. As we have seen, you can test whether the Trinity is biblical by checking whether there is a temple inhabited by the Trinity in the Bible. And there is: the church community is such a temple.

No one but God is meant to be the spiritual presence that dwells in the church community. And Christ and God's Holy Spirit fulfill that role. Father, Son, and Spirit, in one temple, could only be one God. It's a simple demonstration that they together are this temple's God.

Christians Are Temples of the Holy Spirit

When St. Paul and other Christians called themselves and their bodies a "temple of the Holy Spirit," they were making a big claim—that God lived inside them, that they were temples of the true God. Even though they were people—so not a building of stone!—God's spiritual presence was living inside them.

It is an amazing grace given to us to learn this simple thing, because it is the foundation of how Christians in the early church understood the Trinity. What they were saying was that they were temples not only of the Holy Spirit. It was more than that. They were actually temples of the Holy Spirit and Christ, and we will see God the Father come into this too.

Later, I want to show you how we can put a finger on a page of the Bible to say, "There—that is the Trinity, there!"

3. WHAT ANCIENT CHURCHES TAUGHT

We can have some confidence in what the ancient churches taught, not least because they were closer to the time of Jesus' disciples than we are. They had contacts in the most ancient churches where the disciples taught. We need to listen to them.

Later in this book, I will list a lot of ancient Christian writers. For me, the discovery of these writers was a great breakthrough in understanding the Trinity better. Let me explain this personal journey of discovery.

I knew that some critics, such as Jehovah's Witnesses, make the alarming claim that the first Christians did not know anything about the Trinity, and they claim that it took hundreds of years for the church to believe in it. Could the Jehovah's Witnesses be right about that? I did not think so, but I had to find out the reasons. I always want to be able to give an answer to explain my faith, and I needed answers.

Supposing, just for a moment, that the first Christians had nothing trinitarian about them, then there would be a problem as far as I was concerned. After all, why would I believe something about God if, *as Jehovah's Witnesses claimed*, the first Christians didn't believe it? The stakes were high. I was confident that if the Trinity was so central to Christian faith, it could not have been totally alien to the first Christians. Looking for evidence, I listened to what others said and read what they wrote.

Some say that verses in the Bible *suggest* the Trinity to our minds. But these verses contain clues that there is something more than just "suggest," and to my mind the only option is to keep looking and properly uncover what we find, to have a better answer to offer to visiting Jehovah's Witnesses.

From study of books such as John's Gospel, a clear message comes through that Jesus came to show what God is really like. If the Trinity doctrine is true, it could not be right that Jesus would not reveal it in some way. Why would Jesus and the Bible not teach something about a doctrine that was supposed to be so very important? And if they did, there would be at least traces of evidence.

So, this is where we hear from those ancient Christian writers, from a time after the New Testament was written, but much closer to it than we are. And it turns out they had the inside track on how belief in the Trinity does stem all the way back from the earliest churches and the New Testament. Their writings tell us that one of the ways that the early church understood the Trinity was by thinking about God having a temple. They were saying this: that there is a temple where God lives, and in it God the Father, the Son, and Holy Spirit dwell as one. As one, they dwell in their temple. They are the God of that temple. One God in God's temple. What temple, by the way? They meant the Christian community; it was the temple (and even individual Christians are temples too). Lots of ancient Christian writers knew about the Trinity this way: Father, Son, and Spirit, in one temple, could only be one God. Simple, logical. So, if Father, Son, and Spirit dwell as one in the true temple, then they are, quite simply, that temple's God. They are the rightful dweller of that temple. So, that was what I learned: the Trinity is the God of the temple. The Trinity is God. The temple is the church.

In this way, the three-in-one God *was* known to the earliest churches. It is my sincere hope that more people will share what ancient Christians wrote about this. What could be better than to talk about the Trinity in the same way that early Christians did?

This is a line of evidence that we will follow wherever it leads. Careful research unearths what Christians wrote about it in the second century, and in the third century, and in the fourth century. The evidence is there to bring into the light.

In quote after quote, the early church understood the Trinity this way. For now, a small sample of these ancient writers will do, just SS. Augustine, Jerome, and Ambrose, but more later. These names are unfamiliar to a lot of Christians, but they were famous Christian authors. Nowadays, there are many famous Christian writers, from C. S. Lewis to Philip Yancey. But in the early church, SS. Augustine, Jerome, and Ambrose were among the most important and famous authors. Here are some things they said on our subject.

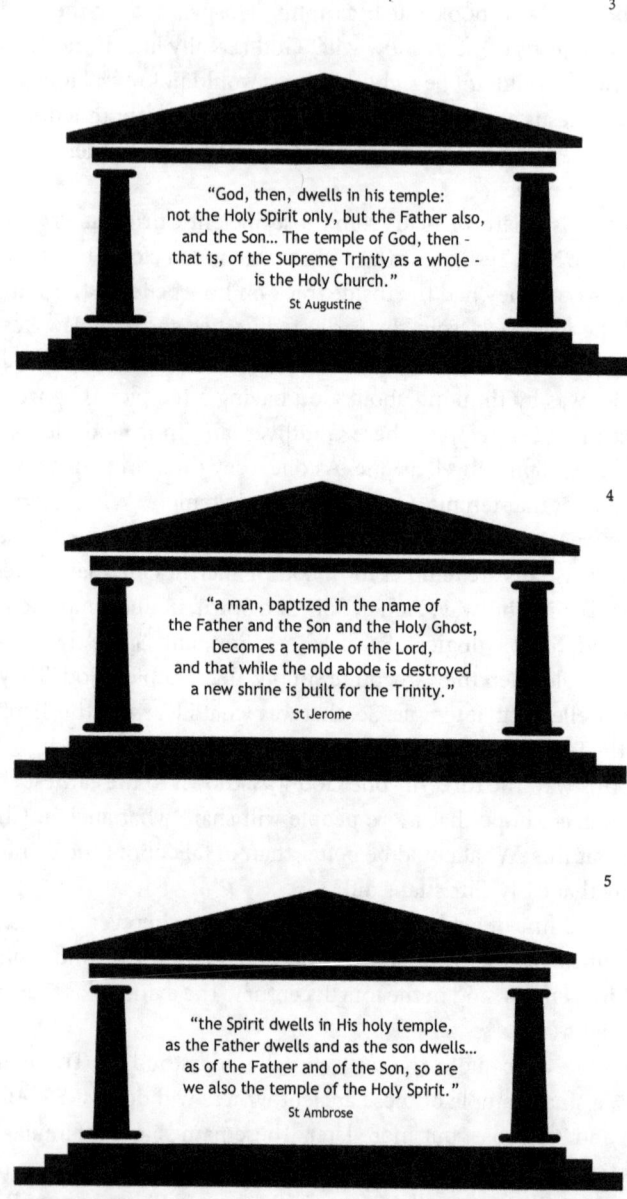

3. Augustine, *Enchiridion*, 56.
4. Jerome, *Dialogue Against the Luciferians*, 6.
5. Ambrose, *On the Holy Spirit*, Book 3, 12, 91–93.

That was clear:

- The church is the temple.
- There is only one true God who dwells in the true temple.
- The Father, Son, and Spirit dwell in the true temple.
- So Father, Son and Spirit—as one—are God. They are the three-in-one God.

This is treasure. Let's dig deeper still.

Where Did They Get Those Ideas From?

It matters to know where their ideas came from. Was it all from Jesus and the first Christians? How can we be sure? To find an answer, we can let them speak for themselves.

The fact is that anti-church skeptics such as Jehovah's Witnesses would be smiling *if* this did *not* go back to the first Christians. They would claim there was still a problem with the doctrine of the Trinity. Finding proof that the first Christians knew this seems to me important enough to share it.

Ancient Christian authors did leave a trail going back to the first Christians and the Bible. They were able to put a finger on a page in the Bible and show people the Trinity. St. Ambrose explains it from the Bible. He says:

> . . . the Holy Spirit has a temple. For it is written:
>
> 'You are the temple of God, and the Holy Spirit dwells in you.'
>
> Now God has a temple, a creature has no true temple. But the Spirit, Who dwells in us, has a temple. For it is written: 'Your members are temples of the Holy Spirit.'
>
> But He does not dwell in the temple as a priest, nor as a minister, but as God, since the Lord Jesus Himself said:
>
> 'I will dwell in them, and will walk among them, and will be their God, and they shall be My people.'
>
> And David says: 'The Lord is in His holy temple.'
>
> Therefore *the Spirit dwells in His holy temple, as the Father dwells and as the Son dwells*, Who says:
>
> 'I and the Father will come, and will make Our abode with him.'
>
> We observe, then, that *the Father, the Son, and the Holy Spirit abide in one and the same*, through the oneness of the same nature.

> Therefore, He Who dwells in the temple has divine power, *for as of the Father and of the Son, so are we also the temple of the Holy Spirit*; not many temples, but one temple, for it is the temple of one Power.[6]

Ambrose is clear about these things:

- The Holy Spirit has a temple, so the Holy Spirit is God.
- Jesus has a temple, as Jesus said: *"I will dwell in them"*—so he is God.
- The Father and Jesus dwell in one and the same temple: "*I and the Father will come, and will make Our abode with him.*"
- This is three persons in one temple. That is to say, Father, Son, and Spirit in one temple: "not many temples, but one temple, for it is the temple of one Power."
- They are one God, what Ambrose calls "one power" with "the oneness of the same nature."

One temple for one God. This is a striking argument. And the good news is that it is drawn straight from what the first Christians said, straight from the Bible. Let's look at these Bible verses to makes sure their meaning was being used properly. The Scriptures St. Ambrose used, in the manner he used, were these:

1 Cor 3:16:	"You are the temple of God, and the Holy Spirit dwells in you."
1 Cor 6:19:	which he sums up as "Your members are temples of the Holy Spirit."
2 Cor 6:16:	"I will dwell in them, and will walk among them, and will be their God, and they shall be My people."
Ps 11:4:	"The Lord is in His holy temple."
John 14:23:	"I and the Father will come, and will make Our abode with him."

These verses are Ambrose's paraphrases, not a published edition of the Scriptures. These Scriptures mean just what Ambrose said they mean. God is a temple-dwelling Trinity. God is Father, Son, and Holy Spirit. We will come back to these same verses many times. The standout feature in Ambrose is that he was especially interested in understanding what St. Paul wrote. So that is what we should do now too.

---

6 Ambrose, *On the Holy Spirit*, Book 3, 12, 91–93.

What St. Paul Taught

In letters written to churches by St. Paul, we can find what the early church writers such as St. Ambrose found. This God is three persons. One God in three persons, who can live in one temple.

Take Paul's letter to the Ephesians, in 2:22 and 3:16–17. We find Paul talking about the Christian community as a "dwelling" place, a temple. And Paul is talking about who lives in this temple:

- God
- and Christ, the Son of God
- and the Holy Spirit

These are Paul's words:

So if the Christian community is built like a temple, who lives in it? Here are Paul's answers:

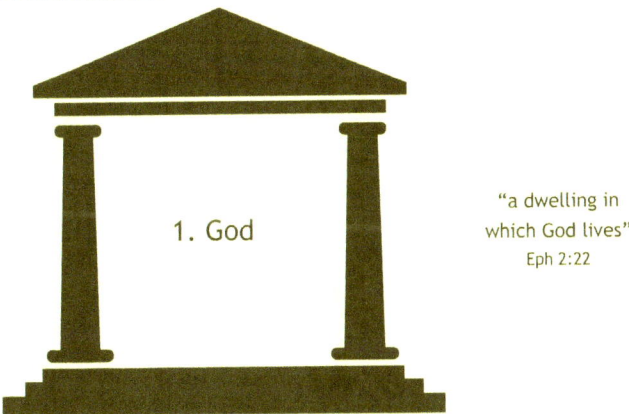

God and his Son and the Spirit—three that live in one temple (that is, in the church community).

It's the temple of the Father, Son, and Spirit. They are its God. Here—in Eph 2:22; 3:16–17—is a place in the Bible where you can put a finger on the page and say, "I see the three-in-one God there." Father, Son, and Spirit in one temple can only be one God.

Remember, Paul was a fervent Jew, and fervent Jews said that there was only one God, the rightful dweller of the temple. "God is one," he wrote in his letter to the church in Rome (Rom 3:30). So this is a good example of where that "one God" attitude fits with the three-in-one God that Paul knows about. That is, the temple-dwelling God.

When Paul spoke about the Father, Son, and Holy Spirit dwelling in a temple, here's the thing: he hadn't changed his mind about it being the temple of only one God. It was still the temple of one God, but Paul's God is a three-in-one God: these three—Father, Son, and Spirit.

A New Twist

We have barely had time to get used to the idea of Father, Son, and Spirit dwelling as one in the temple, when we discover a new twist, a new clue on the map. The emphasis shifts. Now instead of focusing on all three being in a temple, the Bible gives a new emphasis on just two of the three being in the temple: the Son and the Spirit. We will start to see an emphasis on our Father being in heaven, and the Son and the Spirit dwelling in the church. All three always work together, they are never completely separated apart from each other. But the Bible teaches us this special emphasis: one in heaven and two in the temple. And to go deeper in our spiritual understanding of God, we need to go with the evidence a bit further.

This emphasis is in 2 Corinthians, the Son and the Spirit being specially named as being in the church:

Who Paul is talking about	What Paul says	Verse
1) The church community is the temple	"*we are the temple* of the living God"	2 Cor 6:16
2) The Son dwells in it	"Jesus *Christ is in you*"	2 Cor 13:5
3) The Spirit dwells in it	"his *Spirit in* our hearts"	2 Cor 1:22

The true God in the true temple. Paul does this repeatedly in his letters—portraying the Son and the Spirit, these two in particular, as dwelling in the church. He doesn't rule God the Father out of the picture, but the special emphasis is on the Son and the Spirit. In another important statement, Paul writes this:

> *the Spirit of God dwells in you.* Anyone who does not have the Spirit of Christ does not belong to him. But if *Christ is in you*, although the body is dead because of sin, the Spirit is life . . . (Rom 8:9–10 ESV)

This is a breakdown of those words, showing the special emphasis:

Who Paul is talking about	What Paul says	Verse
1) The church community is the temple	"*in you*"	Rom 8:9–10
2) The Son dwells in it	"*Christ* is in you"	Rom 8:10
3) The Spirit dwells in it	"the *Spirit* of God dwells in you"	Rom 8:9

With Paul as our teacher, we settle on the understanding that Jesus Christ and the Holy Spirit dwell in the church community as their temple. Rom 8:9–10 says that believers' lives should be transformed by this good news! Because "the Spirit of God dwells in you" and "Christ is in you." We will learn more about the special emphasis on two of the three persons dwelling in the temple as we go on, picturing God the Father being in heaven especially while Christ and the Spirit are in the temple especially.

Paul expected his church audience to think of itself as a temple and understand his three-in-one God without a lot of explanations. And that means they were already thinking that way. This is the three-in-one God in a language that the early church understood.

And it gets clearer still. Look a bit further on into this chapter. At Rom 8:26 and 34, it says the Holy Spirit prays *for* Christians, communicating to God the Father on our behalf (which is called interceding):

> We do not know what we ought to pray, but the Spirit himself intercedes for us with groans that words cannot express. (Rom 8:26 NIV)

And Jesus is speaking to the Father on our behalf too (Rom 8:34). So in the space of one chapter, we read that Christ and the Spirit both dwell in Christians; and that Christ and the Spirit are both communicating for them to the Father. This means Jesus and the Spirit acting in the same way, getting as personal as each other to our Father God. The Spirit can intercede just as Jesus can intercede because both of them are personal in nature. So, in Rom 8:9–34, we find two crucial proofs of the Trinity:

- Jesus and the Spirit dwell in us as our God—we are their temple and they are our God.
- Jesus and the Spirit are communicating to the Father as one person can to another—all three as personal as each other.

It's why Christians can speak of one God in three persons. It's solid ground of the doctrine of the Trinity of the first Christians. It's God in his temple. We are free to think about the three-in-one God the way the early Christians did, as Paul did, as Ambrose and Augustine and Jerome did.

More detective work is needed. There are still loose ends to tie up. So far, this has mainly been from the New Testament. But what about the Old Testament? After all, the Old Testament was St. Paul's Bible. Did it influence Paul to write such things in the first place?

With the Old Testament open, can we really be sure that we find a three-in-one God in the same way, as God in his temple? What does the Bible really say about this?

This may be a nagging question for some readers. As mentioned, Paul was a fervent Jew, and fervent Jews believed that there was only one true God. Paul believed that. So was it a bit of a jump for him to believe in a three-in-one God? Or did the Old Testament already help him to think this way?

It is a grace given to us to see that Paul was on to something priceless: a way of understanding the three-in-one God that goes right back to truly ancient Old Testament ideas about the temple. It turns out that fervent Jews had already been appreciating Israel's God and temple in a three-in-one way. Paul really had been reading about it in the Old Testament, seeing God's three presences this way: two in the temple and one in heaven. To see that picture, let's travel further back in time to the temple of Israel's King Solomon.

4. THE NAME AND THE GLORY

We need to discover what happened when King Solomon built the ancient temple in Jerusalem. Imagine you can hop into a time-travel machine, and use it to travel back to a time one-thousand years before Christ. The most remarkable events are reported there. Let yourself be gripped by reading about it in 2 Chronicles 5:13—7:3.

Solomon finished building the Jerusalem temple, a fabulous ornate monument, and on its "launch day" he prayed for God to come to be in it. The Glory came. It came like blinding light, like fire from heaven, straight to the temple. The Glory filled it. And not only the Glory. We also read that the "Name" came to dwell in the temple. The "Name" can be read like a code word for God's presence.

Solomon speaks a long prayer, dedicating the temple to God. In his prayer, he talks to God who is in heaven. He asks for God's "Name" to come to dwell in the temple. Solomon prays these words:

> May your eyes be open towards this temple day and night,
> this place of which you said you would put *your Name* there . . .
> Hear from heaven, your dwelling place . . .
> Now arise, O LORD God, and come to your resting place [the temple].

These Scriptures tell us that Solomon's prayer was answered like this:

> When Solomon finished praying, fire came down from heaven . . . and *the glory* of the LORD filled the temple. (7:1 NIV)

But God was still in heaven, hearing prayer, and says:

> . . . if my people who are called by my name humble themselves and pray and seek my face and turn from their wicked ways, *then I will hear from heaven* and will forgive their sin and will heal their land. (7:14 NIV) [7]

This scene unlocks a mystery about the three-in-one God. It is crucial that when Solomon built the temple, "the Name" came to dwell in it. The Bible tells us about it again and again. The Israelites "built you a sanctuary there for your name . . . for your name is in this temple" (2 Chr 20:8–9 NJB).

But who or what is "the Name"? This is something you might never have heard about in church on a Sunday. In the Old Testament of the Bible, the way the early church read it, "the Name" is simply one of the things that God's presence is called. Just "the Name." God's spiritual presence in the temple, as told in many stories in the Old Testament, is named this way. Some scholars would call it God's *alter ego*.[8] Some Jews called it the *Shekinah*. This means the dwelling presence.[9]

Picture the scene in Jerusalem: it as if "the Name" is ushered into the temple by "the Glory." It is a bit like a king being ushered into his palace with a splendid welcome. The Glory comes and the Name is then present, right in the heart of the temple, in its inner sanctuary, the room they called the holy of holies. The Name and the Glory are together. These two are in the temple, two distinctly arriving as God's presence.

We have discovered all three: God and his Name and his Glory. That is the key that unlocks a mystery. It will open up the Trinity in the pages of the Old Testament. The Name dwelled in Solomon's temple, and the Glory filled the temple.

God and "the Name"—two things distinct from each other. It's a vital detail in this story. God was still in heaven while his Name entered Solomon's temple. A distinction between them is right there on the page to be seen. God the Father is the heavenly presence; the Name is the earthly presence of God. There was this particular moment when the Name moved into the temple. It was when God in heaven answered Solomon's prayer that the Name entered the temple.

In this, we find something special and different from pagan temples. Pagan temples had their wooden idols in them. But in the Jerusalem temple,

---

7. For key moments in the story of the arrival of the Name and the Glory, see 2 Chr 6:20–21; 6:41; 7:1, especially reading through 2 Chr 5:13—6:14.

8. Knight, *Biblical Approach*, 14.

9. For instance, 2 Chr 6:1 in *Targum of Chronicles*. Many examples in the Targums are included later.

there were no wooden idols—there was God's spiritual presence instead, called the "Name," who came with the Glory.

So far we have a good match. God is in heaven, while his Name dwells among his people in the temple and his Glory fills the temple. This is alike to what Christians know: God is "our Father in heaven," while Jesus dwells among them, and the Holy Spirit fills them.

But we haven't joined all the dots yet. If the Trinity is the Father, the Son, and the Spirit, we need to do a bit more digging in the Bible to see better how this matches with God, his Name, and his Glory.

A remarkable clue comes from Paul's friend Luke, who wrote both a Gospel and the book called Acts, which tells the story of the early church, the church of Jesus' first disciples. That's where we turn next.

5. THE NAME AND THE GLORY IN THE BOOK OF ACTS

The quest for the three-in-one God takes us to the story of Jesus' first disciples and their church in Jerusalem, as told in Luke's book of Acts. Luke does us a great service. He teaches us how the Name and the Glory are to do with Jesus and the Holy Spirit in memorable ways. As an important bonus, he also shows us what the temple has to do with all of this. He does this in two landmark stories: the story of Pentecost where we learn especially about the Glory; and then the story of Peter and John being persecuted, where we learn especially about the Name. So, first to the story of Pentecost, found in Acts, chapter 2.

The Glory

Many Christians already know about the Glory, more than they may realize. This is because they know about the church's story of Pentecost. This is the celebrated moment when Christians were spectacularly filled with the Holy Spirit. Churches remember this day every year, a few weeks after Easter, when they sing such things as "We want another Pentecost, send the fire."[10] What has this to do with the Glory, you might ask. Both came like fire.

Tom Wright, a widely published historian on the early church, sees it this way. It's a match between the Holy Spirit *filling* the believers, at Pentecost, and the Glory *filling* Solomon's temple. In Wright's words:

> When Solomon built the Temple and dedicated it, it was filled with the cloud which veiled God's presence . . . And Luke,

---

10. Booth, "Thou Christ."

> writing the story [Pentecost], wants us to think: this is the glory of the Lord coming back to fill the Temple![11]

Wright also says:

> at the heart of Pentecost, in Acts . . . the coming of the Spirit is all about the launching of the new Temple.[12]

This remarkable insight reveals how the Glory and the Holy Spirit are matched together. So, a temple being filled with the Glory amounts to the same as being filled with the Holy Spirit. Both ways, whether we are talking about a stone building or a church community being filled, it is a temple and it is being filled.[13]

In church life, learning about being filled with the Holy Spirit is an important and well-known personal step. Many Christians can quote popular Bible verses about it:

> they were all filled with the Holy Spirit (Acts 2:4 ESV)

> be filled with the Holy Spirit (Acts 9:17 ESV)

Temples of the Holy Spirit—that's what Christians are. A temple, just as much as the ancient stone one that was filled with the Glory. It's a telling match in so many ways. Both of these stories happened in Jerusalem. Both happened in kinds of temples. Both were about being filled. First, a temple filled with the Glory (Solomon's temple)! And second the church, a temple filled with the Holy Spirit! Being "filled" with the Glory equates to being "filled" with the Spirit. And both came like fire.

It is a rewarding finding, to see this connection between the Glory and the Holy Spirit. This connection is a clue for finding the three-in-one God in the Bible. And what a clue! We need to remember these two pictures: a picture of the Glory like fire filling Solomon's temple; and a picture of the Holy Spirit coming like fire, filling Christians.

Luke does something really interesting with the story here. The visible Glory is seen by some in the church community not once but twice. First, at Pentecost (Acts 2:1–4). Second, at the death of the first Christian martyr Stephen (Acts 7:55–56). Before Stephen dies, he sees into heaven and sees the visible Glory there. These two sightings of the Glory sit like bookends

---

11. Wright, "New Law, New Temple."
12. Wright, "Spirit of Truth."
13. On the link between Spirit and Glory, see Bonnington, "New Temples in Corinth," especially page 157.

around stories to do with the temple—in between them another story is told, a story about the Name in the temple.

So far, remember these two matches in how the story is told:

God = God the Father

The Glory = the Holy Spirit

Next we add the third piece of the puzzle:

The Name = Jesus

The Name

Luke has an eye on the ancient past, on the story of Solomon's temple, to help us, bringing the Old Testament picture of the three-in-one God right into Christian thinking. The history of the first churches, Acts moves quickly from one gripping story to another. In chapters 3 to 5, it tells us of two men who have been Jesus' disciples—Peter and John—upsetting the establishment at Jerusalem's temple. What caused offence? They kept preaching about "the name of Jesus" in the temple. That ruffled feathers within the establishment. The brave apostles were warned about it, punished for it, but kept going back to the temple and telling people about "the name of Jesus."

Clue: Words and Numbers

There is here an extraordinary clue. To lead us to identify Jesus with "the Name," Luke uses a biblical words and numbers game. It is in this report of Peter and John caught up in controversy at the temple. If we really want to see what Luke is doing, we have to count words.

Quite a few of the inspired writers of the Bible made use of words and numbers games. They are gems to own if you can locate them. Ancient readers were more aware of these games than most modern readers are.

Luke does it by picking two Greek words: the word *onoma* which means "name"; and the word *hieron* which means "temple." What makes it so telling is that in this story (in Acts chapters 3 through 5) Luke wrote the word *onoma* (name) referring to Jesus, and the word *hieron* (temple) precisely twelve times each.[14] Not more, nor less. Twelve times each, in Acts 3–5, in this story. So that's:

---

14. "Name" in relation to Jesus occurs here twelve times: Acts 3:6, 3:16 (twice), 4:7, 4:10, 4:12, 4:17, 4:18, 4:29, 5:28, 5:40, and 5:41. "Temple" occurs twelve times in: Acts

- *onoma* (name) referring to Jesus—12 times
- *hieron* (temple)—12 times

Mere coincidence is easily ruled out. It's not just that twelve is a significant number in the Bible, which it is, or just that we are interested in these words. It's clearly not a coincidence because, after using these words in this story twelve times, Luke hardly uses them the same way at all in the chapters that follow. The word *hieron* disappears and does not turn up again until much later, in chapter 19. *Onoma* in connection with Jesus doesn't show up again until chapter 8. So why does the story of the controversy in the temple make such a measured use of these two words?

One conclusion is inescapable: here in this story based around the temple, in Acts 3–5, both words are used twelve times each, in a special way with a special meaning. But what is it?

This is how we can work it out. The number twelve matters because it is about "Israel." (This was common knowledge—Israel was famous for having twelve tribes.) So:

- Having this word "temple" *twelve times* means that the temple which Luke is thinking of is a temple that has something to do with Israel.
- As well as "temple," seeing the word "Name" *twelve times* in regard to Jesus means that Luke is telling us something about Jesus and the Name that dwelled with Israel, in the temple.

We know that the temple of Solomon was the dwelling place of the Name. What might surprise us in Luke's clue is this: it's the Name *in connection with Jesus* twelve times. The verses where the disciples preach "in the name of Jesus" are examples of that.

It's an eyebrow-raising way of connecting the Name with Jesus! Mixing in the "Name" of Jesus twelve times whips up a whole new recipe out of our "temple" and "Name" ingredients. Mix in the fact that the number of Jesus' apostles at the birth of the church is also twelve and it's got extra spice.

These "twelves" might not seem much on their own, but they are a whole new recipe together. They serve up these messages, something new about the temple and something new about the Name:

- Jesus is the Name
- Israel has a new temple, the church community
- Israel's new temple is the dwelling place of the Name of Jesus

---

3:1, 3:2 (twice), 3:3, 3:8, 3:10, 4:1, 5:20, 5:21, 5:24, 5:25, and 5:42.

As such, Jesus is the spiritual presence who has a rightful claim on everything the temple stood for.[15] It is harking back to when the Name dwelled in Solomon's temple. Luke's book is indicating that the Name with the right to dwell in the temple is the Name of Jesus. In Christian experience, what it means is this: Jesus' *spiritual presence* dwells in the church community.

By weaving into his story the "Name" and "temple" twelve times each, Luke has made a big statement. It's a big development in the story of the Bible. When the author, Luke, thinks of "the Name" in Solomon's temple, he thinks of Jesus. That is, Jesus dwelling in the temple. The big message? The Name has a new home—in Jesus' people.

Luke has done a subtle attack on any idea that Herod's stone temple would be the home of God, his Name, and his Glory. Was it still the home of God? That is in doubt, according to Acts 7:48, where Stephen's speech (like Solomon's prayer—2 Chr 6:18) says the temple is too small for God. But was the stone temple still the home of the Name? Not according to Acts 3–5, where the Name is the Name of Jesus, which dwells in the church community, not Herod's temple. But, was the stone temple still the home of the Glory? Not according to Acts 2:1–4, where Pentecost springs the surprise that the return of the Glory to Jerusalem comes not in the stone temple but in the church community. The Name and the Glory had moved out of the stone temple, and into the church community, a living temple.

Luke has done away with the idea that the Jerusalem temple was the home of God, his Name, and his Glory. That honor now went to the church community. The Christians were reading the stories of Solomon's temple in brave new ways.

And Luke is shedding light on the identities behind the Name and the Glory. They are God's Son and his Spirit:

God = God the Father
The Name = Jesus
The Glory = the Holy Spirit

There are reasons for having confidence in this match. Both sides of it are biblical pictures of God's spiritual presence in a temple:

- The church's Trinity—God, Son and Spirit
- Solomon's Trinity—God, Name, and Glory.

So many matches: both models have to do with a temple. Both models feature the moment of a temple being filled—by the Glory, or indeed filled by the Spirit. Two models so alike:

15. Wright, *New Testament and the People of God*, 368.

Solomon built a temple	A church community is a temple
1) God	Our Father
is in heaven	is in heaven
2) The Name	The Name of Jesus
dwells in the temple	dwells in the church
3) The Glory	The Spirit
fills the temple	fills the church

It is a match made in heaven. You could think of it like a makeover. The New Testament has taken what we knew about God, his Name, and his Glory, and given it a makeover, and presented to us the Father, the Son, and the Spirit. A makeover that is inspirational in every sense of the word.

This is more than just a thought to remember. This is a key. Turning the key opens up messages in the pages of the Bible and leads us to the Trinity—in the New Testament *and* in the Old Testament. And in this way we learn about how the first Christians could have faith in a three-in-one God. We are well on our way to understanding the Trinity in a way that they could.

So, if the true temple (in the ancient days of Israel's kings) was the temple built by Solomon, who was its rightful dweller? It was God, dwelling *in the form of his Name and his Glory*. And now to the New Testament: if the true temple is the church community, who is this temple's rightful dweller? It is God *in the form of his Son and his Spirit*.

We have very good reasons now to want to find out more. So, there is nothing better than to dig deeper into the stories of the Name and the Glory in Solomon's temple, starting with the high point of the story of Israel in the Old Testament, the glory days, when the stone temple was dedicated to God.

6. THE NAME AND THE GLORY IN THE OLD TESTAMENT

A good place to look, to find out more about God, is: God's house. We find Jerusalem's temple called "the place where your glory dwells" and "the dwelling place of your Name" (Pss 26:8 and 74:7 NIV).

Let's look again at the Name and the Glory close up, through the story of Israel in the Old Testament, through the good times and bad times of Israel and its temple, and its most holy inner room, a sanctuary for God's presence. Scripture tells of a moment of terrible judgment at the hands of Israel's enemies for the temple of God's Name:

> They burned your sanctuary to the ground;
> they defiled *the dwelling place of your Name*. (Ps 74:7 NIV)

In another Scripture about the temple and the Glory, better times:

> I love the house where you live, O LORD,
> the place *where your glory dwells*. (Ps 26:8 NIV)

So, both the Name and the Glory lived in the temple. Hardly spoken of in churches, but known to scholars, the message of the Old Testament is that the Name and the Glory dwelled in the temple. The author of the Book of Revelation knew this about the temple, and wrote about a temple in heaven just like it, where God's Name and his temple are threatened by blasphemy. But a temple full of God's Glory just the same:

> God's temple in heaven was opened, and the ark of his covenant was seen within his temple . . . [the beast] opened its mouth to utter blasphemies against God, blaspheming his name and his dwelling . . . and the sanctuary was filled with smoke from the glory of God . . . (Rev 11:19; 13:6; 15:8 ESV).

Let's look at the Old Testament backstory of the Name and the Glory, one at a time.

The Name

The Name is a personal spiritual presence, with a dwelling place, a home. Many Scriptures say it:

> And rejoice before the LORD your God at *the place* he will choose as a *dwelling* for his *Name* . . . (Deut 16:11 NIV)

A question that helps us to get the point here is this: who needs a dwelling, who needs a home, according to that Bible verse? Is it God, or is it his Name that needs a home? Answer: it is the Name. That is what the Bible says here. God's spiritual presence needs a home. God's presence is a person.

There are plenty of examples in the Old Testament where the Name is a word for God's presence:

> a dwelling for my Name (Neh 1:9 NIV)
>
> [The Israelites] built you a sanctuary there for your name . . . for your name is in this temple (2 Chr 20:8–9 NJB)
>
> we give thanks, for Your Name is near. (Ps 75:1 NIV)

It is even possible to read these words as if they were about Jesus' presence. The Bible speaks of the church as a house built for Jesus' presence, a place where he dwells, where Jesus is near to Christians.

The Glory

What about the Glory? We already gathered that Solomon's temple was filled by the Glory, like Christians are filled with the Holy Spirit. But there is a deeper question about the Glory: the Holy Spirit is a person in Christian belief—so is there a sign in the Old Testament of the Glory being a person? It is only fair that we should ask.

And yes, there is a sign. The Glory is sometimes shown like a personal figure, such as in this vision of the Glory on God's throne in the temple:

> High above on the form of a throne was a form with the appearance of a human being . . . This was the appearance of the likeness of *the glory* of the LORD. (Ezek 1:26–28 NJB and NIV joined up)

This shows the Glory as God's presence. And what's more, a kind of presence with a distinct identity too, as a person has. This picture of the Glory fits with the Holy Spirit having a distinct identity of its own, as a personal presence, as a person.

It will be important that we remember that the first Christians were able to see the Holy Spirit as a person. We see this is so when the Holy Spirit personally speaks a detailed instruction to the disciples in Acts 13:2–4 (NIV):

> the Holy Spirit said, "Set apart for *me* Barnabas and Saul for the work to which I have called them."

The Holy Spirit calls himself personally "me" and "I" there. The Spirit even personally specifies the things to be understood by those listening, in a way that only a person would have done. Jesus predicted this relationship with the Holy Spirit. He said:

> when he, the Spirit of truth comes, he will guide you into all truth. He will not speak on his own; he will speak only what he hears, and he will tell you what is to come. (John 16:13–14 NIV)

That is how the Holy Spirit of the Bible speaks, as a person, just like God the Father and his Son Jesus are persons.

All of this means that when we come to the Old Testament and the stories of Solomon's temple, we see that God's Name and Glory are personal presences. They cannot be impersonal, because God does not have an impersonal side to him. It is in the New Testament that their identity is fully revealed, as the Name is matched with Jesus, and the Glory is matched with the Holy Spirit.

The Name and the Glory—Persons in the Trinity

God is three persons. God is three-in-one. That is true if we call it God and his Son and his Spirit. It is true if we call it God and his Name and his Glory. It is still one God, and it is still a God of three personal presences.

It is the God who dwells in the temple, who fills the temple, as his Name and his Glory. Just in case some are finding it a bit difficult picturing the Name and the Glory as persons, compare them with Jesus and the Holy Spirit. What goes for Jesus and the Spirit goes for the Name and the Glory. Remember what we learned in Rom 8:9–34. There, we read that Christ and the Spirit both dwell in Christians; and that Christ and the Spirit are both communicating for them to the Father. So:

- For Christians, Jesus and the Spirit *dwell* in us as God—we are their temple and they are our God (together with the Father).
- Jesus and the Spirit are *communicating* to the Father.

There are conversations going on inside God, conversations between the Father, the Son, and the Holy Spirit. We can take those truths over to Solomon's temple and understand the Name and the Glory better. We can picture the Name and the Glory sent by God, dwelling in the temple, and communicating back to God.

God's Inner Conversations

Communicating like that illustrates that the Son, and the Spirit, and the Father are distinct from each other, like voices are. This communication doesn't split them apart into completely separate beings. They are one. Communication is what is happening inside God: this is the nature of God, inner communication between the three persons. The Son and the Spirit make requests to God the Father for us.

Human beings pray and communicate because we are born in God's image: we are doing what God does. But hold on, someone might say. We pray to the Father and we are separate from God. So how can Jesus not be separate from God, since he prays too? But actually, communicating with the Father is not what makes someone separate from God. It is only that we are *part of creation* that makes us a separate kind of thing from God. There is a dividing line. On one side of the line is God, and on the other side is creation. We are part of creation, and so we are on the other side of the line from God. There has been only one person who has been part of both sides of this divide: Jesus, being God and coming into creation in human form.

Some people face this with a bit of confusion at first. They are puzzled to see Jesus pray to God the Father on one hand, and yet think that we can call Jesus himself God. Jehovah's Witnesses have made fun of this, saying God can't pray to himself, but that is just a trick statement. There are three persons in God. Jesus doesn't pray to himself, he prays to God the Father, just as the Spirit does.

They are God together. That doesn't mean that the Son and the Spirit can't pray, can't intercede, can't plead on our behalf to the Father. They can. They can do all that, and still be God together. We know they are one. Remember that they dwell in the church. It's their temple and they are its God.

But if we are puzzled to see Jesus pray to the Father, we just need to take a moment observing God. Observing is always the place to start. Remember that the bumblebee used to confuse scientists who couldn't understand how a bumblebee's tiny wings could lift its bulky body off the ground. But they observed it in a fresh way with modern digital cameras that could show the wings flapping in super-slow-motion. Then everyone could see how bees fly, and it's an amazing thing to see.[16]

With observing the Trinity, we can be hampered, like scientists who once couldn't see how a bee really flaps its wings and lifts its little body into the air. What has hampered us is to do with how we think about people. We tend to think of ourselves as separate private individuals, each with private thoughts that we can keep from each other. But we miss something if we think Jesus and his Father are like that. Something different is going on with them. For looking at the Trinity in close-up, our super-sharp camera is the Bible. The clue is in the story of the Name and the Glory in Solomon's temple again. Seeing the Name and the Glory is like seeing the bumblebee's wings in slow motion. We can observe that the Trinity is one, all the more clearly, just as we can observe the bee more clearly. Looking at the Name and the Glory, they aren't private individuals who can keep their thoughts from each other and from God. They are one. They have this relationship with each other, and the same time they are one. This gives us the right idea about

---

16. A bumblebee can move its wings independently of each other, and they tend to flap forwards and backwards more than up and down, moving the air around them as they need. And they flap furiously! None of this could be seen until modern cameras revealed it.

God. So, looking at the Father, Son, and Spirit, they are not like completely separate private individuals who can keep their thoughts from each other. They are as one.

Let's go in even closer, picturing God's Name and Glory dwelling in Solomon's temple. Part of the scene is that Israelites were praying facing towards the temple. And on the Israelites' behalf, the Name and the Glory in the temple are there, bringing them closer to God. It is through the Name and the Glory dwelling in the temple that the Israelites have contact with heaven. The Name and the Glory are always in touch with God the Father in heaven—they are always one together, they never lose their connection with each other. Think of the Name and the Glory communicating back to God in heaven. And through them, all the prayers of Israel are going up to heaven; just how we speak of the prayers of Christians going up to heaven through Jesus and the help of the Holy Spirit.[17]

Just as we can picture Jesus and the Spirit communicating with the Father on our behalf, so we should picture the Name and the Glory communicating just the same. Because God, his Name, and his Glory are what the Father, the Son, and the Spirit are.

And they are one. We are right to picture the Father and Son talking to each other, just not as completely separate private individuals. Remember how God and the Name are one. God the Father and his Son are one. They can communicate with each other, and still be God together.

I wrote that with observing comes understanding, like observing the bumblebee flying. The more we observe about God and his Name and his Glory, the more our understanding of the Trinity will come. One important lesson that we will keep hold of is that God, his Name, and his Glory can't ever be pulled apart, split off and divided from each other to have totally separate existences. Why say so?

First, it's God and his own Name. Second, it's God and his own Glory. They can only ever be one God. God and his Glory cannot be pulled apart, split off, and divided from each other to have two totally separate existences, and so the same goes for God and his Spirit. They are one, God and the Spirit of God. No one should have any quibble with that. Even when the Spirit intercedes in prayer to the Father, they are still one.

The same goes for God and his Name, God and Jesus.

---

17. Leithart, seeing the temple and the Name as very integrated to the point where they are virtually inseparable, speaks of the "mediatorial" role that the temple plays in Kings. Prayer is made "toward this house," and the house serves as an interchange between Israel on earth and Yahweh in heaven. Leithart, "Placing the Name."

7. THE MYSTERY OF WHERE GOD LIVES, AND AN IMPORTANT CLUE

Many Christians are confused about where God dwells. Is God on earth or in heaven? The confusion fades when we discover the three-in-one God of the temple. And this turns out to be another important clue to the existence of the Trinity in the Bible.

When asked, some Christians can be heard offering not one but three different answers to the question of where God lives. Three very different answers. But we shouldn't be confused by this. Each of the three answers reveals something about where God lives, as the Bible describes it.

One answer given is that God lives *in heaven*. People giving this answer can't be faulted, because Jesus' teaching was to pray to "our Father in heaven" (Matt 6:9). So, we can settle for this emphasis on where the Father is—in heaven.

The second answer is that God can be found *everywhere*. This is really different from saying God is in heaven. This is saying that God can be found here on earth *and* in heaven. But this answer cannot be faulted either because in the book of Jeremiah, the Lord says:

> Am I only a God nearby, and not a God far away? Can anyone hide in secret places, so that I cannot see him? Do I not fill heaven and earth? (Jer 23:23–24 NIV)

The third answer about where God lives is this: believers say that God is present in their hearts, saying that they are temples of the Holy Spirit who dwells *inside them*. So the Bible says:

> Do you not know that you are God's temple and that God's Spirit dwells in you? (1 Cor 3:16 ESV)

Those three answers put God in three different locations at the same time: here inside the believers; but also there in heaven; and also everywhere worldwide. Three different answers because all three answers are in the Bible, and all three are needed to explain the whole picture of where God dwells.

It is especially the Holy Spirit—and the Glory as a sign of the Holy Spirit—that the Old Testament pictures as having a worldwide presence. So Christians usually are talking about the Holy Spirit when they are talking of the presence that is everywhere. So whereas we generally say that the Father lives in heaven, we say that the Holy Spirit can be found everywhere in earth and heaven.

The "everywhere" answer has to do with Jesus too, as he dwells in the church community, spiritually present in the church through the Holy Spirit, when Christians are together.

What's the Difference?

As temples of the Holy Spirit, the Christian sense of God's inner presence is different from the sense of God being present in the rest of creation, such as in a garden. Why is there a difference?

The Bible leads us to expect a difference, otherwise it would be meaningless to make any point at all about God entering the temple of Solomon, or the Holy Spirit filling people. That is to say, the way in which God was *inside* of the temple must have been different from the way God was *outside* the temple. There must be a difference between God entering the temple of Solomon or not. There was something different about the temple experience, something about God being at home there. People would notice the difference.

And there would be no point to Pentecost if there were no difference whether the Holy Spirit was *inside* or *outside* of people. When experiencing the Holy Spirit, there must be a difference between being filled and not being filled. That is why we need to understand how the Bible talks about where God lives. And answers come with understanding God as three-in-one.

This God is present all over the world, but when he comes to make his home somewhere, or in someone, it introduces a more personal quality to the experience. The difference has a more direct impact on people's lives. Christians today speak of their own experience of God's presence in ways that are in tune with everything we have thought about. First, they are conscious that they pray to "our Father *in heaven*" as Jesus taught them to, so they know about God the Father being there. Second, they experience the inner presence of the Holy Spirit and Jesus *in their hearts* and *in the church*. Third, they know God's Spirit is present working *in the whole world*—they may even sense his presence in a garden or another place—and they know that this is something outside of them, more than just their inner experience. No other God is like this, like the three-in-one God. The Bible especially pictures them this way: present in heaven, and locally and worldwide at the same time.

Of course, we must remember that God is not limited. There is nowhere in creation that the Father and Son could not be present through the Holy Spirit. All three can be omnipresent. They are always working together, never separated from each other. But there is a special emphasis. Jesus said to pray to "our Father in heaven," so it would be no good to try to write about an "everywhere" God, but ignore this special emphasis on where the

Father is: heaven. Jesus expected us to understand something about the Father from this. He expected Christians to respect it when they address the Father in prayer. Although the Father can be present everywhere through his Holy Spirit, the Bible's special emphasis is on the Father being in heaven.

Where Does God Live in the Old Testament?

Let's turn again to the landmark story of the launch of the Jerusalem temple. This is in 2 Chr 5–7. Solomon prays to God:[18]

- "May your eyes be open towards this temple day and night, this place of which you said you would put your Name there . . . Hear from *heaven, your dwelling place*"
- "Now arise, O LORD God, and come to *your resting place* [the temple]"
- When Solomon finished praying, fire came down from heaven . . . and the glory of the LORD *filled the temple* (2 Chr 6:20–21; 6:41; 7:1 NIV)

Where is God in that scene?

- God himself listens *from heaven* to Solomon's prayer
- but his Name dwells *in the temple in Jerusalem*; and
- and his Glory fills *the temple*.

Of those three things, let's start with the first: God in heaven.

In the story, God was still in heaven hearing prayers—before and after the Glory fills the temple (2 Chr 6:23–39). So, when we add it all together, this story tells us about the three presences not all being in the same place at the same time. One in heaven, two in the temple:

- God in heaven
- the Name and the Glory in the temple

Where Does God Live in the New Testament?

It's worth another look at the question of where God dwells according to the New Testament. God was still in heaven, before and after the Name and the Glory were sent into Solomon's temple, and this gives us a clue. We have

---

18 2 Chr 5–7: "Glory" appears four times; "Name" thirteen times; "dwell/dwelling" seven times. It is important to read the whole of 2 Chr 5:13—7:1 to get a sense of how important the Name and the Glory are to Solomon's temple.

great matches from looking at where God and his Name and his Glory live, and where the Father and his Son and his Spirit live.

We can see the match in what Jesus taught about praying to "our Father in heaven." Just as when Solomon prayed, it is the same when Jesus prayed: God the Father is still the same God in the same place doing the same thing—in heaven hearing prayers.

It is an unmovable feature of the Bible: the distinct presences of God: two spiritual presences on earth, one in heaven.

Like two halves of a treasure map, the detailed matches make more sense when seen together:

Solomon built a temple	*The church community is a temple*
1) God in heaven	God the Father in heaven
hears prayers	hears prayers
2) The Name	Christ
dwells in the temple	dwells in the church
3) The Glory	The Holy Spirit
fills the temple	fills Christians
(and is everywhere in earth and heaven)	(and is everywhere in earth and heaven)

The conclusion is unavoidable. We have two models of a three-in-one God, to do with the temple. They match in detail after detail. Little wonder that it was so natural for Paul to speak of Christians as temples with Christ and the Spirit dwelling in them—it would have had a familiar ring to Israelites who knew about the Name and the Glory.

As we go on to the next part, we can take with us an especially important thing. We can put a finger on a page of the Bible, in 2 Chr 6–7, read the story of Solomon's temple, and say, "I see a three-in-one God there!" The standout verses where we find the details in the story are 2 Chr 6:20–21, 6:41, and 7:1.

8. HOW COULD THREE BE ONE?

We have answers to some of the questions we started this book with. The early church did not have to wait hundreds of years to decide to believe that God was three-in-one: one God, three personal presences. They already had faith in that, back in the days of Jesus' disciples. We hear it in the New Testament, which has the language of their time, the language of the temple. The words are different from the complicated language of the creeds that Christians say in Sunday services today. So, getting back to the words of the disciples is vital, if we want to know what they knew about God, to discover *their* idea of a triune God.

But some people struggle with the idea that God can be three and one at the same time. If we are to really understand the Trinity, then we can't avoid talking about this.

Help is at hand in what we have learned about the Name and the Glory. In the Old Testament picture, this could only be one God:

God + his Name + his Glory = one God

God plus his Name plus his Glory equals one God. Not three gods. The three are one. After all, we are talking about God and *his own* Name and *his own* Glory. So these three can only ever be one God. It's not someone else's name, not someone else's glory. So this is not three separate gods. It's one God. That's the first thing to keep hold of.

Now look what we can do with this:

God + his Name + his Glory = one God

Therefore:

God + his Son + his Spirit = one God

See how the match works? This match means one clear thing: three are one. God and his Son and his Spirit are one God. They are three persons, three spiritual presences[19]: but together they are one God.

In taking hold of this, we now possess something that many Christians have asked for and not been given: a way of picturing a three-in-one God that can be found in the Bible. This is the scene: Solomon's temple, with its majestic high walls, being filled with the Glory, bringing with it a spiritual presence called "the Name" into the temple's holiest inner room; and as part of the scene, while they enter the temple, we still have God remaining present in heaven hearing prayers. This is a way of picturing the three-in-one God. A scene where God has three personal presences, one in heaven, two in the temple: God, his own Name and his own Glory. The three-in-one God of the temple: for God and Name and Glory, read instead Father and Son and Spirit. In New Testament language, we can replay the scene. Only the words change. The temple is the church.

This is the scene: the church community, a living temple being filled with the Holy Spirit, and with the spiritual presence of Jesus, and we still

---

19 Three presences: the word "presence" is a really useful translation of the Greek word *prosopon*. It is a biblical word that speaks of the three "presences" of God: as the Father, the Son, and the Holy Spirit. *Prosopon* is also the word for "person." More on this later. Cf. Bates, Birth of the Trinity, 89.

have God the Father remaining in heaven hearing prayers. It is a picture of a Trinity of presences, one in heaven, two in the church community.

And we have a personal dimension, because we know that Father, Son, and Spirit are three persons who communicate to each other. So, Scripture gives us grace to see that God, his Name, and his Glory are three persons communicating with each other.

9. IT'S PENTECOST AND THE CHURCH IS A NEW TEMPLE

In plain sight in the pages of Scripture we find the three-in-one God. In that light, a lot of things in the Bible make new sense. Questions such as these are answered:

- How is Pentecost the start of a new temple?
- How does the church compare with Solomon's temple?
- Is Jesus really God's presence?

How Is Pentecost the Start of a New Temple?

Let's turn back to the story of Pentecost, when the believers became temples of the Holy Spirit. This is what Tom Wright wrote about when he said, "at the heart of Pentecost, in Acts . . . the coming of the Spirit is all about the launching of the new Temple."[20]

Now, for the first time, let's look at the words in the book of Acts that describe the moment when the believers became temples of the Holy Spirit, "filled" with the Holy Spirit, a scene of tongues of fire from heaven:

> And suddenly there came *from heaven* a noise like a violent rushing wind, and it filled the whole house where they were sitting. And there appeared to them tongues as of fire distributing themselves, and they rested on each one of them. And they were all *filled with the Holy Spirit* and began to speak with other tongues, as the Spirit was giving them utterance. (Acts 2:2–4 NIV)

It echoes the dedication scene of Solomon's temple, where these events are reported:

---

20. Wright, "Spirit of Truth."

> When Solomon finished praying, *fire* came down *from heaven* ... and the glory of the LORD *filled the temple* (2 Chr 6:20–21; 6:41; 7:1 NIV)

This was the Glory coming, and they were the new temple. Again, like two halves of a treasure map, the clues make more sense together:

In Solomon's temple	*At Pentecost*
from heaven	from heaven
the Glory of the LORD came with fire	tongues as of fire
and filled	filled
the temple	each one of them

How Does the Church Compare with Solomon's Temple?

The idea of the launch of a new temple is important to help us understand the switch from the old way of talking about God, his Name, and his Glory to the new way of talking about God, his Son, and his Spirit.

And with it, something important about the church community. It is not meant to be a second-rate temple. It is ideally on a par with Solomon's temple, and the presence of Christ and the Holy Spirit as magnificent as the presence of the Name and the Glory there. This means the church can be absolutely magnificent as a community.

Is Jesus Really God's Presence?

About the Trinity, one question that many people really want an answer to is this: could Jesus truly be God? The answer is yes. Picture the three-in-one God of the temple. The "Name" is God's spiritual presence. And this spiritual presence, the Name, is Jesus. This means that Jesus is God's presence. So we can rightfully say that Jesus is God.

In the picture of Pentecost in Acts, we will find another clue. It is Jesus who pours out the Holy Spirit on the believers. Jesus is doing something that God alone can do—give God's Holy Spirit. In the Old Testament, we see a similar picture, where it is the Name who pours out the Spirit. Jesus and the Name do one and the same thing because they are one and the same.

There is a case of this in a scene not long before Pentecost, when Jesus gives the disciples a foretaste of what is to come. Jesus is actually pictured *breathing out* God's Breath, God's Spirit. Jesus is doing something that God alone can do. Jesus is the God who breathes his Holy Spirit into the believers, the God of Israel:

> he breathed on them and said to them, "Receive the Holy Spirit" (John 20:21–22 ESV)

A trail of evidence stretches out in front of us, in the pages of the Bible. It is inviting us to follow it wherever it leads. Of course, we could have been content with what we read in Paul's letters, teaching how the church is the temple of the three-in-one God. We could have settled for SS. Augustine, Ambrose, and Jerome saying the same. We could even have settled for seeing that the New Testament and Old Testament both have a model of a three-in-one God based around the temple. We could have settled for knowing about the Name and the Glory.

But like detectives in a movie, a lot of people may feel a question nagging at them. It is time to listen to that question. It is whether Jesus taught his disciples about a three-in-one God. This seems essential. So while we already know the fundamental facts for understanding the triune God of the Bible—and we can be more confident that we can put a finger on a page of the Bible and say, "I see a three-in-one God there"—allow me to tell you how Jesus prepared his disciples to understand this too.

10. WHAT JESUS TAUGHT

If the Trinity is such a central and important doctrine as the church says, then we should be alert to what Jesus teaches on it. If you read a lot of books on the Trinity, you find they have virtually nothing to say about this. This does not satisfy some Christians, and rightly so, because we are on a quest for answers. So let's take this investigation further.

We can make progress, because now we understand better what to look for. To find the three-in-one God of the Bible, we need only to look in Jesus' teachings for what he knew about the three-in-one God of Solomon's temple. And when we open the Bible, it is right there in the place where it should be.

Jesus knew the old ways of speaking about God's presence in the temple: that God had a presence there at the same time as a presence in heaven. Here is one time that Jesus spoke about God's presence being both on earth (in the temple) and in heaven:

> he who swears by *the temple* swears by it and by *the one who dwells in it*. And he who swears by *heaven* swears by God's throne and by *the one who sits on it*. (Matt 23:21–22 NIV)

We are very fortunate to have these words. This is an education in how to think of God's presence. Here are two special dwelling places for God: in heaven and in the temple. Jesus' words line up right with what the Old Testament says, in Ps 11, about one God, two dwelling places:

Jesus speaking: Matt 23:21–22 NIV	Ps 11:4 NIV
he who swears by *the temple* swears by it and	
by *the one who dwells in it*.	The LORD is *in his holy temple*;
And he who swears by *heaven* swears by God's *throne*	The LORD is *on his heavenly throne*.
and by the one who sits *on it*.	

God is in two special places: "The LORD is in his holy temple" and also "The LORD is on his heavenly throne." This was the understanding of the temple and heaven that Jesus had—and this is what he expected his followers to understand—the two places, with God in heaven and with *God's Name* in the temple, as Solomon prayed:

> . . . praying in your presence. May your eyes be open towards *this temple* day and night, this place of which you have said *you would put your Name there*. May you hear the prayer your servant prays towards this place . . . Hear from *heaven your dwelling place* . . . (2 Chr 6:19–21 NIV)

Jesus' disciples were already primed by the temple stories of the Old Testament, ready to appreciate the three-in-one God of Israel, the God of the temple. This would change their lives forever. To get them ready, Jesus laid the ground, step by step. This is what he taught his disciples:

Step 1	Jesus reveals his role as the temple's God, returning to his temple to bring Glory fire.
Step 2	He teaches his plan: the temple of the body.
Step 3	He teaches that in this new temple, he himself and the Spirit will dwell.
Step 4	He does new things with the language of the Name and the Glory for this new kind of temple.
Step 5	His followers become temples of the Holy Spirit, a community in which Christ is spiritually present.

Step 1—Jesus Reveals His Role as the Temple's God, Returning to His Temple to Bring Glory Fire

To understand the three-in-one God as the disciples did, we need to learn from a trail of clues about the three-in-one God left by Jesus. One of the first clues is that Jesus came on the scene in the role of God himself returning to his temple with fire. A sign that Jesus' followers learned to think of him this way is in John's Gospel. Calling Jesus by his famous title "The Word," John's Gospel tells us that

> The Word became flesh, and tabernacled for a while among us.
> We have seen his glory . . . (John 1:14 NIV, author's adaption)

These words put us right on the trail. It's to do with finding the words "tabernacle" and "Glory" put together like that.[21] This is exactly the sort of clue we need.

First, to remind ourselves what a tabernacle was: it was a temple in a tent basically. The words tabernacle and Glory put together are like a spark to a flame. They are explosive together. To understand why, we need to ask a simple question: what God does this Glory belong to? The simple answer, you might be thinking, would be that this Glory belongs to the God of Israel. The answer in John's Gospel is startling. It is this: the Glory and the tabernacle belong to Jesus. His tabernacle, his Glory. He is this God. His own Glory is in the temple of his own body.

In other words, Jesus is John's God. He is Israel's God, stepping into our world. He is a temple: but he's also the divine presence too, the presence in his temple.

So, we can take it that Jesus' followers understood step 1. That is: Jesus revealed to them his role as their God, with his own temple and his Glory. His Glory is like fire. We shall see in a later chapter how the words of Jesus and John the Baptist led the disciples to this conclusion.

Step 2—Jesus Teaches His Plan: the Temple of the Body

Jesus' disciples would understand the temple in a new way. As for the Jerusalem temple, Jesus was downgrading it slowly. While it still stood, it was still meant to be dedicated to God. But Jesus said that it had lost its good reputation and was headed for destruction:

- It had become "a den of robbers" (Luke 19:45–46)
- Every stone of it would come down in ruins (Luke 21:5–6)

---

21. Skarsaune, *In the Shadow of the Temple*, 328.

So instead of a big stone house for God, there would be a new kind of temple. Jesus got the message across to them:

> he was speaking about the temple of his body (John 2:21)

It was coming. Out with the old, in with the new. A new kind of temple. That is what they learned in step 2.

Step 3—Jesus Teaches That in This New Temple, He Himself and the Spirit Will Dwell

Jesus teaches that the Jerusalem temple would be destroyed by others. And he teaches something that for the disciples was a new thing. The life-changing teaching was the idea of the body being a temple. First Jesus spoke about his body as a temple. Then he spoke about the disciples also being this new kind of temple. This is what Jesus makes them realize: they learn this idea off him. Each one of them was to know this: that their body was a temple. So it is not just that Jesus' own body was a temple. It is more than that: they all had to be a temple.

And he teaches about the three-in-one God, by way of teaching that in this new temple (in his people), he himself and the Spirit will dwell.

Making a match between what happened in Solomon's temple and what happens in the church, Jesus leads his disciples towards these triune truths:

At Solomon's temple	In the church community
1) God in heaven hears prayers	God the Father in heaven hears prayers
2) The Name dwells in the temple	The Son dwells in the church
3) The Glory fills the temple	The Holy Spirit fills believers

This is his teaching: that he himself would dwell in his church personally, as a spiritual presence:

> For where two or three have gathered together in my name, I am there in their midst. (Matt 18:20 NASB)

This is electric, lighting a fire in believers from that day to this. Why did Jesus say this? It was for the disciples to know *where* Jesus himself would spiritually be present in days to come—he would be spiritually dwelling among them as in his temple. Jesus is making a dazzling statement equating himself with the presence in the temple. He is calling his disciples a temple, and he is calling himself the divine presence in it. This is a crucial clue about how he taught his disciples to think about the three-in-one God of the temple.

PEOPLE LIKE YOU CAN UNDERSTAND THE TRINITY 45

These ideas all go back to the story of the launch day of Solomon's temple, the day when the Name came to dwell in the temple.

When we turn to John's Gospel, we again find Jesus talking about himself dwelling spiritually in his disciples. But this time he goes even further, with a triune truth. We see the disciples learning from Jesus that when they became temples, they would be temples of all three persons of the Trinity: the Father, the Son, and the Holy Spirit. It is the night before Jesus' death, at supper, when they learn this:

	Jesus speaking
About the Father	"If anyone loves *me*, he will keep my word, and *my Father* will love him, and *we will come to him and make our home with him*" (John 14:23)
About the Son	"*that I may be in them*" (John 17:26 NIV)
About the Holy Spirit	"he dwells with you and *will be in you*." (John 14:17)

Remember what St. Ambrose wrote about the Trinity? He was quoting one of those verses, John 14:23. He was explaining how the whole Trinity was the God of the temple. These words of Jesus in John's Gospel add a lot to our appreciation of the three-in-one God dwelling in a temple of believers.

"Hold on," you might be thinking. "Jesus said to pray to 'our Father *in heaven*,' so why is Jesus now saying that *the Father* will dwell with believers *on earth*?" It will make sense, fortunately! The Father is in heaven, of course, but he is not limited. The Holy Spirit can be present in all creation and the Father can too if so he wishes. There will be more about this later.

So, in the three steps so far, the disciples have learned this from Jesus:

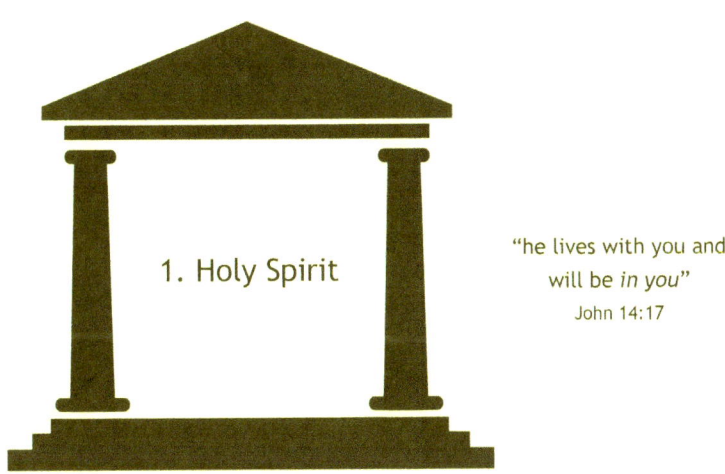

- Jesus had come to them as their God (they spoke of Jesus' temple, Jesus' Glory).
- They learned to think that "my body is a temple."
- Their bodies would be temples of the spiritual presence of the Father, the Son, and the Holy Spirit.

And now that the Jerusalem temple was declared an unfit place for the Name to dwell in, that left the way open for the new kind of temple to be a fit place for the Name, not a "den of robbers."

Step 4—Jesus Takes the Language of the Name and the Glory and Fits It to This New Kind of Temple—People's Bodies

If Jesus' body is a temple, what does that mean for talking about the Name and the Glory? After all, we know that if there is a true temple, then the Name and the Glory should dwell in it. What does Jesus say about this? The answer to that tells us more about how Jesus taught about the old ways of Solomon's temple. In a famous prayer, Jesus speaks to his Father about

> the name you gave me (John 17:11 NIV)
>
> *and*
>
> the glory that you gave me (John 17:22 NIV)

This is temple talk. When Jesus says "the Name you gave me" and "the Glory you gave me," he is saying that he is the true temple in which God's Name and Glory live. He is the one who spoke of the temple of his body.

It's a temple with the Name and the Glory: that is what Jesus' body is. And this is the next step: his disciples must become temples of the Name and the Glory too. This is bringing the stories of Solomon's temple to life in a new way.

Jesus prays "that I may be in them" (John 17:26). When believers become a temple, then the double presence of the Name and the Glory is shared with them, passed from Jesus into them, in unity. Like Jesus, believers become temples of the Name and the Glory. This happens simply by being one with him.

So in these steps, Jesus has taught his disciples that Jerusalem's temple would fall and a new kind of temple was already on the way. This new temple would be a home fit for the Name, as Solomon's temple once was when first built as a holy place. Jesus has taken the language of the Name and the Glory to fit it to this new kind of temple, the believers' own bodies. This is the temple in which Father, Son, and Spirit would dwell, as Jesus taught them. It is the temple of God, his Name, and his Glory.

Step 5: Jesus' Followers Become Temples of the Holy Spirit, in Which Christ is Spiritually Present

So Jesus has promised it. He has prayed for it. Now it happens—the disciples become temples. Near the end of John's Gospel, we read of that moment when they become temples of the Holy Spirit:

> he breathed on them and said to them, "Receive the Holy Spirit."
> (John 20:21–22 ESV)

This was a foretaste of what was soon to come upon all believers at Pentecost. At Pentecost, the Holy Spirit came upon a house full of believers, came like the fiery Glory. That done, the spiritual presence of Jesus dwells in the church community. So, they are now a temple.

We can welcome the evidence of the New Testament, which is that the first Christians were primed by the temple stories of the Old Testament, and prepared by Jesus to know what was happening when their Father in heaven made them a spiritual temple which Jesus and the Holy Spirit dwelled in. They were prepared to appreciate the three-in-one God, the Trinity.

	What Jesus revealed	Verse
Step 1	Jesus reveals his role as the temple's God, returning to his temple to bring Glory fire.	John 1:14
Step 2	He teaches his plan: the temple of the body.	John 2:21
Step 3	He teaches that in this new temple, he himself and the Spirit will dwell.	John 14:17, 23; 17:26
Step 4	He does new things with the language of the Name and the Glory for this new kind of temple.	John 17:11, 22
Step 5	His followers become temples of the Holy Spirit, a community in which the Trinity is spiritually present.	John 20:21–22

11. WHAT TREASURE HAVE WE FOUND?

This first chapter has been a whistle-stop tour meeting the triune God in the Bible. What can we take away with us from this chapter? God is a temple-dwelling Trinity. God is Father, Son, and Holy Spirit.

We have another memorable phrase for the Trinity: it's God, his Name, and his Glory. It's a story of God in heaven, with his double presence on earth, in God's temple. It's God in heaven hearing prayer, and his Name dwelling in the temple, and his Glory filling the temple. That Old Testament pattern carries over into the New Testament. This is God and his Son and his Spirit. It is the Father in heaven, plus his Son dwelling in the church, his Spirit filling the church.

We have two models of a three-in-one God, both to do with the temple. Once, it was a stone temple. Now, God dwells in a temple of believers. The first Christians understood perfectly well that the God of Solomon's temple was alive in their experience, where it meant the church community being a temple of the Holy Spirit and of Christ. Jesus is the Name that dwells in the church. The Holy Spirit is God's Glory that fills the church.

That is why St. Paul could write this:

> *the Spirit of God dwells in you*. Anyone who does not have the Spirit of Christ does not belong to him. But if *Christ is in you* . . .
> (Rom 8:9–10)

We can remember that as a page in the Bible—Rom 8:9–10—where you can put a finger and say, "I can see the Trinity, the God of the temple there." It is the lived experience of believers, to know the three-in-one God of the temple in this way, dwelling in them. The temple helps us to remember that God, Son, and Spirit in one temple can only be one God.

Three Persons in One

God is three in one. It means three persons in one God: after all, God and his Name and his Glory are not three gods! These three can only ever be one God: it's his own Name and his own Glory. They cannot be pulled apart, split off, and separated to make three gods. God does not give his Glory away, or his Name! We have learned this easy-to-remember way to explain it:

> God + his Name + his Glory = one God
> This is a three-in-one God.
> *Therefore:*
> God + his Son + his Spirit = one God
> This is the same God: a three-in-one God.

The Old Testament helps us to remember that God is one. The New Testament helps us to remember that God is one in three distinct persons who communicate to each other. It is three, and they are one God.

The three are distinct from each other in Solomon's temple too: it is God's Name present in the temple on earth, whereas God is in heaven hearing prayers at the same time. This is what we have found then: God, his Name, and his Glory are three persons, not one. They are a three-in-one God.

Some strange ideas occur if we forget that there are three persons in the Trinity. An old heresy shows how people can get it wrong. Its mistake is in saying that Jesus is the Father; and that Jesus is also the Holy Spirit—as if there was only one person and not three. This is nonsense. For instance, we see in the Bible where Jesus and God the Father talk to each other, one to another. Saying that Jesus and the Father are the same person is a mistake; it is the opposite of what the Trinity is about. It is about relationships between the Father and the Son and the Holy Spirit.

The right thing to say is that they are distinct from each other. So, believing in the Trinity means we see that the Son is not the Father. The Father knows who is his Son. And the Son knows who is his Father. They never get this confused.

And the Holy Spirit itself knows that it is not the Father or the Son. All three of them know who they are and how they differ from each other. They are three persons—Father, Son, and Holy Spirit.

Now, when we correctly lay our picture of the Father, Son, and Spirit on top of our picture of God, his Name, and Glory, our vision of them is clear. It is like laying a see-through picture on top of another picture. On one sheet you can see where an artist has drawn the outlines of the people in the picture. You can see through it, and see underneath that on the other sheet the artist has colored them in. So with the two see-through sheets on top of each other, you see the outlines of the people nicely colored in, and you can see the whole picture properly.

It's like that. When we lay our picture of the Father, Son, and Spirit on top of our picture of God, his Name, and his Glory, now we see the picture better. We have mapped Father, Son, and Spirit on top of God, his Name, and his Glory. Now it is clearer than ever. What do we see? Since we know that Father, Son, and Spirit are three personal presences, now we see more clearly that God, Name, and Glory are the same three personal presences. And we see something else. Since we know that God, his Name, and his Glory are one God, now we see more clearly that Father, Son, and Spirit are the one God. The same one.

St. Jerome wrote:

> ... a man, baptized in the name of the Father and the Son and the Holy Ghost, becomes a temple of the Lord, and that while the old abode is destroyed a new shrine is built for the Trinity ...

These early church ideas go back to Jesus, and Jesus' way of talking about these things goes back to Solomon's temple.

In this book, we will cover a lot more ground. If you have ever wondered if the Father and the Son are equal or not, that will be answered. If you have wondered how Jesus could be both man and God at the same time, that will be answered. We will use what we have learned about the Name and the Glory to explain this. It is something that can be understood. It is not a mystery beyond reason.

This first chapter has given you all the basics you need to better understand the Trinity. It is time to pick up the threads of the story in more detail and depth, time to follow a treasure trail in Jerusalem two thousand years ago. It begins with Jesus' disciples harking after Israel's glory days and waiting for a miracle. It is the story of Pentecost, in the book of Acts written by St. Luke.

Reflection and Application

- Why is it right to say that, for the Father and his Son and Spirit, the church is their temple?
- Why does it matter to show that the Trinity is only one God?
- How can talking about the three-in-one God of the temple help you to be more confident talking about the Trinity to people?

- How might you show a Muslim that the Trinity makes sense when seen as the Trinity of God, his Name and Glory? How could you show a Muslim that this is one God, not three gods?
- How might you show a Jehovah's Witness that the Trinity makes sense when seen as God, his Name, and Glory? How could you show them that this is one God and three persons?
- Using the Trinity of God, his Name, and his Glory, how might you show a Jewish person that the Trinity looks just like the God of Solomon's temple, the God of Israel?
- Can you find a page in the Old Testament and the New Testament where you can see the three-in-one God?

Chapter 2

The 3D Launch of the Church

1. WAITING FOR DAYS OF HOPE AND GLORY

Just weeks after the death and resurrection of Jesus, in a house in Jerusalem, his core followers, the faithful few, were gathered. Luke's Acts says there were about 120 of them there (Acts 1:15), just like there were 120 priests sounding trumpets at the dedication of Solomon's temple (2 Chr 5:12–14).

A new movement was ready to be born, one that would take believers into the streets with Jesus' message. Its momentum has led Christians with an amazing degree of self-sacrifice to bring free assistance to the needy in remote places without hope of earthly reward. All of this momentum can be traced back to one unique day.

Jesus' Jewish disciples were patiently waiting, as he had instructed them. Waiting for God to do something that would bring a new hope to his people Israel. Expectations were high.

Some had believed it would mean the corrupt ruling elite in their land would be brought down. This elite included one of the notorious Herods and his heavies; and the cruel soldiers from the Roman Empire and their collaborators; money-grabbing priests and their cronies who dominated the Jerusalem temple. This whole system, this rotten den of thieves, would be brought crashing down. With such a victory over evil, Israel would be in charge of its own future in its own land again, practicing God's true religion, with Jesus as King. The peoples of the world would be impressed and come to worship Israel's God.

At least some of the disciples had thought it would be like that. But Jesus had begun to challenge any suggestion that his people's problems could be answered that way. He also opposed any suggestion that a violent solution would do. There would be a new way, one that would still fulfill everything that Israel was truly meant to be, a shining light to the world, that would show God's pattern for how to live. Avoiding violence, Jesus had gone against the tide of people's expectations. Jesus made sure he brought his disciples round to his way of thinking.

Like other religious Jews, they knew what the ancient glory days of Israel had looked like. We need to know about them.

The Glory Days

Solomon—King David's son—had built a shining stone temple a thousand years before Christ was wearing out sandals. A unique building, a great achievement of a great king, a house for their God to dwell in. Not only did Solomon get the job of temple-building started and finished; it was he who prayed the prayer that officially handed over to God this sanctuary. This was the stuff to make a nation proud. These were stories that Israelite parents would tell their children, and their children's children. They told it like this—the scene of Solomon and the temple:

> Then the temple of the LORD was filled with a cloud... for the glory of the LORD filled the temple of God. (2 Chr 5:13–14 NIV)

> Then Solomon said, "The LORD has said that he would dwell in thick darkness. But I have built you an exalted house, a place for you to dwell in forever." (6:1–2)

God replied, naming his presence that would dwell in the temple—"the Name":

> "I have chosen Jerusalem for my Name to be there." (6:6 NIV)

Solomon prays towards heaven again, taking God's point that the Name would come to the temple:

> "May your eyes be open towards this temple day and night, this place of which you said you would put your Name there... Hear from heaven, your dwelling place." (6:20–21 NIV)

> "Now arise, O LORD God, and come to your resting place." (6:41 NIV)

> As soon as Solomon finished his prayer, fire came down from heaven... and the glory of the LORD filled the temple. (7:1)

In a spectacular fashion, God had moved into the house. But then God spoke, saying he would continue to hear prayers in heaven, and famously said this about tough times ahead:

> ... if my people who are called by my name humble themselves and pray and seek my face and turn from their wicked ways, then I will hear from heaven and will forgive their sin and will heal their land. (7:14)

As the temple was the dwelling place of the Name, God had an extra comment to make to Solomon:

> I have chosen and consecrated this temple so that my Name may be there forever... But if you turn away... I will uproot Israel from my land, which I have given them, and will reject this temple which I have consecrated for my Name. (7:16–20 NIV)

It is a fascinating end to an account of a conversation between God and Solomon.

When that great fiery light, God's Glory, hit the temple, it shone so brightly that the temple's priests bowed their faces to the ground. That was spectacular enough, and God had clearly signaled that he had made this house his own. What was really significant to the lives of ordinary Israelites was this: it meant that God's people would be able to come near to him, closer to his presence, in the courts of the temple.

With the mysterious Name being ushered into the house by the fiery Glory, *the temple had become the house of God, his Name, and his Glory.* These were Israel's glory days.

2. HOW THE CHRISTIAN COMMUNITY BECAME A TEMPLE AT PENTECOST

Who was living in the Jerusalem temple in the days of Jesus' disciples? And, come to that, how can we be sure that Jerusalem's temple mattered to them at all?

Answers come quickly when we see how the disciples' patient waiting was rewarded, during the Jewish religious festival of Pentecost.

Jesus' disciples wanted the sacred experience of knowing the true God in the true temple. They were sure that this would be part of how he was going to restore the glory days to Israel. But they had been learning from Jesus that things were going to happen in a new way, without anyone admiring the slabs of a stone house.

It was the day of Pentecost. It was the birth of an era with a new kind of temple: people as *temples of the Holy Spirit*. It meant every Christian could say, "My body is a temple." The true God would have his home in people's hearts, not only in a stone building. It would change their world forever.

As we have seen, this day is reported in the Bible's book of Acts like this:

> And suddenly there came from heaven a noise like a violent rushing wind, and it filled the whole house where they were sitting. And there appeared to them tongues as of fire distributing themselves, and they rested on each one of them. And they were all filled with the Holy Spirit . . . (Acts 2:2–4 NIV)

This scene scatters clues in our path, and one by one we will gather them.

To appreciate why these events are so significant for understanding the three-in-one God, and how it made them temples of the Holy Spirit, we need to take a step back and learn more about the disciples' thoughts—especially about temples.

3. TOUGH QUESTIONS FOR THE FIRST CHRISTIANS TO ANSWER

A thousand years before the days of Jesus' disciples, King Solomon got his answer to prayer. As we read, God made his newly built temple into his dwelling place, his home on earth. It was remembered as the day the Glory came, what some call the Shekinah Glory, meaning the Glory that dwells.[1] Jesus' disciples were familiar with these memories.

But God was not limited to a stone temple. God's own spiritual presence could go further by dwelling in a church community, because a community could expand far beyond the size of a stone temple and take God's presence out into the whole world. They were walking talking temples.

It was a revolutionary way for them to think about the temple and about themselves. But they could make a case for it. Apart from a temple, there were other ways of having a sacred space. A community could be a place for God to come to. He could live inside each person's body as a perfectly proper temple. If this was true, Jerusalem's temple was not now

---

1. Shekinah means "dwelling." The Name and the Glory both dwell in the temple. So it would be right to speak of the Shekinah Name and the Shekinah Glory. The Shekinah Name is the Name dwelling in the temple—think of Jesus. And the Shekinah Glory is the Glory dwelling in the temple—think of the Holy Spirit.

unique as it had once been. That was incredibly offensive to Jerusalem's religious authorities, because their stone temple was uniquely special at the heart of their whole way of life.

Who was responsible for spreading these ideas? It was Jesus of Nazareth in the first place. All of these ideas were around when he was wearing out footwear in Galilee, and he personally made sure his disciples got a hold of it. Of course there was nothing wrong with a stone temple so long as the true God was dwelling in it. But an even better temple would be a walking, talking one.

Becoming Temples

But what had they expected it to look like when it happened, when they became temples of the Holy Spirit? Did they think it would be anything like Solomon's day when the Glory filled his stone temple? The disciples were learning by first-hand experience at Pentecost.

It was a momentous spiritual experience. By comparison, at Herod's great stone temple up the road in Jerusalem, nothing quite like this seemed to be happening. So let's do the detective work on the clues it has scattered before us.

Pentecost Clues: Tongues of Fire Stand for the Glory

This is the first big clue to the three-in-one God in the book of Acts. Luke's words present to us the Glory-style tongues of fire as a sign of the Holy Spirit's presence:

> And there appeared to them tongues as of fire distributing themselves, and they rested on each one of them. And they were all filled with the Holy Spirit (Acts 2: 3–4 NIV)

They had become temples of the Holy Spirit. The Holy Spirit had got inside them, it filled them. It is a scene of the same kind as the Glory filling the old temple. There is no mistaking who Luke has identified the Glory with. With his account of Pentecost, Luke has locked the Glory onto the Holy Spirit.

As we saw earlier, the respected historian Tom Wright puts it like this:

> When Solomon built the Temple and dedicated it, it was filled with the cloud which veiled God's presence . . . And Luke, writing the story, wants us to think: this is the glory of the Lord coming back to fill the Temple![2]

2. Wright, "New Law."

You needed the Glory to come to confirm the launch of a new temple. Now the Glory-style fire—the tongues of fire—was doing just that, by resting on them.

Just like the Glory fire coming upon Solomon's temple, the tongues of fire came and rested over the disciples. Just like the Glory filled the temple, the Spirit filled them as mini-temples. So that is a clue in the bag about the Glory. The sight of the Glory is a sign of the presence of the Holy Spirit. Why wouldn't it be? So, what does this tell us about the Trinity? Well, if we are checking Scripture in depth to see if God, and his Name and his Glory—the three-in-one God—are the same as the Father, and his Son, and his Spirit, one of the three links gets a tick here: the Glory-Spirit link.

This story is celebrated by churches around the world every year on the anniversary of Pentecost. But this was a big change in the disciples' culture. The Jerusalem temple had represented a past Golden Age and their greatest hopes. Jesus wanted to set their sights higher. Aware of their thoughts one time, he said, "something greater than the temple is here" (Matt 12:6). To push the point, he also said, "something greater than Solomon is here" (Matt 12:42). He wanted them to raise their hopes to new heights for a new future. He was taking the idea of the temple to a whole new level.

4. CLUE AFTER CLUE ABOUT THE GLORY

The Holy Spirit is linked with the Glory. If we have any doubts about whether this is really a convincing link, we should do what a detective should do before packing up our bags and moving onto the next part of the trail: check it against other evidence.

The evidence comes from further back in time, a thousand years before Solomon. We find it in the days of Moses, the great Israelite guided by God's presence who led his people out of slavery in Egypt towards the promised land. Incredibly, there is a close relation between things Moses saw and what the disciples saw at Pentecost.

Pentecost Clues: the Glory Rested on the Mountain

Here is Luke's Pentecost scene again, and notice the words in italics:

> And suddenly there came from heaven a noise like a violent rushing wind, and it filled the whole house where they were sitting. And there appeared to them tongues as of *fire* distributing

themselves, and they *rested on* each one of them. And they were all *filled* with the Holy Spirit . . . (Acts 2:2–4 NIV)

With a bit of detective work, we can see why it matters that the fire "rested" on them. We know where Luke got the word from, and how it has to do with the Glory.

In the story of Moses, we read that "*the glory* of the LORD *rested on* Mount Sinai" (Exod 24:16 NASB). In a strong echo of this, Solomon invited God to come to his "*resting* place" in the temple. It's no coincidence that the word "rested" crops up another time, at Pentecost. It is used like a code word telling us that the tongues of fire—resting on the disciples—were a new sighting of the Glory.

The word "rest" goes back to the very idea of a temple being God's home on earth. If a person rests in their home, their dwelling, then it means much indeed, to say that God does so at his home. Sinai, where God's Glory "rested," served as a place where God would be "at home." Moses could go and meet with him there. The mountain called Sinai was a sort of temple.[3] Indeed, according to Exod 15:17, a mountain could be what a temple is, a sacred place where God wants to dwell. And there is a pattern we have seen before: God comes down to his temple but at the same time is still in heaven too. The Bible tells the story: "You came down on Mount Sinai and spoke with them from heaven" (Neh 9:13). God is in two places at once, which is always the case when God has a temple, dwelling on earth, speaking from heaven:

- "You came down on Mount Sinai [*on earth*] and
- spoke with them from *heaven*."

Sinai and the church community are both kinds of temples and are resting places for what?—for God's Glory. Here is how those pictures match up:

Acts 2:2–4	Exod 24:16
tongues as of *fire*	the *Glory* of the LORD
rested on	rested on
each one of them.	Mount Sinai.

It happened more than once. The Glory also appeared over Moses' handmade temple, the ritual tent called the "tabernacle." The Glory rested over it (Exod 40:38).

---

3. Leithart, *House for my Name*, 83–84.

Carry that thought over to Pentecost, and you have the meaning of the tongues of fire resting on the disciples. This was the Glory and they were the new temple.

Pentecost Clues: the Glory Filled the Tabernacle

There is another piece of evidence we can check this against. At Pentecost, when the tongues of fire rested on them, "they were all *filled* with the Holy Spirit." We know another inspiration for Luke's choice of words, about being "filled." It's to do with the Glory again.

In the story of Moses, we read that "the glory of the LORD *filled* the tabernacle" (Exod 40:34). Once more, it's no coincidence. At Pentecost, it is used like another code word telling us that the Holy Spirit *fills* just as the Glory *fills*. Here is how these pictures match up:

Acts 2:2–4	Exod 40:34
they were all	the tabernacle was
filled	*filled*
with the Holy Spirit	with the Glory

In a way, the stories have got "'temple" written all over them. The disciples' Pentecost is one big echo of these ancient scenes. It is not as if Luke didn't know this when he was writing it down.

Step by step, God and his Glory are coming into better focus in the story of Pentecost. The Glory is accounted for in person in the Holy Spirit.

Church Life Today

This Pentecost link between the Glory and the Holy Spirit has never been forgotten by the church. Many Christians today ask the Holy Spirit to fill them. And while they may not literally expect to see the Glory-fire in their church meetings, they do express their excitement about the Holy Spirit with that kind of language. Hymns and songs about receiving the Spirit picture it as the Glory coming, including a well-known Pentecost hymn.[4]

To know God's presence as an inner experience, to know the Holy Spirit filling them and the Glory resting on them: this is something that Moses and King Solomon would have longed to experience. The disciples' Pentecost event was all of that, a revolution, compared to what happened

---

4. Booth, "Thou Christ."

in the stone-built house of God in the older days. The dwelling place of the Glory no longer needed to be built by hands.

5. THE BREATH OF GOD

On the treasure trail leading to God and his Name and his Glory, we are picking up new clues that Luke scattered in his report of Pentecost. Notice the words in italics:

> And suddenly there came from heaven a noise like a violent *rushing wind*, and it filled the whole house where they were sitting. And there appeared to them *tongues as of fire* distributing themselves, and they rested on each one of them. And they were all filled with the Holy *Spirit* and began to speak with other tongues, as the Spirit was giving them utterance. (Acts 2:2–4 NIV)

Sometimes when you turn familiar evidence over in your hands, a new clue can jump out at you. Here we come back to where Luke wrote "tongues of fire" and "rushing wind."[5] We know an inspiration for this choice of words. This is from the book of the prophet Isaiah:

> See, the Name of the LORD comes from afar,
> with burning anger and dense clouds of smoke;
> his lips are full of wrath,
> and his *tongue is a consuming fire*.
> His *breath* is like a *rushing torrent* ... (Isa 30:27–28 NIV)

There are striking similarities with Luke's report.

In Isaiah, the "tongue is a consuming fire."[6] In Acts, there are "tongues of fire."

In Isaiah, there is a rushing torrent of "breath." In Acts, the noise heard is like a "rushing wind."

In Isaiah, the Name of the Lord with the rushing breath and tongues of fire comes from "afar." In Acts, heaven is the source.

---

5. See Beale, *Temple and the Church's Mission*, 205.

6. See also 1 En 14:8–22, a book popular in ancient times, mentioning tongues of fire in a different way.

Pentecost Clues: the Divine Breath is the Holy Spirit

Let's start with what Isaiah calls the "breath" and Luke calls the "rushing wind." Something that these words have in common is a connection with the Holy Spirit.

The Holy Spirit is sometimes called the Breath of God. There are even hymns about the Holy Spirit such as "Breathe on me, Breath of God."[7] The churchgoer who has sung these songs has already spoken out loud this connection with the Holy Spirit and the divine Breath.

Another thing the words have in common is that "breath" and "spirit" and "wind" are one and the same word in the languages in which the Bible was written.[8]

If we place these things side-by-side, the similarities stack up like this, linking the Spirit, the Glory and Breath of God:

At Pentecost (Acts 2:1-4)	In Isaiah (Isa 30:27-28)
the divine Breath, the Spirit	the breath
with a noise like a rushing wind	like a rushing torrent
and with the tongues of fire	with the fiery tongue
from heaven	coming from afar

Pentecost Clues: the Word "LORD"

We come now back to the Name:

> See, *the Name* of the LORD comes from afar,
> with burning anger and dense clouds of smoke;
> his lips are full of wrath,
> and *his tongue* is a consuming fire.
> *His breath* is like a rushing torrent ... (Isa 30:27–28 NIV)

---

7. Hatch, "Breathe on me."

8. The word "spirit" describes not only the Holy Spirit, but the Father and Son too. "God is spirit" (John 4:24). In talking about Jesus, the connection between "spirit" and "breath" is seen in 1 Cor 15:45. The apostle Paul writes that Jesus has become "life-giving breath" to believers. (Many translations render this "a life-giving spirit" which muddies the meaning.) It is a picture of Jesus breathing life into his people, a mirror image of the Genesis story: God in the Garden of Eden breathing life into Adam. The first Adam *received* God's breath. The last Adam (that is, Jesus) is the *giver* of God's breath. (Elsewhere, Jesus and the Holy Spirit are included in the identity of Yahweh, setting them apart from created "spirits" such as angels.)

One of the clues about the Name in this quote from the book of Isaiah is the four-letter word in capitals, "LORD." It is to do with God's personal name. Isaiah tells us this name—but it is not at first obvious in some Bible translations.

Sometimes, a clue on a trail consists of code words. To crack this particular code, the key is this: in this translation, "LORD" is written in capital letters. It is a message to those in the know, saying that when Isaiah wrote it in his original language, he wrote down the personal name of God, a name which is also made up of four letters: *YHWH*. Where we read "LORD" in capital letters, it means that the Hebrew word is *YHWH*. It is God's personal name in the Old Testament. If we spell it out as we say it, we usually write it "Yahweh" (or "Jehovah" in older English).[9]

The first line actually tells us that "the Name of Yahweh comes from afar" and we will see how very useful this is shortly.

If we put Isaiah's words under the spotlight, there are three things we can tell apart:

1. Yahweh ("the LORD")
2. the Name of Yahweh
3. the fiery tongue and breath

Once again, this is a picture of the three-in-one God.

As for the first two, we need to tell them apart. We wouldn't have a "Name of Yahweh" if we didn't have a Yahweh. The "Name of Yahweh" exists because Yahweh exists, so let's keep an eye on them as two things. Let's do detective work. Let's ask the questions: why doesn't Isaiah say simply that "Yahweh comes from afar"? Why was it necessary for him, instead, to say "the *Name of Yahweh* comes from afar"? Isn't that a peculiar thing to say?

In Scripture, there are times like this where you can tell apart "the Name of Yahweh" from Yahweh as two distinct persons. It is the "Name of Yahweh" who is coming, as distinct from Yahweh.

In this Scripture, the Name has personal characteristics that sound like the way the Bible talks about God—with imaginative words like a poem, not literal, not like a photograph. The Name's mouth is the focus of the picture: his "lips are full of wrath," his "tongue is a consuming fire," and his "breath is like a rushing torrent." It is the Name who has "burning anger."[10] The

---

9 This is explained in the introduction in the NIV translation, for example.

10. In the Targum of Isa 30:27, the personal characteristics of "the Name" are given even more color, saying that the Name will slay the mighty, for instance. Uzziel, *Chaldee Paraphrase*, 101.

Name is described in a pretty fearsome way to show him putting Israel's archenemy, Assyria, on the run.

Although "the Name" can be found many times in the Bible, churches hardly talk about this fact. But if we dig deeper, we can uncover a lot of information about him.

We have been thinking about the true identity of the "the Name of Yahweh" as being Jesus. There is another hint of that here. This is because we should expect "the Name of Yahweh" to be behind the scenes at Pentecost, the rushing noise, the tongues of fire, all signs of the Name at work. And here is how Luke tells it, locking the Name onto Jesus. He reports that when these strange things are happening in Jerusalem on the day of Pentecost, Jesus is behind the scenes in heaven causing it. Peter says that Jesus "has received from the Father the promised Holy Spirit and has poured out what you now see and hear" (Acts 2:33 NIV). We'd expect it to be the Name doing this. It's Jesus doing it. The Name is being revealed as Jesus.

Jesus is pouring out the Holy Spirit from heaven, and immediately on earth the disciples are filled with the Spirit. This is immediate because, according to the Bible, heaven is not some place far away from us. Heaven and earth are joined together, not completely separate.

Do we have enough evidence there to unmask "the Name" as Jesus? Yes, but if there is any doubt, we can check this against the details about the "breath," and its link to the Spirit. You don't get the "breath" without someone to breathe it out. As for Isaiah, it is the Name who breathes out the breath, the rushing breath. As for the church era, who breathes out the Spirit into Christians? A check in the Scriptures tells us exactly who: Jesus. In that preview of the Pentecost experience that we saw earlier, he does exactly that:

> he breathed on them and said to them, "Receive the Holy Spirit."
> (John 20:22 ESV)

There is the divine Breath, coming from his mouth. Just as from the Name's mouth. The biblical truth is that breathing out the divine Breath, the Holy Spirit, into the church, isn't something that just anyone can do, because it is God's Breath for God to breathe out. In the Bible it is God's Name (in Isaiah) and God's son Jesus who do this.[11] So, we started by seeing that, at Pentecost, someone is breathing out the Holy Spirit upon the church. We have confirmation that it is Jesus, the only candidate to be the Name. What's more, the same John even calls Jesus "the Name":

---

11. Otherwise, the nearest thing to that is when God breathes out the breath of life into Adam in Gen 2:7. But that is not necessarily the same thing as breathing out the Breath of God, the Holy Spirit.

It was on behalf of the Name that they went out (3 John 7, this author's translation)

To recap, you don't get the tongues of fire without the Name being behind it (in the Isaiah Scripture). In parallel, at Pentecost, you don't get the tongues of fire without Jesus being behind it. The new and old scenes are alike. We can see our checks about Jesus and the Name at a glance:

Jesus at Pentecost (Acts 2:1–4 and 32–33)	The Name in Isaiah (Isa 30:27–28)
The Father's	Yahweh's
Son	Name
pours out the divine Breath, the Spirit	pours out the divine Breath
with a noise like a rushing wind	like a rushing torrent
and with the tongues of fire	with the fiery tongue
from heaven	coming from afar

The prophet Isaiah foresaw it. The disciples experienced it. The three-in-one God is found in the pattern:

1) Yahweh is	the Father
2) the Name of Yahweh is	the Son
3) the Glory-style fiery tongue and breath are a sign of	the Holy Spirit

If we may sum up the answer to this question: what is the relation of the "Name of Yahweh" to Yahweh? We can answer that it lines up with the "Son of God" to "God." Like this:

Yahweh	God
the Name of Yahweh	the Son of God

One thing that troubles some Trinity-seekers is this idea that Jesus is "God." But the evidence has so far served up two of the reasons why Jesus is known as God to Christians:

- Jesus—as God—breathes out the Breath of God upon people, the Holy Spirit.[12] Only God can breathe out the Breath of God—his own breath. Jesus does so, and it follows that he is, in a vital sense, to be considered God.

---

12. More evidence is given in Peter's speech. In Acts 2:17–18, it is God who says "I will pour out my Spirit." The Greek word for "I will pour out" is *ekcheo*. In verse 33, using that selfsame word, Peter says that it is Jesus who has "poured" the Spirit out. Therefore, we take Jesus to be God in action there.

- Along with that, no one but God is entitled to be identified as the "Name" of God. It is quite a revelation that Jesus has this identity. It follows that he is God in a very real sense.

And there are more clues to Jesus being the Name still to be gathered up. We will see this as Luke describes that famous controversy that erupts in the story of Peter and John at the Jerusalem temple. There are more clues to be found.

6. A TEMPLE FOR MY NAME

On the trail of God, his Name, and his Glory, one clue in our possession is the biblical principle that there has to be a true temple for the Name to be present in. The Bible often speaks of this:

> build a house for my Name. (2 Sam 7:13 NIV)
> a dwelling for my Name. (Neh 1:9 NIV)

The Israelites
> built you a sanctuary there for your name . . . for your name is in this temple. (2 Chr 20:6–9 NJB)

That had been important in the Old Testament era. After Pentecost, after "temple" developed from being a stone building to being a church community, new stories carry a similar meaning—a true temple is a home for the Name. Luke takes this vital code word for the presence in the temple and locks it onto Jesus.

Peter and John at the Temple

It started not very long after Pentecost. Peter and John got caught up in a controversy about Jesus and Jerusalem's temple. The story is in Acts, chapters 3 through 5. We briefly touched on it. Let's go deeper.

A disabled beggar being carried to the temple is healed "in the name of Jesus" through the actions of Peter and John. The healed man's excitement attracts a crowd in the temple courts.

Peter tells the crowd that the man was healed through the name of Jesus, and that Jesus has been raised from the dead. Surprisingly, Peter and John get taken off and locked in jail for preaching this, but are released after having a word with the authorities.

Free again, they carry on as before, and the Holy Spirit sends them back to the temple to preach their message. The authorities are angered again, and the apostles are hauled in to be punished for preaching "the name of Jesus" in the temple:

> They called the apostles in and had them flogged. Then they ordered them not to speak in the name of Jesus, and let them go. The apostles left the Sanhedrin, rejoicing because they had been counted worthy of suffering disgrace for *the Name*. Day after day, in the temple courts and from house to house, they never stopped teaching and proclaiming the good news that Jesus is the Christ. (Acts 5:40–42 NIV)

The way that this speaks of "the Name" is striking enough. Here Jesus is the one Luke has in mind when he speaks of "the Name." After all that we have learned, that might not come as such a surprise. But this is just the tip of an iceberg.

Clue: "Everyone who calls on the Name of the Lord will be saved"

Let's go deeper. In Luke's report of Peter's preaching at Pentecost, after the crowd heard his explanation for the outpouring of the Holy Spirit, Peter began identifying the name of Jesus with the name of Yahweh. Here is how.

In Acts 2:21, Peter quoted the prophet Joel: "everyone who calls on the name of the Lord shall be saved" (Joel 2:32). This first clue is where Peter says "Lord." Joel's original wording in Hebrew says "Yahweh," but Jewish readers would sometimes say "Lord" instead. The Lord *is* Yahweh. And Peter says that Jesus is the Lord that Joel is talking about. But could Peter really be saying that the Lord Yahweh is Jesus? Yes, he could. Peter locks the word "Lord" onto Jesus: "God has made him both Lord and Christ, this Jesus whom you crucified" (Acts 2:36).[13]

"Everyone who calls on the name of the Lord will be saved," says Peter. Whether you call him Yahweh or Jesus, it is the same Lord. The name of Yahweh is taken up in the name of Jesus. This is how it matches up:

---

13. Here is a trinitarian pattern: Jesus is identified as Yahweh God; and at the same time, the talk is about what "God" did to Jesus (making him Lord and raising him from the dead). This is typical of how the Bible makes its distinction between the Father in heaven and his presence on earth. It is the same sort of arrangement as when God chose a home for his Name and put his Name in the temple. The effect of God acting towards his earthly presence is a common thread.

Joel 2:32 says	*Peter says*
"Everyone who calls on the Name of Yahweh will be saved"	"Everyone who calls on the Name of the Lord will be saved"
	"God has made this Jesus Lord"

That's not all. A phrase such as "everyone who calls on *the name of the Lord* shall be saved" (Acts 2:21) fits a bigger picture of connecting the Name of the Lord and the Name of Jesus. For instance, "they were baptized in *the name of the Lord* Jesus" (Acts 19:5).

Some of the devoutly religious—and frankly a bit touchy—people in Peter's audience may have been shocked and surprised to hear Peter using Scripture like this. But with little or no thought for his own safety, he presses the point further, mentioning the healing of the beggar:

> by the name of Jesus Christ of Nazareth, whom you crucified, whom God raised from the dead—by him this man is standing before you well. This Jesus is the stone that was rejected by you, the builders, which has become the cornerstone. And there is salvation in no-one else, for there is no other name under heaven given among men by which we must be saved. (Acts 4:10–12 ESV)

Peter is emphatic. He speaks of Jesus' name as the *only* name that saves people. In the light of Joel's words that were about Yahweh's name being the name that saves people, Peter is really nailing his colors to the mast. For Peter's purposes, the name of Jesus is equivalent to the name of Yahweh.

So in many ways, the phrase "the Name of Yahweh" is locked onto Jesus. Right at the start of the church, Jesus is identified with the Name.

Twelves

Earlier we saw how Luke's telling of Peter and John's adventure in the temple uses the word "temple" twelve times, and "Name" twelve times in connection with Jesus. In connection with Jesus, the word Name (the Greek word *onoma*) comes up in phrases like this: "in the name of Jesus Christ"; "by the name of Jesus"; "through the name of your holy servant Jesus." With his twelves, Luke believed he was weaving something special into the story. It was all part of saying that God, his Name, and his Glory have relocated from the stone temple to the church community. Let's go further than earlier.

Jewish readers knew the words temple and Name belonged together—that God had "a temple built for my Name." The number twelve was loaded with Jewish meanings too. Here are key facts about it in the Bible. Famously there were twelve tribes of Israel who were descended from Israel's twelve father figures. Jesus followed the pattern in choosing twelve apostles (including Peter and John), which was like putting a flag in the ground to announce a fresh start for God's people. That is why Rev 21:14 describes the promise of a "New Jerusalem" like this: "the wall of the city had twelve foundations, and on them were the twelve names of the twelve apostles of the Lamb" ("Lamb" being a title for Jesus).

Twelve, the number of apostles: it was an important symbol of hope for the church community, in believing that God's work was restarting. (Matt 19:28 and Exod 24:4 make this link obvious.) So they were in a new era. It was time for Israelites to re-commit themselves, united, to God's work, with the twelve disciples of Jesus blazing the trail. Twelve was an important number to them.

Luke is leading us to think not only about the Name in terms of Jesus, but also about the temple in terms of Jesus' twelve disciples. So although he uses the word temple twelve times, it is not Herod's temple that Luke is keen on. The believers are the temple he cares about, filled with the Spirit, with the Glory resting on them. The words Name and temple remind us that the life of Israel in this way should include a true temple dwelled in by the Name. It is the *name of Jesus* that Luke is placing in such a temple.

And, as if the sequence of twelve wasn't enough in itself, Luke gives us a little more in the way he crowns the story with the twelfth and final occurrence of Name. Coming exactly at the climax of the drama, it differs from the eleven before it, as it reads simply "the Name."

It's a nice little finish to his name/temple game, but that's not all. It coins a phrase—"suffering disgrace for the Name"—a phrase that passed into common use in early Christianity. That's the sort of impact most writers can only dream of having. For centuries afterwards, Christians used his phrase—"suffering for the Name"—as a tribute to those who were paying a heavy price for following Jesus. (We will see a few examples of this later.)

Here is how it is wrapped up and sealed in the twelfth and final "temple" and "name":

> They called the apostles in and had them flogged. Then they ordered them not to speak in the name of Jesus, and let them go. The apostles left the Sanhedrin, rejoicing because they had been counted worthy of *suffering disgrace for the Name*. Day after day, in the temple courts and from house to house, they

never stopped teaching and proclaiming the good news that
Jesus is the Christ. (Acts 5:40-42 NIV)

The trail is giving up its secrets to us. Luke planted these things in his work to be found. He is doing it not to show off his deep knowledge of the Old Testament. He is triggering us to think about Jerusalem's temple, built for God's Name. And it's a new message. Thinking of "the Name" as present in the old stone temple finds a match in thinking of "the Name" as to do with Jesus, who—what's more—was now spiritually present with his twelve disciples, and with all of the people of his church.

This new temple was the church community, built on a foundation of the twelve disciples; with the name of Jesus in the heart of their group. And the message doesn't end there: it's about Jesus living in the hearts of all Christians to this day.

This is where we have got to. There is no mistaking whom Luke has identified the Glory with. With his account of Pentecost, Luke has locked *the Glory* onto the Holy Spirit. And Luke has locked *the Name* onto Jesus. The words Glory and the Name are now fixed onto the Holy Spirit and Jesus. We are seeing the three-in-one God of Solomon's temple rediscovered.

7. CLUE: THE STORY OF STEPHEN AND THE GLORY

Stephen: one of the most celebrated disciples in the book of Acts, brave and not afraid of controversy. Despite strong pressure against him, he preached passionately that Jerusalem's temple could not be regarded as an adequate temple. This was one more thing that the temple's religious authorities did not want to hear. This is the story of how Stephen became the first Christian martyr.

Luke says Stephen was full of the Holy Spirit—he was a temple of the Holy Spirit (Acts 6:5; 7:55). As he reports Stephen's dying moments, it says Stephen was able to see into the spiritual realms—he saw the Glory in the true heavenly sanctuary. We can discover more about the three-in-one God from this.

Like Jesus before him, Stephen faced wrongful accusations about what he stood for. Stephen never said, as some of his accusers claimed, that Jesus threatened to destroy the temple and traditions of the Jewish people. Far from it. Jesus had said that enemies would destroy the temple. There was a negative judgment to be made about Jerusalem's temple, but not in the way Stephen's accusers told the story.

Forced to face his accusers, he delivered a strong reply. The very first words from Stephen's mouth go like this: "Hear me, brethren and fathers! The God of glory appeared to our father Abraham" (Acts 7:2).

It is fitting that the first thing mentioned in Stephen's speech is "the God of glory." Like bookends, at the other end of Stephen's story, the Glory of God will be seen by him.

He gives his Christian thoughts on the temple in Acts 7:46–50, with an important mention of King David

> who enjoyed God's favor and asked that he might provide a dwelling place for the God of Jacob. But it was Solomon who built the house for Him. However, the Most High does not live in houses made by men. As the prophet says: "Heaven is my throne, and the earth is my footstool. What kind of house will you build for me? says the Lord. Or where will my resting place be?" (NIV)

There is something of a riddle here, as to whether God was or was not in the house built for him. It is solved only when we understand the three-in-one God.

God the Father was not seeking a "resting place" on earth for himself, but for his Name. In this way, God's presence had been in Solomon's temple (2 Kgs 19:14–15). The visible assurance of this was that Solomon's temple was filled by the Glory.

But Stephen obviously held to the church teaching that the stone temple was far from being the limit of God's plan for his presence on earth. Stephen himself was an example of the new kind of temple, being a man filled with the Holy Spirit.

We don't know if he finished what he wanted to say. He met a swift end. In his dying moments, Stephen's intriguing revelation was this:

> But he, full of the Holy Spirit, gazed into heaven and saw the glory of God, and Jesus standing at the right hand of God. And he said, "Behold, I see the heavens opened, and the Son of Man standing at the right hand of God." (Acts 7:55–56 ESV)

This snapshot of heaven brings into focus so much of what we have learned. The triune God is there before Stephen's eyes as heaven is opened. In the Glory we have a sign of the presence of the Holy Spirit—Luke has established that at Pentecost. We also have Jesus present.[14] And God the Father is enthroned in this scene—we are aware of that because it says Jesus

---

14. Beale, *Temple and the Church's Mission*, 220 n1.

is at the right hand. That means at the right hand of God's throne in heaven. As Heb 8:1–2 says, Jesus

> sat down at the right hand of the throne of the Majesty in heaven
> . . . the sanctuary, the true tabernacle set up by the Lord, not by man. (NIV)

So here we have a complete picture of the Trinity. Stephen was seeing the true heavenly temple where Father, Son, and Spirit were now present together.

Reflection and Application

- What are the signs that Pentecost is the launch of a new temple?
- In the story of Pentecost, and the story of Peter and John at the temple (Acts, chapters 3 through 5), how does the book lock the Glory onto the Holy Spirit, and lock the Name onto Jesus?
- What messages is Acts giving out by revealing the church, at Pentecost, to be a temple of the Name and the Glory?
- Should Christian communities think of themselves as a home of the Name and the Glory?

Chapter 3

A Time-Traveler's Guide to the Name, the Glory, and the Temple

1. TRAVELING BACK IN TIME

That "the Name" dwelled in Solomon's temple was a hot topic amongst the ancient Israelites. It is time to tell their story, of a time centuries before Jesus was wearing out footwear in Galilee.

As God's people, the Israelites had a very special place for the Name in their religious life:

> Sing to God, play music to his name (Ps 68:4 NJB)

We get much evidence for this in the Old Testament. In a trail of clues, it becomes clear that all roads lead to the three-in-one God. We find verses like this one:

> They burned your sanctuary to the ground;
> they defiled the *dwelling place of your Name*. (Ps 74:7 NIV)

Notice how, instead of saying God lived there, this verse says the Name lived there. This is what we are getting used to: the Name lived there in God's place; God put his Name in the temple, while in heaven God remained and heard prayers.

The temple was celebrated as the home of the Glory too:

> I love the house where you live, O LORD,
> the place *where your glory dwells*. (Ps 26:8 NIV)

It's a way of talking about the Glory that is on a par with how the Name is spoken of. They dwell as a double presence in the temple: God's double presence, in God's temple.

For many Christians today, the ancient temple barely attracts attention. But it is difficult to overdo saying just how very important it was for God's people back then. On page after page of the Old Testament, its prestige shines. It was the most sacred place for Israelites practicing their religious devotions, their prayers, and their sacrifices.

Even the story of how the temple was built takes up many pages of the Bible. We are told it was something that King David wanted to see built, but it was his son Solomon who got the green light to start. That is why we call it the temple of Solomon—although this was God's house, not King Solomon's! There, only God, his Name, and his Glory commanded worship.

The Israelites felt more confident about living up to expectations of them—as the people chosen by God's grace to become a light to the world—when his presence was in their temple. And the faithful ones mourned later when his presence was gone from the temple, heartbroken, knowing his judgment, the harsh reality of the temple being razed to the ground by Israel's enemies. That was the dramatic situation described in Ps 74.

This is one of many story twists involving the Name. As if in a time machine, we can leap backwards to an even earlier time, the days of Moses, to pick up the story from there.

Moses and the Name and the Glory

Moses had a memorable encounter with the Name and the Glory, which is told in Exod 33:18–23. Here we learn how God and his Name and his Glory could be told apart in those days. It could be one of the earliest recorded descriptions of the three-in-one nature of God in Scripture.

It was the worst of times for Moses. The Israelites had sinned before God by worshiping a false idol, a golden calf. This had left real doubts about how this holy God could be present with this wayward people any longer. With a hard journey to the promised land ahead, Moses was concerned that he would not be able to lead them effectively unless God's presence still accompanied them.

Moses wanted to actually see God, to reassure himself that God's presence was still there and would go with them. God gives Moses the promise he wants: "My Presence will go with you, and I will give you rest" (Exod 33:14 NIV).[1]

---

1. There is a strong hint of Christ's presence in this scene, as Jesus equated himself

Moses wanted more reassurance. A surprising conversation takes place between him and God.

He makes this request of God: "Now show me your Glory." But God replies to him, "I will make all my goodness pass before you, and *will summon the Name*, Yahweh . . . but you cannot see my face" (Exod 33:19).[2]

Since God summons the Name, we can tell that God and his Name are distinct from each other, but closely related. Why did God summon the Name? So that the Name would be with the Israelites.

But what is this about God's "face"? It is associated with the Glory. This was God's advice to Moses:

> There is a place near me where you may stand on a rock. *When my glory passes by*, I will put you in a cleft in the rock and cover you with my hand until I have passed by. Then I will remove my hand and you will see my back; but my face must not be seen. (Exod 33:21–23 NIV)

Something is curious in this: Moses was denied a direct view of the Glory, of God's "face." But the Name did not present the same problem.

The Name would be summoned by Yahweh God. This was God's answer. This was how a holy God solved the problem of being present with his wayward people on their journey. Yes, his Glory was too much for them to bear up close now, but his Name was not too much. The appearance of the Glory is so dramatic that it can tend to keep people at a distance, hiding their eyes. But the Name is a facet of God that his followers can feel they are getting closer to, for a closer relationship with God.[3] We hear an echo of this in Ps 75:1: "We give thanks, for your Name is near" (NIV). The Name was meant to be near.

We see the three-in-one God right here on a page of the Old Testament—in Exod 33:19–23, even if it is disguised in translations. God summons his Name. The Name is distinct from God, and the Name is distinct from the Glory too. But these three—God and his Name and his Glory—have a connection that is very close together with each other. It is a three-in-one God.

So Moses had his answer. He had learned a little earlier that the Name would be with them, as God had said, "See, I am sending an angel ahead of you to guard you along the way and to bring you to the place I have

---

with this by using God's words, saying "I will give you rest" (Matt 11:28).

2. Many translations say "proclaim my Name" instead, but without doing justice to the sense of the verse. "I will summon the Name" is in keeping with how the same Hebrew word "summon," or "call upon," is used elsewhere in the Hebrew Bible.

3. McConville, "God's 'Name' and God's 'Glory,'" 153–57.

prepared. Pay attention to him ... since *my Name is in him*" (Exod 23:20–21 NIV). It is clear—the Name would be going with them. Since the Name could dwell in an angel, it could also dwell among God's people. That much needed to be understood. The Name was needed to accompany the Israelites and dwell among them.

This is what we can take away from those scenes: God summons his Name; he calls upon his Name to go where he wants, to reassure his people; having the Name means having the presence of God in the way that God wishes.

God's wishes are laid out clearly in an account of Moses' words in Deut 16:11, with two translations of it here for added clarity:

> And rejoice before the LORD your God at *the place* he will choose as a *dwelling* for his *Name* ... (NIV)
>
> You must rejoice in the presence of Yahweh your God, in *the place* where Yahweh your God chooses to give his *name a home* ... (NJB)

Nine times in Deuteronomy, God says it: he wants a home for his Name to dwell in, for being among the people.[4] It is an upbeat message that his people should rejoice, because his presence is at home with them.

Moses and the Voice Out of the Fire

There are different roles for God in heaven and his Name on earth. In heaven, God plays a leading role in sending his presence; that is, choosing a place on earth for his Name to dwell.

The idea of God being in both heaven and earth at the same time becomes more and more important in these reports. A good impression of this can be gained from Moses' words to the Israelites about God:

> *From heaven* he made you hear his voice to discipline you.
>
> *On earth* he showed you his great fire, and *you heard his words from out of the fire.*
>
> ... he brought you *out of Egypt by his Presence* and his great strength ... (Deut 4:37 NIV)

This confirms God's presence has been with them on earth. The voice is an attention-grabber. It comes out of the midst of the fire (because that was where God's presence on earth was[5]), but it is just as much linked to heaven (because that was where God was controlling affairs from).

---

4. Deut 12:5, 11, 21; 14:23–24; 16:2, 6, 11; 26:2.
5. Wilson, *Out of the Midst of the Fire*, 68–69.

The fire, a sign of his presence, also has a link with the Glory, which was described like this:

> To the Israelites the glory of the LORD looked like a consuming fire ... (Exod 24:16–17 NIV)

It's a little glimpse of the three-in-one God: the Father in heaven, and meanwhile on earth the Glory present with his voice, with his presence.

This scene was almost like a blueprint for Solomon's temple where God listens in heaven, while his Name dwells in the fiery Glory in the stone temple.

In the desert days of Moses, life was mobile. God's presence dwelled at the tabernacle tent, and they could "up sticks" and take this tent with them all the way to the promised land. The Israelites traveled and God went with them.[6] Even after their arrival in the promised land, God's house was not permanent. A thousand years later, in King David's day, that was still the situation. God spoke about this state of affairs:

> Go and tell my servant David, 'This is what the LORD says: Are you the one to build me a house to dwell in? I have not dwelt in a house from the day I brought the Israelites up out of Egypt to this day. I have been moving from place to place with a tent as my dwelling.' (2 Sam 7:5–6 NIV)

God's words continued with a promise that King David's son Solomon would get the green light to start the building work:

> He is the one who will build a house for my Name. (2 Sam 7:13 NIV)

Without a permanent temple, the Israelites had been making their sacrifices to God in sacred places in the landscape:

> The people, however, were still sacrificing at the high places, because a temple had not yet been built for the Name of the LORD. (1 Kgs 3:2 NIV)

All that was about to change. A house would be built for the Name. So, by means of our time machine, we can leap forward to that day when King Solomon had finished building in Jerusalem. Solomon was ready to say his historic prayer. This at last was God's house. At that moment, from heaven, God speaks to Solomon:

---

6. Stevenson, *Power and Place*, 122.

> Since the day I brought my people out of Egypt, I have not chosen a city in any tribe of Israel to have a temple built for *my Name to be there*; nor have I chosen anyone to be the leader over my people Israel. But now I have chosen Jerusalem for *my Name to be there* . . . (2 Chr 6:5–6 NIV)

The opening of the temple, God's house, was a decisive step forward. Built of solid construction in a permanent place, it could offer something that Moses' tabernacle never could when it was on the move. Now God's people far and wide would know where to go in order to visit the house built for the Name—Jerusalem.

These were the glory days. 2 Chr 5–7 describes in vivid detail, right in the heart of the story of God's people, one of the most ancient descriptions of the three-in-one God of the temple. It is worth seeing these Scriptures again:

> Then the temple of the LORD was filled with a cloud . . . for the glory of the LORD filled the temple of God. (2 Chr 5:13–14 NIV)

> Then Solomon said, "The LORD has said that he would dwell in a dark cloud; I have built a magnificent temple for you, a place for you to dwell for ever." (2 Chr 6:1–2 NIV)

God said:

> I have chosen Jerusalem *for my Name to be there*. (2 Chr 6:6 NIV)

Solomon prays towards heaven again, taking God's point that the Name would come to the temple:

> "May your eyes be open towards this temple day and night, this place of which you said *you would put your Name there* . . . Hear from heaven, your dwelling place." (2 Chr 6:20–21 NIV)

> "Now arise, O LORD God, and come to your resting place." (2 Chr 6:41 NIV)

> When Solomon finished praying, fire came down from heaven . . . and *the glory of the LORD filled the temple*. (2 Chr 7:1 NIV)

God's presence had now taken up residence there. But then God replied, saying he would continue to hear prayers in heaven, with the famous promise:

> . . . if my people who are called by my name will humble themselves, and pray and seek my face and turn from their wicked

ways, then will I *hear from heaven* and will forgive their sin and heal their land. (2 Chr 7:14 NIV)

Such then are the glory days, with God in heaven and his double presence in the temple, the Name and the Glory. This spectacular temple, shining bright and beautiful in Jerusalem, became a place where creativity flourished, and new songs were written to offer praise to God and also to his Name. Here are some examples of these inspirational creations:

> *I will praise God's name* in song . . . For God will save Zion . . . and those who love his name will dwell there. (Ps 69:30–36 NJB)

> I will bow down toward Your holy *temple*. And *give thanks to Your name*. (Ps 138:2 NASB)

> We give thanks, for *your Name is near*. (Ps 75:1 NIV)

When his people were facing towards the temple building high up on the temple mount, bowing down, they gave praise to the one living in it, present in the form of his Name.[7]

> Sing to God, *play music to his name* . . . Father of orphans, defender of widows, such is God in his *holy dwelling* . . . *your temple* high above Jerusalem. (Ps 68:4–5, 29 NJB)

Ps 138 again:

> I will bow down towards your holy *temple* and will *praise your name* . . . for *you have exalted above all things your name* and your word. (Ps 138:2 NIV) (Remarkably, Jesus has since been called both "Name" and "Word.")

In the Psalms, there is plenty more celebration of the Name.[8] And the Psalms were meant to be read, or sung, in the tabernacle or temple, the most fitting place to celebrate God's presence in that era.

2. THROUGH THE KEYHOLE

We can pick up another clue about the Name at the Jerusalem temple. Every home has some furniture, not least of course a chair! But there were no beds, no chairs for visitors, in the temple sanctuary—even the priests didn't

---

7. Gieschen, "Divine Name," 122.

8. E.g., Pss 76:1–2; 96:1–8; 99:1–3; 102:12–15. Also, Pss 13:5 (NJB); 66:1; 72:17–19; 115:1 may be noted where a temple context is not explicit.

stay in it. They only worked there. It was uniquely the house of God alone, present in the form of his Name and Glory.

So, in God's house, the temple of Solomon, there was one seat only. It was the throne of God.

We need to go through the keyhole, so to speak, for a closer look at this. Surrounding the temple building there were massive courtyards, for gatherings at religious festivals. They called these the temple courts. A visitor entering the courts would find himself facing the stunning temple building, which was called the holy place. Inside the holy place, away from visitors' eyes, priests would be at work, performing their religious duties. And the priests would look to the far end, where they would see the door leading into the most sacred room, called the holy of holies.

Normally, the Jewish high priest, and he alone, would go into the holy of holies. This inner sanctum contained the ark of the covenant, that sacred box (famously in an Indiana Jones film). On top of that box was a precious thing, the mercy seat. It was the throne for Yahweh—a permanent feature in the holy of holies—like a mirror of the Father's throne in heaven. The mercy seat was flanked by two finely made models, which were in the shape of winged creatures called cherubim.

In the space above the mercy seat, the Glory of God would supernaturally make its appearance, too bright for any mortal being to gaze upon directly. Only the high priest was allowed to stand next to it. Even he could not gaze on the Glory. Its light was known as a mysterious sign of God, as if taking his seat there, through his presence.

The Name, the Temple, and the Throne

As the Name and Glory were nothing less than the earthly presence of Yahweh God himself, Yahweh himself could be said to be present:

> Hezekiah took the letter from the messengers' hands and read it; he then went up to the Temple of Yahweh and spread it out before Yahweh. Hezekiah said this prayer *in the presence of Yahweh*, 'Yahweh Sabaoth, God of Israel, *enthroned on the winged creatures*, you alone are God . . .' (2 Kgs 19:14–15 NJB)

The Old Testament is brimful with excitement about God's presence in the temple. In the same breath, the psalm-writers could praise the Name and speak of the temple or its throne:

> he sits enthroned between the cherubim . . . let them praise your great and awesome name. (Ps 99:1–3 NIV)

> ... praised be the name of Yahweh! ... supreme over the heavens his glory ... His throne is set on high ... (Ps 113:3–5 NJB)

The Name, the temple, and the throne: they are mentioned together so many times. At least they were in Israel's glory days, but they were not to last. It is time to get back in our time machine and travel forward in time again to see Israel's fortunes change.

3. THE END OF THE GLORY DAYS

The Name and the Glory were the beating heart of Israel's best days. In the good times, the Name dwelled gloriously in Jerusalem's temple. But, after Solomon's reign, time began to run out on the glory days. The triumphs of King David and Solomon gave way to centuries of depressing decline. There was disobedience to God at the very highest ranks of society. It was a nation in a downward spiral of disorder.

There is a trail of clues about the Name to gather here. Through the good times and the bad times, the Israelites were reminded of one thing especially: Jerusalem was the place chosen by God for his Name to dwell in. That was a crucial part of the story.

Early signs of problems for Israel began with Solomon himself, when his heart turned against God towards idols. God's judgment was to split Solomon's kingdom, taking most of the twelve tribes of Israel away from him.[9] God said he would still leave something for Solomon's family:

> I will give one tribe to his son so that David my servant may always have a lamp before me in Jerusalem, the city where I chose to put my Name. (1 Kgs 11:36 NIV)

They were troubled times. Solomon's son, King Rehoboam (Israel's king for the years 930–913 BC) had a shaky start. But after accidentally stirring up rebellion against himself, he humbled himself, and 2 Chr 12:13 (NIV) says he continued as king "in Jerusalem, the city the LORD had chosen out of all the tribes in which to put his Name." All was not yet lost. The Name still dwelled in Jerusalem's temple.

Indeed, half a century later when the crown was held by King Jehoshaphat, the power of God to protect his people was still evident. Praying to "God who is in heaven," the king remembered that in this land the Israelites "have built you a sanctuary there for your name ... for your name

---

9. So it became north and south kingdoms, with the north kingdom being called Israel. The south kingdom—where the Jerusalem temple was—became known as Judah. I will refer to people of Judah as "Israelites," as in the Gospels.

is in this temple" (2 Chr 20: 6–9 NJB). The faithful still knew that God was in heaven and that his earthly temple was a home for the Name.

But the nation continued to lose its shine. Our time machine can take a leap forward to the days of the prophet Isaiah (who lived about 747–716 BC). Isaiah was concerned about God's people—they were naively wishing that Egypt would save them from defeat by a dangerous foreign nation, Assyria. It was with these words, now familiar, that Isaiah wrote that the Lord's Name could overcome Assyria:

> See, the Name of the LORD comes from afar, with burning anger and dense clouds of smoke. (Isa 30:27 NIV)

Despite the offered help from the Name, their conduct failed their nation's standards. To see this, our time machine steams ahead to the days of the disastrous King Manasseh (697–642 BC) who brought shame on the nation. He got embroiled in the worship of pagan gods. In Jerusalem's temple, he placed a wooden pagan idol:

> He took the carved image he had made and put it in God's temple, of which God had said to David and to his son Solomon, "In this temple and in Jerusalem, which I have chosen out of all the tribes of Israel, I will put my Name for ever." (2 Chr 33:7 NIV)

This carved idol was a serious offense to the faithful; the temple had been intended as a home for the Name, not a home for any man-made idol.

This sort of idolatry would be pushed away and then come back again like a bad penny. God's people did not stay true to God's ways consistently as a group. A time came when God decided to act in judgment and allow the nation's enemies to come and wreck and ruin Jerusalem. As a sign that the blessing of his presence was departing, he allowed their enemies to destroy Solomon's temple. God no longer treated it as the home of the Name.

But he had given plenty of warning first. He had tried to win them back to his own heart, even though they would not have it. The prophet Jeremiah here takes center stage in the Jerusalem temple (609 BC).

God told Jeremiah to stand in the temple, and he made himself heard there. He had the unenviable task of warning the Israelites that the Name had once left a previous home—called Shiloh—because of the people's disobedience. This is the picture:

> This is the word that came to Jeremiah from the LORD: "Stand at the gate of the LORD's house and there proclaim this message . . . Has this house, which bears My name, become a den of robbers to you? But I have been watching! declares the LORD. Go now to the place in Shiloh where I first made *a dwelling for my*

Name, and see what I did to it because of the wickedness of my people Israel." (Jer 7:1–12 NIV)

Jeremiah's message was pretty stark: a true temple cannot be a den for robbers, or else it would be destroyed and the Name would be gone from it. The temple's visitors were meant to find themselves near to the Name, not near to robbers. (Jesus would one day use Jeremiah's words again to make the same point to a different generation, as we will see later.)

But the Israelites paid little attention to Jeremiah. His warning words turned into grim reality. Solomon's temple was destroyed by the nation's enemies, and many of their people were taken away into exile as prisoners. It was no longer a home for the Name.

The prophet Ezekiel wrote about the crisis by describing a vision he had concerning the Glory. Just as the Name would no longer have a home in Solomon's temple, the Glory left too. The story is told in chapters 9 through 11 of the book of Ezekiel. His vision shows the Glory moving out of the temple's holy of holies. Then it goes from the threshold of the temple, out to the gate. It leaves Jerusalem and heads east towards a mountain. (This is likely the Mount of Olives, where Jesus spent so much time.)

Hope Returns

The exiles, far from Jerusalem, never forgot the spectacular temple they had lost. And so they kept writing about it.

Like all generations of God's people, they wrote and cherished many books about their faith as well as their sacred Scriptures. In the modern day, believers might have books next to the Bible on their shelf by authors such as C. S. Lewis or Philip Yancey. Some of the popular books from ancient times have survived and can be read today. They tell a bitter story of events that followed Jeremiah's warnings.

One is the book of Judith. It makes plain the concern of the faithful few, those who cherished the presence of the Name at the temple:

> For they intend to defile your *sanctuary*, and to pollute the *tabernacle* where your *glorious name* resides (Jdt 9:8 RSV)

Another book of the exile era went by the title of Tobit. It told believers what to pray for: "Thank the Lord as he deserves and bless the King of the ages, that your temple may be rebuilt with joy within you"; and he had a vision of what all the peoples of the world would do when the temple got rebuilt. They would "dwell *close to the holy name* of the Lord God" (Tob 13:10–11 NJB).

That was the hope they clung to: to dwell close to the Name, just as it had once been.

But it seemed a distant hope at best. At that time they were in a foreign land, with no temple for their God to dwell in, no house built for the Name.

They showed their commitment by composing more Psalms about it. They prayed for a day when they could go back and rebuild it. They used the word "Zion" to remember their land by. They harked back to the temple not just as a ruin, but rather as it had been in the glory days—the place for the throne, and for the Name and the Glory. They wrote about it like this:

> But You, O LORD, are enthroned forever . . .
> Nations will fear *the name* of the LORD,
> and all the kings of the earth will fear *your glory*.
> For the LORD builds up Zion;
> *he appears in his Glory* . . . (Ps 102:12–16 ESV)

The prophet Ezekiel too had a vision of a future in which God would return to the temple. There is a telling version of it in an ancient Greek translation. It says: "the house [the temple] was filled with the Glory of the Lord." And God says to Ezekiel:

> thou hast seen the place of my throne, and the place of the soles of my feet, in which *my name shall dwell in the midst of the house of Israel* for ever. (Ezek 43:5–7, LXX)[10]

The Name and the Glory were going to make a comeback.

The people's spirits were lifted when a new leader came on the scene by the name of Nehemiah. He had the vision and the talent to get Jerusalem's temple rebuilt. His hope was that God's people would be able to return from exile abroad and gather in Jerusalem again. In prayer, he asked God to honor an ancient promise to Moses. That is, if this scattered people turned to their God, then God would "gather them from there and bring them to the place I have chosen as a dwelling for my Name" (Neh 1:9).

It would be a major building project. To make matters more complicated, the Israelites in exile needed planning permission from their foreign lords and masters. They got it in a decree, which King Cyrus of Persia wrote, and King Darius approved.

Their decree, surprisingly, had a prayer in it, saying what should happen if anyone tried to stop Nehemiah from rebuilding the temple. It's about the Name again:

---

10. See Brenton, *Septuagint*.

> May God, who has caused his Name to dwell there, overthrow any king or people who lifts a hand to change this decree or to destroy this temple in Jerusalem. (Ezra 6:12 NIV)

So even foreign kings had heard of who should dwell in the Jerusalem temple—the Name had international recognition. The exiles must have been talking about it.

So Jerusalem got its second temple built. But surprisingly there is no confirmation in the Old Testament that God's presence ever returned to it. Something was wrong. We find that the story of God's people was up and down at best, with many lows when the nation turned away from their God.

Optimism remained though centuries passed. Hope persisted that God would return to the temple in the form of the Name. It appears wistfully in another popular book of that era, called *The Psalms of Solomon*. The seventh psalm in it says:

> Make not Thy dwelling afar from us, O God ... Thy name dwelleth in our midst ...[11]

It was a way of harking back to the old days. Notably, there were Jews who grew dissatisfied with the way things were run at Jerusalem's second temple. Some of their rabbis came to think that God's Glory never returned to it.[12] There had been time enough for this to happen. Things had looked promising since Nehemiah's day when rebuilding began on the temple, and even in Jesus' day when it was still being renovated by Herod! But the new temple never saw the glory days of Solomon's temple.

Even after centuries of disappointment, the hope and expectation grew that God's Name and Glory would dwell in his temple again. But some in Jesus' day had begun to look for a temple that would go beyond the limits of a stone building. The new hope was for another way for God's presence to come to his people.

And into this atmosphere of expectation, Jesus came. We will shortly see how he stoked up the hopes of his disciples for the glory days.

---

11. In the eighteen *Psalms of Solomon*, not to be confused with the later forty-two *Odes of Solomon*, or the biblical Psalms.

12. See Green, *I Believe in the Holy Spirit*, 36. Green cites T. Sota 13:2 and b. Yoma 21b (writings of rabbis in the centuries after Jesus).

Reflection and Application

- From Moses in the desert, to Solomon's temple in Jerusalem, the Name and the Glory were both present, but what differences were there between them?
- Why was it a national trauma to the Israelites that the Jerusalem temple was destroyed, and was no longer a home for the Name?
- How does seeing the temple as the home of the Name help us to thread together the stories of the kings of Israel and Judah?

Chapter 4

3D Letters to Christians

1. LETTERS FROM ST. PAUL

As we have traveled along the trail, we found an easy-to-use definition of God. It is to do with God's temple, and it is the simple answer to a simple question: who is the rightful dweller of the true temple? The rightful dweller of the true temple is, by definition, God. If you have found the true temple and you have found the rightful dweller in it, then you have found God.

So, what would St. Paul's approach to this question be? He found the Christian community to be a true temple. And his answer would be that God and Jesus and the Holy Spirit dwell in it. Together, these three as one, they are the rightful dweller of the true temple. Just as it was with God's Name and his Glory—when they were the rightful dwellers in Solomon's temple—so it is with Father, Son, and Spirit as rightful dwellers in the church.

Let's look a little bit at the story of Paul. He came to this subject from a background where the Jerusalem temple loomed large over everyone. A contemporary of Jesus (but initially independent of the church), Paul had lived in Jerusalem as an Israelite. He would have known its temple like the back of his hand. When we first encounter Paul, he is known by his other name, Saul (Acts 7:58).

Just a few years after the crucifixion and resurrection of Jesus, Saul was a persecutor of the church. First he cut a callous figure, looking after the cloaks of those who were stoning Stephen to death. (That was their vicious reaction to Stephen's challenging message about the limitations of Jerusalem's temple.)

Within a short time, Saul's life was turned around. He became a follower of Jesus, and became better known by the name Paul (Acts 13:9). No longer a persecutor of the church, he famously wrote treasured letters to a number of churches. His words contain revealing insights into God, and what the temple meant to him.

As we saw earlier, one thing in particular Paul knew from his religious upbringing: the temple was God's house, and no one else's. It was a place where priests went to work and serve. The sanctuary was not where they lived: they had to make do with quarters in the outsides of the temple premises. Anyone but God dwelling in his temple was regarded by Paul as a blasphemous idol. And there is someone he calls "the Lawless One" who could do the unthinkable:

> He opposes and exalts himself above every so-called god or object of worship, so that he takes his seat in the temple of God, declaring himself to be God. (2 Thess 2:4, NRSV)

The very idea was a scandal to Paul. He would not have envisaged anyone dwelling in the true temple but the true God. This becomes key for understanding Paul: when he talks about the church community as God's temple, he is very clear about the divine presence which inhabits the church community—it's the true God. And he names those who really play the true God's part—Christ and the Holy Spirit. Paul is sure that they are true dwellers of the true temple. It is a three-in-one understanding of God. We see this frequently in Paul's letters, especially in the few examples below.

Paul's Letter to the Romans

"God is one," Paul wrote in Rom 3:30. One God in God's temple is what he would expect. But this is a three-in-one God. Paul declares that Jesus and the Holy Spirit dwell in this temple, the church community. This is all in his letter to the Christians in Rome. Rom 8:9–10 says believers' lives should be transformed because "the Spirit of God dwells in you" and likewise "Christ is in you." This takes believers to be a temple, as the place where the Son and Spirit dwell.

Two presences—Christ and the Spirit—in one temple. It is a familiar echo of God's double presence in Jerusalem's ancient temple: the Name and the Glory. This is how the three-in-one God is the God of the temple: whereas God is in heaven, two presences are in the temple. The pattern of the temple has been rediscovered in a new way by the early Christians and named as the heavenly Father, plus the double presence in the temple—that is, Christ and the Holy Spirit in the church community. This is the Trinity on a page in the New Testament. We looked at Rom 8:9-10 in more detail earlier, so let's look at another letter.

1 Corinthians

In Paul's letters to the Corinthian Christians in Greece, he memorably uses this classic language: "your body is a temple of the Holy Spirit within you, whom you have from God" (1 Cor 6:19). Here is what we find in 1 Corinthians:

Who Paul is talking about	What Paul says	Verse (NIV)
The church community is the temple	"you yourselves are God's temple"	1 Cor 3:16
1) God	"God's temple"	1 Cor 3:16
2) His Son	"When you are assembled in the name of the Lord Jesus . . . and the power of our Lord Jesus is present"	1 Cor 5:4
3) His Spirit	"your body is a temple of the Holy Spirit, who is in you"	1 Cor 6:19

2 Corinthians

In 2 Cor 6:16, Paul says "we are the temple of the living God." A temple for Jesus, for in 13:5 Paul says "Jesus Christ is in you"; the NJB translation puts it this way—Christians are "people in whom Jesus Christ is present." And in 1:22 it says that God "put his Spirit in our hearts" (which Paul underlines in 5:5).

So there it is again. Christ and the Spirit indwell the believers, the church. We see that God, his Son, and his Spirit are—as one—this temple's God. It's their temple to dwell in, and they are its God. In table form:

Who Paul is talking about	What Paul says	Verse (NIV)
The church community is the temple	"we are the temple of the living God"	2 Cor 6:16
1) God	"the living God"	2 Cor 6:16
2) His Son	"Jesus Christ is in you"	2 Cor 13:5
3) His Spirit	"his Spirit in our hearts"	2 Cor 1:22

Paul memorably finishes this letter in 13:14 by blessing the church with the triune God:

> May the grace of the Lord Jesus Christ, and the love of God, and the fellowship of the Holy Spirit be with you all.

This is one of the verses we can always point to, for anyone who wants to see the Trinity in the Bible.

Ephesians

Paul says God's people are "a holy temple in the Lord"—"a dwelling in which God lives by his Spirit" (Eph 2:21–22 NIV).

Paul's meditation on the temple and the members of the Trinity reaches a climax in this blessing upon his readers:

> For this reason I bow my knees before the *Father* . . .
>
> that according to the riches of his glory, he may grant you to be strengthened with power through *His Spirit in your inner being*,
>
> so that *Christ* may *dwell in your hearts* . . .
>
> that you may be *filled* with all the fullness of *God*. (Eph 3:14–17)

Here it is summed up—the church community is the temple of the Trinity:

Who Paul is talking about	What Paul says	Verse (NIV)
The church community is the temple	"you are being built together to become a dwelling in which God lives by his Spirit"	Eph 2:22
1) God	"a dwelling in which God lives"	Eph 2:22
2) His Son	"so that Christ may dwell in your hearts"	Eph 3:17
3) His Spirit	"his Spirit in your inner being"	Eph 3:16

Once again, Paul finds both Christ and the Spirit dwelling in the true temple, the church community. It's their temple.

Filled

In this letter, Paul says that believers should be "filled" with the Spirit (Eph 5:18). It is an echo of when the Glory filled Solomon's temple. Paul is calling for a trinitarian experience of God, and here this is all about God's presence dwelling in his temple and his Glory filling his temple.

The Name and the Glory

In Ephesians, we also get some insight that Paul had an interest in connecting Jesus with God's Name. It is in another prayer:

> that the *God* of our *Lord Jesus Christ*, the Father of *glory*, may give to you the *Spirit* of wisdom . . .
>
> he raised him from the dead and *seated him* at His right hand in the heavenly places [that is, on heaven's throne] . . .
>
> *above every name that is named* . . . (Eph 1:17–21)

What this is saying is that Jesus was raised above every name as he was enthroned in heaven. This leaves only the highest name for him—the name Yahweh.[1] It is a name shared by both the Father and the Son. It is very reminiscent of the words of Ps 138:2: "you have exalted above all things your name."

These are glimpses of the key themes of Solomon's temple—God, Glory, Name, throne, temple.[2]

Believers to this day pray after the fashion of Paul's prayers. They pray to be filled with the power of the Holy Spirit and for Jesus to dwell in the church community. By praying in that way, Christians have sought to continue being temples of the three-in-one God from that day to this. These triune truths have never been lost. This is what the church has always been doing.

In Ephesians, Paul reminds us what a true temple is all about—a sacred space for humanity to meet God.

Philippians: the Name Enthroned in the Glory

Picture this: in Solomon's temple, in the holy of holies, the mercy seat was God's throne, and above it the Glory shone brightly. God's presence was enthroned in the Glory fire. It was truly the temple of God, his Name, and his Glory. And this was a mirror of heaven's sanctuary with God's throne. Where can we find a picture like it, of heaven's sanctuary?

There is an ancient song, a hymn that puts Jesus at the center of this kind of picture. In it, he is returning (after his resurrection) to the heavenly sanctuary, to occupy the throne of God, to be seated in the Glory, to be hailed by everyone in the world as having God's Name. This is a lot to take in. Let's see how the Bible paints it, in Paul's letter to the church in Philippi.

The powerful song says this about Jesus:

---

1. Bauckham, *God Crucified*, 34.
2. Gieschen, "Divine Name," 130.

> He humbled himself, became obedient unto death, even to the death of the cross.
>
> For which cause *God also hath exalted him*, and hath *given him a name that is above all names*:
>
> That in the name of Jesus every knee should bow, of those that are in heaven, on earth and under the earth:
>
> And that every tongue should confess that *the Lord Jesus Christ is in the glory* of God the Father.
>
> (Phil 2:8–11, Douay-Rheims 1899 American Edition translation)

This is a picture of Jesus being enthroned on God's throne, with God's Name, in God's Glory, in heaven. It's like a scene in the holy of holies in the temple, with the highest place, the highest Name, the throne, and the Glory.

The Highest Place—God's Throne

It describes how Jesus, back from the dead, is lifted aloft by his Father to the highest place. What is the highest place? It is the Father's throne in the heavenly sanctuary. There is nowhere higher. For a check that Christians could believe Jesus shares this throne, we can turn to Rev 3:21, which reports Jesus saying, "I also conquered and sat down with my Father on his throne." This is a temple scene, and Jesus features in it.

The Highest Name—God's Name

Paul's song says that Jesus was named with "the name that is above every name" (v. 9). What is the name that was above every name? It is God's name, Yahweh. There is no name higher. We know where Paul's words come from. They were inspired by Isa 45:22–24.

> every knee will bow;
>
> by me every tongue will swear.
>
> They will say of me, "In the LORD [Yahweh] alone are righteousness and strength." (Isa 45:22–24 NIV)

Paul's brave song takes these ancient words about Yahweh God to be about Jesus:

What Isaiah says	What Paul says
every knee will bow	every knee should bow
by me every tongue will swear	every tongue should confess
In the LORD [Yahweh] ...	that the Lord Jesus Christ...

If you look closely, you can once again see "Lord" used like a code word there. See, in the Isaiah verse, the word "LORD" in capital letters, standing in for God's name *Yahweh*. So "Lord" is code for *Yahweh*. Paul's song puts it to good use to talk about Jesus as Lord.[3] This is to talk about Jesus as Yahweh.[4] In this picture, the scene of Jesus' enthronement in heaven, everyone is bowing to Jesus as Yahweh God.[5]

It is a breathtaking scene. The highest place, the highest name, shared by Jesus with his Father.

Enthroned—in God's Glory

Finally, perhaps the most crucial thing. This throne is the place of the Glory. The song reaches a climax by picturing Jesus enthroned in the Glory. It says: "Jesus Christ is Lord *in the glory of God the Father*."[6] It literally means this: "Jesus Christ is Yahweh in the Glory." Like in the temple's holy of holies, here the Glory is present at God's throne, and here is Jesus pictured in that very Glory. It's as the Name in the Glory, as in Solomon's temple.[7]

What a song this is—a song of the three-in-one God!

Colossians

Paul touches on some of his favorite themes in this letter. The true temple is all about the divine presence in it: "Christ in you, the hope of glory" (Col 1:27 ESV). The church community is this temple; it is "built up in him" (2:7).

Paul has remarkable things to say about the dwelling place of God. In this letter, he comes at it from a different angle. He focuses on Jesus' body as the temple of God: "In him, in bodily form, lives divinity in all its fullness" (2:9 NJB). God's presence in Jesus is the heart of the story.[8] This is a glimpse

---

3. As for calling Jesus "Lord/Yahweh," Paul does something similar in Rom 14:6–11 when he repeatedly calls the Father "God," and Jesus "Lord," meaning Yahweh as in Isa 49:18 and 45:23.

4. Often in the New Testament, Scriptures that are uniquely about Yahweh—and no one else—are taken to be about Jesus.

5. We will later see how Jesus was given this name both before and after the resurrection when we look at John 17:11.

6. Many translations say "to the glory" but John Wesley's translation, like the Douay Rheims translation, is accurate to the Greek, saying "in the glory." The Greek word in this verse translated by others as "to" is actually *eis*. *Eis* means "in" primarily, and in this context that is surely the better translation.

7. We will see this theme about the Glory again when we look at the Gospels.

8. The same point is made in Col 1:19.

of an idea we will see more of: that Jesus is both the divine presence and the temple at the same time.

What goes for Jesus' "body" goes for the church community. God's people are in spiritual union with Christ as part of his Body. Jesus' body is a temple, so the church body is a temple—God's idea is that all his fullness will dwell in the church community through Jesus.

God and Christ and the Spirit Dwell in the Church

There are more clues about how the three-in-one God is the God of the temple. These clues are found in the Greek words being used in the Bible to mean "dwell." The brave martyr Stephen said that God does not "dwell" in houses made with human hands (Acts 7:48). Stephen used a particular word, a Greek word, to say "dwell." This Greek word is *katoikeo*. The main part of the Greek word *katoikeo* is *oikeo*. It has to do with houses. After Stephen, the word was used by Paul to talk about "housing" God the Father, Jesus, and the Holy Spirit. It is a profound truth about the three-in-one God of the temple.

> Paul, about God: In Col 2:9, God "dwells" (*katoikeo*) in Jesus' body. In 2 Cor 6:16, God "dwells" (*enoikeo*) in his people. So God does some "dwelling," as one who dwells in a temple.

> Paul, about Jesus: Christ "dwells" (*katoikeo*) in his people (Eph 3:17).

> Paul, about the Holy Spirit: the Spirit "dwells" (*enoikeo*) in Christians (Rom 8:11).

So, Christ and the Spirit and God do this dwelling—this *oikeo*—in the church community. This insight can be traced through Paul's letters like a trail on a treasure map, leading to the three-in-one God of the temple.

What Have We Learned From Paul?

Paul, we have learned, saw the importance of honoring the temple as God's house. He saw the church community as a temple, a temple for the Trinity, as the dwelling place of God's Son and Spirit. He was very aware of the double presence of Christ and the Holy Spirit, just like the emphasis in Solomon's temple was on the double presence of the Name and the Glory. And more so, when Paul emphasizes being filled with the Holy Spirit, it is an echo of Solomon's temple being filled with the Glory.

It all comes back to this easy-to-use definition of God: if you have found the rightful dweller of the true temple, then you have found the true God. And we have found a Bible answer: it is the three-in-one God, the Trinity, which dwells in the true temple.

St. Paul's legacy of triune teaching was taken up by later writers of the church. These writers said that the people of the church community are a temple. They are the people

> in whom is the Trinity of the One Divinity—Father, Son, and Holy Spirit.[9]

Next we come to a dazzling display of knowledge about God, his Name, and his Glory, in the letter to the Hebrews.

2. ANOTHER POSTBAG FROM THE BIBLE

We are fortunate to have more letters written to the early church, with attention-grabbing evidence of the three-in-one God of the temple.

Hebrews: Name and Glory

A memorable scene awaits us in the first lines of Hebrews. It's a reminder to us of Phil 2:9–11, where we saw Jesus enthroned in the Glory, and with "the name that is above every name." Throne, Name, Glory—these themes come back again and again.

Hebrews was written to people who knew about being a true temple (Heb 3:6). It is full of references to the tabernacle/temple.[10] But first, we learn more about God, his Name, and his Glory.

On the Glory: Heb 1:3 says that Jesus is *"the radiance of the glory* of God." It's a brave claim to make. It is far more than saying that Jesus reflects God's Glory, like God's people are said to do. It is a statement about Jesus himself—he *is* the radiance. It's a loud echo of the temple scene in Ezek 10:4 (NIV), which says: "The cloud filled the temple, and the court was full of *the*

---

9. Tertullian, *On Modesty*, XXI, 16.

10. Also, Hebrews makes Jesus to be the High Priest of the true tabernacle or temple (8:1). As priest, he brings the sacrifice (10:12), but also his body *is* the sacrifice (10:10). His flesh is the temple's veil (10:20), but he is also the one who passes through the veil (6:19–20). Jesus is just about everything in relation to the temple, across the New Testament. He is the temple—but he is also the cornerstone of the temple (Luke 20:17–18). God and his Lamb are the temple—but are also the divine presence dwelling within the temple (Rev 21:22).

radiance of the glory of the LORD." Hebrews is picturing Jesus in that kind of scene. We should think of Jesus akin to the radiance emerging from the fiery Glory that filled the temple.

On the Name: Heb 1:4 says that Jesus "inherited the Name." What does this mean? From whom did the Son inherit the Name? It's simple: the heavenly Father. His heir, the Son, inherits the name of his Father. This name is Yahweh. These are the verses:

> [God] has spoken to us in the *Son*, whom he appointed *heir* of all things . . .
>
> who being *the radiance of the Glory* and the stamp of what God is . . .
>
> sat down *at the right hand of the Majesty in the highest,*
>
> . . . having become better than the angels as much as differing from them,
>
> he *inherited the Name.*
>
> For to which of the angels has *God* ever said, "*You are my Son*, today I have begotten you." (Heb 1:2–5, author's translation)

This is a triune God scene. It features the Father and the Son, bound together with the Name and the Glory. And it is about the coronation in heaven of Jesus as King of the Jews. Take the last phrase, "You are my Son, today I have begotten you." These are the ritual words spoken when crowning the King of the Jews, just as in Ps 2:7.[11] Those words are prophetic, leading to Jesus sitting *at the right hand of the Father in heaven*. This means we are at the scene of God's throne in heaven, where God the Father is saying these words. It is what is spoken over the King of the Jews taking his throne. This time it is Jesus.

Jesus has more kingly status than any earthly royal with his inheriting the name Yahweh.[12] The one to whom the name "Yahweh" is given *is* Yahweh. It's his identity, shared with the Father, like inherited genes. Jesus has this name. His rightful place is enthroned in the midst of the Glory at the right hand of the Father in the heavenly sanctuary. We are looking at the three-in-one God of Solomon's temple, with the Name locked onto Jesus:

---

11. This meaning is revealed in another psalm too, as part of a series of titles for the king, at the enthronement of King David (Ps 89:26–27). This coronation meaning is also in 1 Chr 22:10, for the enthronement of King Solomon.

12. Hebrews recognizes the Father and Jesus *and* the Holy Spirit as Yahweh too. By quoting Old Testament words about Yahweh, they recognized the Holy Spirit speaking as Yahweh God (Heb 10:15–17); and God the Father recognizes Jesus as Yahweh God (Heb 1:10); the angels also worship Jesus as Yahweh God. (Heb 1:6, which quotes an ancient Greek version of Deut 32:43.) Yahweh is a name shared by all three as one God.

What Hebrews is talking about	What Hebrews says	Verse
The Father's Son	"the Son, whom he appointed heir . . .	Heb 1:2
The Son is the radiance that shines from the Glory	the radiance of the Glory . . .	Heb 1:3
The Son is enthroned in heaven	sat down at the right hand of the Majesty in the highest . . .	Heb 1:3
The Son has God's Name	he inherited the Name . . ."	Heb 1:4

1 Peter

As we come to the letter 1 Peter, let's cast our minds back to the book of Acts, the stories of the first Christians. There, we found what happened to the apostles Peter and John when they were flogged for preaching about Jesus:

> They called the apostles in and had them flogged. Then they ordered them not to speak in the name of Jesus, and let them go. The apostles left the Sanhedrin, rejoicing because they had been counted worthy of *suffering disgrace for the Name*. Day after day, in the temple courts and from house to house, they never stopped teaching and proclaiming the good news that Jesus is the Christ. (Acts 5:40–42 NIV)

Peter never forgot this lesson, and it shows. In 1 Peter, it is obvious that suffering for the Name was a part of life that had not gone away:

> If you are *reviled for the name of Christ*, you are blessed . . . he is not to be ashamed, but is to glorify God *in this name*. (1 Pet 4:14–16 NASB)

While his fellow sufferer John wrote about other experiences in a similar way:

> It was on behalf of *the Name* that they went out receiving no help from the gentiles. (3 John 7, author's translation)

1 Peter turns the spotlight on the church community being a temple of God's presence, and shows what the Name and the Glory can be to the life of the church. In 1 Pet 2:4–9, Jesus' followers are a temple, "living stones" of "a spiritual house." Peter really hits his stride in chapter 4:

> . . . at the revelation of *His glory* you may rejoice with exultation. If you are *reviled for the name of Christ*, you are blessed, because the *Spirit of the Glory* and of the Deity *rests* on you . . . but if

anyone suffers as a Christian, he is not to be ashamed, but is to glorify God in *this name*. (1 Pet 4:13–16 NASB adapted by author, taking the Greek literally: "of the Glory and of the Deity.")

The Glory was upon Peter because he suffered for the Name, with John in the temple.

Moving on from the Name, let's see what this says about the Glory. Let's focus on the word "rested," starting with the Glory resting on a mountain that itself was a kind of temple to them:[13]

- "*the glory* of the LORD *rested* on Mount Sinai." (Exod 24:16 NASB)
- Peter, at Pentecost, saw "*tongues of fire*" which "*rested* on each one of them." (Acts 2:3 NASB)
- "*the Spirit of the Glory* and of the Deity *rests* on you."[14] (1 Pet 4:14, author's translation)

What Peter had seen at Pentecost—the Holy Spirit as the Glory-style "tongues of fire" resting on his fellow believers—makes an appearance in his letter: "the *Spirit of the Glory* and of the Deity *rests* on you." The believers are a spiritual house, a temple (1 Pet 2:5) and their status as a temple is sealed when the Glory rests on them.[15]

Putting it all together, the familiar triune links and patterns are there: Spirit/Glory, as well as Jesus/Name, and the temple as a place for the Glory to rest.[16]

It is hard to resist the impression that Peter was inspired to write these things by his experiences reported in the book of Acts, when he suffered for the Name. It is as though, in his memories, he has one eye on the Glory at Pentecost, and another eye on the Name that caused such controversy in his clash with temple authorities.

There is a final twist. It is Jesus' Glory where it says "his glory" (1 Pet 4:13). What a loaded phrase! Peter was one of those who had already

---

13. Beale, *Temple and the Church's Mission*, 105–7.

14. J. B. Rotherham's translation rightly has "the Spirit of *the* glory," a rare translation that reflects the definite article which is there in the Greek (*tes doxes*). The definite article is purposeful; it is *the* Glory, linked to the Holy Spirit. See Michaels, *1 Peter*, 265. Hence, it is translated by this author as "the Spirit of the Glory and of the Deity."

15. A case can also be made for Isa 11:2 being in the background. In it, the Spirit rests (with no mention of the Glory).

16. That Peter considered God, Jesus, and "the Spirit of the Glory" to be one God is corroborated by the following evidence from the book of Acts and 1 Peter: he identified the Holy Spirit as God (Acts 5:3–4); and he applies to Jesus a Scripture that was written exclusively about YHWH, making Jesus Peter's God (1 Pet 2:4–8 alluding to Isa 8:13–14).

had a glimpse of it—Jesus' Glory—at the scene of Jesus' supernatural transfiguration on a mountain. We shall see this later.

Now it is time to turn from Christian letters to the Gospels, to take a deeper look at how Jesus prepared the disciples to understand these things.

Reflection and Application

- How might the Glory at the temple of Solomon help us to understand why Paul talks about being filled with the Holy Spirit?
- Paul tells churches that Christ dwells in them and the Spirit dwells in them and fills them. What ways can churches today respond to that message?
- What signs are there that Paul's belief in one God included Father, Son, and Spirit as one God?
- How do Paul's thoughts on Christ and the Spirit dwelling in the church help us to think about the holiness of the church as a temple? (Read Rom 8, or 1 Cor 3, or 2 Cor 6.)

Chapter 5

The Gospels in 3D

1. PREPARE THE WAY

As we saw earlier, Jesus' disciples were primed by the temple stories of the Old Testament to understand the three-in-one God of Solomon's temple. Then Jesus prepared his disciples for a deeper understanding. He did this in steps.

Step 1	Jesus reveals how he will fulfill the role of the temple's God, returning to his temple to bring Glory fire.
Step 2	He teaches his plan: the temple of the body.
Step 3	He teaches that in this new temple, he himself and the Spirit will dwell.
Step 4	He does new things with the language of the Name and the Glory for this new kind of temple.
Step 5	His followers become temples of the Holy Spirit, a community in which Christ is spiritually present.

We will see how these things unfold as we go through the story of Jesus' ministry.

The Story of Jesus' Ministry—Beginnings

Mark's gospel story—the story of Jesus—starts at the River Jordan. It begins with the Israelite prophet John the Baptist, in his hard-to-ignore way preparing crowds to welcome Jesus.

The very first words of Mark's Gospel tell us that ancient prophesies were coming true in the moments when John the Baptist and Jesus came on the scene. These prophetic words reappear in all the Gospels. They signal an understanding of the old ways of Solomon's temple, the ways of the three-in-one God. This is how Mark starts:

> The beginning of the Gospel about Jesus Christ, the Son of God.
> It is written in Isaiah the prophet:
> "I will send my messenger ahead of you, who will prepare your way,
> "a voice of one calling in the desert,
> 'Prepare the way for the Lord, make straight paths for him.'"
> (Mark 1:1–3 NIV)

In that way, Mark's Gospel begins with quotes from the Old Testament and an eager sense of anticipation of good things to come. The first half of the quote comes from the book of the prophet Malachi (Mal 3:1), the second half from Isaiah (Isa 40:3). Both writings date from several hundred years before Christ. They are about one hope: God returning to his temple among the Israelites with Glory fire. Since this Gospel gives pride of place to these quotes, we will do so too.

Like two halves of a treasure map, Mark has fitted these quotes together. They map out a journey that we will follow. On the way, we will detect memories of Solomon's temple in the map's clues. There is more in these Scriptures than you see in those short quotes.

The prophecies speak of God returning to Israel—in fact, to his temple. The very first thing that Mark is establishing is that Jesus is this returning God. This is daring stuff. We need to understand how he shows this.

For many Christians today, this may at first seem a surprise, as it is much more common to hear of Jesus' future return, his "second coming," if people are talking about him returning. It is the letters of St. Paul that especially think of this future hope: "For the Lord himself will come down from heaven" (1 Thess 4:16 NIV). But it is perhaps not so surprising that those writing the Gospels want us to understand that when Jesus came as in the Gospels, this too is the coming of God to his people. In other words, by Jesus coming in the flesh, God's presence returned to his people. This is a story of the triune God's presence.

The Messenger

Here at the start of the story of Jesus, a question needs an answer: in that day and age, what hope and expectations did the Israelites have? Some Israelites were looking forward to seeing God's spiritual presence in his temple again in all its splendor. After all, it was not enough that they had a rebuilt temple in Jerusalem. What about the Glory? Things didn't look quite like the old times of Solomon's temple. Was something missing at the rebuilt temple?

Some Israelites were anticipating that someone born of David's line would be the new King of the Jews. Their messiah. He would bring back Israel's glory days, they thought. Many readers will be familiar with this idea from things heard at Christmas in the nativity story and carols.

Some thought that Jesus then really would be the one to bring back the glory days. "Messiah" is an Israelite word. It means "anointed one." This religious phrase was more or less code for Israelite king, one who would put the world to rights for them. This hope goes deep in the Old Testament.

But what if these two things were combined? What if the Messiah and the temple presence of God were rolled into one, in one man?

And another question: how could God return in this land if God the Father was still in heaven? The answers had to be triune answers. In the Old Testament, the answer was that God's Name and Glory came to Solomon's temple while God himself was still in heaven hearing prayers. The Name and Glory in the temple were a personal visitation of God's presence. How would it work if this presence came in the form of a man?

Were any Israelites expecting God to return in such a personal way? At least one person was—the prophet John the Baptist. And not only him. John's father, Zechariah, had been told to expect God to come, not just a man! The story is that Zechariah was met in Jerusalem's temple by an angel, who made a big prediction that John would play a trailblazing role in their nation and stoke up people's expectations of God's return. The angel had put it this way:

> Many of the people of Israel will he [John] bring back to *the Lord their God*. And he [John] will go on *before the Lord* . . . (Luke 1:16–17 NIV)

This joins the dots. First to come would be the messenger (John the Baptist), and then comes God himself. This message takes us back to words from before this Zechariah, before this angel, back again to the prophecy in Malachi that is so key.

John played his trailblazing role around the beginning of Jesus' ministry years. People found John living in his desert wilderness. Just to confirm about John's role, Luke telling the story uses the same words of Isaiah to describe John's preaching as a voice in the desert:

> A voice of one calling in the desert, 'Prepare the way of the Lord;
> make straight paths for him.' (Luke 3:4 NIV)

So the Malachi and Isaiah prophecies were being talked about. Like two halves of a treasure map, they predicted John the Baptist and Jesus, how John comes first, then Jesus. The two halves side by side:

Mal 3:1–2 (NIV)	Isa 40:3–5 (NIV)
(The Lord speaks about sending his messenger, who is John the Baptist)	(John the Baptist is calling out as the messenger)
"See, I will send my messenger,	"A voice of one calling:
who will prepare the way	"In the desert prepare the way
before me (the "me" is the Lord)	
Then suddenly *the Lord* [Jesus] you are seeking	for *the LORD* [Jesus]
will come	make straight in the wilderness a highway for our God..
to his temple . . .	
he will be *like a refiner's fire* . . ."	And *the glory* of the LORD
	will be revealed.'"

There is a lot of valuable treasure there. Piece by piece, let's investigate how we know that some expected the return of God—this provides a vital clue, as it is God returning as to his temple with Glory fire.

- Luke was aware that Israelites would know this Isaiah verse, and would know how this was actually about the *Lord God* coming after his vocal messenger who is doing the calling: "A voice of one calling: "In the desert prepare the way for the LORD; make straight in the wilderness a highway for *our God.*"" (Isa 40:3 NIV)[1]

- The quote from Isaiah contains a familiar clue, the four-letter word LORD. This is to do with God's personal name. Not at first obvious in some Bible translations, but it is a challenge we have seen before. Where we read LORD in capital letters, it means that Isaiah's original Hebrew word is *YHWH*, God's own personal name in the Old Testament, spoken as Yahweh. That is, *YHWH* with the letters A and E added, making Yahweh. With this simple code cracked, we discover

---

1. The placing of the speech marks is as in the NIV translation.

this: John the Baptist, as foretold by Isaiah, was preparing the way for Yahweh God to come.

It may still be a surprise to some that John could be expecting God to come. So, as careful as detectives, let's look at the clues. If there is any doubt that John really ought to have been expecting God to be coming, here is how we check. We turn from Isaiah to Malachi who gives us two clues:

- Malachi speaks of the "me" who would come to his temple. Who has the right to speak of the temple as their own? Only God. God was coming.
- Malachi proclaims that the one speaking of coming was "the Lord of Hosts" (Mal 3:1)—an Old Testament title that belongs to God and God alone. (Some Bible translations represent "Lord of Hosts" with the words "Lord Almighty.") God was coming.

As the gospel story unfolds, we need to be alert to recognize the one coming after John, because that person can then be recognized as John's God, as Yahweh. Where and when did this person arrive?

The evidence shows that John and Jesus knew that these Scriptures were about them, with John saying that Jesus was the one to come, and Jesus agreeing. In the Gospel of John, John the Baptist makes his position clear. (The Gospel of "John" author was a different "John" from John the Baptist.)

- In the Gospel of John 1:23–33, the Baptist is speaking publicly about himself, saying the Isaiah words: "I am the voice of one calling in the desert, 'Make straight the way for the Lord.'" This was attention-grabbing. It is obvious that John strongly believed that he was the one preparing the way, and so we are ready to see him tell who comes after him.
- The next day John spots Jesus and makes an announcement: "This is the one I meant when I said, 'A man who comes after me has surpassed me because he was before me'" (John 1:30 NIV). And John points out Jesus. So all eyes are now on Jesus. John has identified him as the one expected to come.
- John points out Jesus as a man, but then he throws something explosive into the mix. John adds the crucial message that Jesus "will baptize with the Holy Spirit" (John 1:33 NIV). This makes Jesus not only a man, but much more too. As we have seen earlier, only one person can pour the Holy Spirit on people—only the Name of God does this.

It is a telling clue, to reveal Jesus' identity as the Name of Yahweh—for no one provides God's Holy Spirit except Yahweh God himself in the form of his Name. Luke's Gospel fills in a crucial detail that fits alongside what John said about Jesus:

> He will baptize you with the Holy Spirit and with fire . . .
> (Luke 3:16 NIV)

The extra detail about fire is just the sort of clue we need. There is background to this clue in the Malachi prophecy. In it, God speaks:

> See, I will send my messenger, who will *prepare the way before me. Then suddenly the Lord you are seeking will come to his temple . . . he will be like a refiner's fire.* (Mal 3:1–2 NIV)

And there, in Malachi, we see a mention not only of the fire but of the temple too. This hits the mark. It's about the three-in-one God of the temple. Descriptions of God coming to his temple with fire are familiar to us—we saw how it happened at Solomon's temple when we read about God's Name and his Glory. John the Baptist is saying that Jesus has got the ability to baptize with spiritual fire.

Imagine the stunned looks when he confidently picked out Jesus as the one bringing fire. He was picking out Jesus as his God, returning to Israel to baptize with fire. John's eyes could see that Jesus embodied everything that the return of Israel's God should be. John's eyes could see what many since have seen: that Jesus was Malachi's God.[2] So, to be sure, John was not expecting anyone else to come after this: he had identified the right person—Jesus. He boldly uses the Scriptures!

As mentioned, two ancient predictions fit together like the two halves of a treasure map:

- Malachi predicted God coming with fire.
- Isaiah predicted: "And *the glory* of the LORD shall be revealed."

The Glory and the refiner's fire: they point to the same thing—the power and presence of the Holy Spirit, the Spirit whom Jesus was bringing. So this was to be fulfilled. John said it:

- Jesus "will baptize you with the Holy Spirit and *with fire . . .*"

John had nailed his colors to the mast. He was letting everyone know it. Jesus was bringing fire as Yahweh: Glory fire, Holy Spirit fire.

See how it has all fitted together:

---

2. John Calvin, *Institutes of the Christian Religion*, I.13.10 (p. 88 of the 1845 Beveridge translation). Cf. Bates, Birth of the Trinity, 89.

Mal 3:1–2 NIV	Isa 40:3–5 NIV	The Gospels
(The Lord speaks about sending his messenger, who is John the Baptist)		John the Baptist says:
"See, I will send my messenger,	"A voice of one calling: "In the desert	"I am the voice of one calling in the desert . . .
who will prepare the way	prepare the way	'Make straight the way
before me		for the Lord.'"
		John spotted Jesus and made this announcement: "This is the one I meant when I said,
Then suddenly *the Lord* you are seeking will come	for *the LORD*	'A man who comes after me has surpassed me because he was before me.'"
	make straight in the wilderness a highway for our God..	
to his temple . . .		
he will be *like a refiner's fire* . . ."	And *the glory* of the LORD will be revealed."	Jesus "will baptize you with the Holy Spirit and with fire."

Let's just take stock and summarize the thrust of the prophecies of Isaiah and Malachi. Taking them together, which is what Mark does, the return of Yahweh God to his true temple would be heralded by the return of the Glory, by an awesome fiery power, one that would bring his people back to holiness. In that much, it sounds a lot like the spectacular scene of Solomon's temple. This sounded like it was about the glory days coming back.

Many Israelites had been waiting for something like this to happen for centuries, since the days when the Glory left Solomon's ruined temple. Isaiah and Malachi had written to encourage people in these hopes. Now that John the Baptist was playing the messenger, acting out his part in the prophecies, the signs were that the glory days really were coming back. John didn't hold back when it came to stoking up people's expectations.

And he only cranked it up higher with his talk of Jesus baptizing with the Holy Spirit and fire.[3]

---

3. To unpack John's religious language a little more: the word "baptizing" means "immersing" in something. People were being immersed in water by John. But, greater

We have John the Baptist to thank for joining the dots together, tying the story of Jesus to the prophecies. It takes us right to the heart of who the true temple belongs to, who should be in the true temple. Right where you would expect the Name of God to be, you find it's Jesus that he's talking about.

The prophecy of Jesus bringing fire was fulfilled at Pentecost, in the book of Acts. It is well to pause and recall what happened at that Pentecost:

- It is a moment where we see heaven and earth joined together, when Jesus pours out the Holy Spirit from heaven. This puts us in touch with one of the truths of the true temple: it was the place where heaven and earth were joined together.

- Jesus from heaven pours out the Spirit into the new temple—the community of believers. And this teaches us where God's presence can be found. There is Jesus in heaven with God the Father. And at the same time, when Jesus pours out the Holy Spirit, Jesus' spiritual presence is flowing from heaven to earth. And so we find Jesus and the Spirit dwelling in the church community, just as the Name and the Glory dwelled in the temple.

This moment of pouring out the Holy Spirit is a key to understanding the three-in-one God. That's Pentecost. But John the Baptist would not live to see it. He would miss seeing how tongues of fire at Pentecost fulfill these prophecies. Dark days were coming for him.

2. JOHN THE BAPTIST'S CRISIS

Events in John the Baptist's life took a dramatic turn for the worse. He was taken into King Herod's custody and locked up in prison. He had spoken out too loudly and too often for the liking of Herod's sister-in-law about matters concerning her and Herod's close and dubious relationship.

In his cell, John's hopes all seemed far away. This didn't look like the glory days of Israel. He began to question his own convictions about Jesus. John hadn't been expecting anyone else to come but Jesus, but now he had doubts. Was the return of Yahweh embodied in Jesus, or had he got it very wrong?

While he still had contact with his friends, John asked them to go to Jesus. In his moment of crisis, John wanted to hear Jesus' side of the story. So his friends go to Jesus with the question, "Are you the one who is to come, or should we expect someone else?" (Luke 7:20)

---

still, they were going to be immersed in a heavenly fire, he was saying.

To answer these doubts, Jesus says this:

> The blind receive sight, the lame walk, those who have leprosy are cured, the deaf hear, the dead are raised, and the good news is preached to the poor. (Luke 7:22 NIV)

To those in the know, those who knew the Jewish Scriptures, these words of Jesus were the confirmation John wanted. And here is how: Jesus is quoting ancient words about Yahweh. They were again from the prophet Isaiah:

> . . . your God will come . . . He will come and save you. Then will the eyes of the blind be opened and the ears of the deaf unstopped; then shall the lame leap like a deer, and the tongue of the mute sing for joy. (Isa 35:4–6)

God wasn't still on his way, he was already here, in the form of Jesus. He uses these words—which tell of Yahweh God coming and healing in these ways—to describe himself going about his business.

He also reassuringly recognizes John's role in preparing the way for him. Jesus says this about him:

> This is the one about whom it is written [in Malachi]: "I will send my messenger ahead of you, who will prepare your way before you." (Luke 7:27 NIV)

Jesus is the first person in the Gospels to quote this Malachi verse directly (apart from the angel in Luke 1:17 and Mark himself starting his Gospel with it) and he used it to say that John had got it right. So, his friends could take the answer back to him—John need expect no one else to come, despite John's crisis.

These Scriptures were about John and Jesus. This was crucial. The Malachi Scripture was loaded with the message of God's return to his temple with fire. By publicly backing John, Jesus was nailing his colors to the mast too: the temple and the fire were his own. John's historic announcement—that Jesus was the one—was intact. This is step one: John and Jesus have revealed to their disciples that Jesus fulfills the role of the temple's God, coming to bring Glory fire with him.

Since John and Jesus said so, Jesus' followers took this onboard. As a check against this, we can take St. Paul's words: "John baptized with the baptism of repentance, telling the people to believe in the one who was to come after him, that is, Jesus" (Acts 19:4 ESV).

It is a dramatic insight into Jesus' own awareness of how he embodied God returning to his people. It's an exceptional thing for someone to think about himself.

But just how was Yahweh embodied in Jesus? It has to do with the Name being embodied in Jesus. (This comes to the fore later.)

About the same time that Jesus had spoken with John's disciples, the people were saying, "God has come to help his people" (Luke 7:16 NIV). They were starting to perceive what John had first believed about Jesus.[4]

John tragically was murdered in Herod's prison, and now the weight of the story falls squarely on the shoulders of Jesus.

From here, we will pick up a scrapbook of scenes from his life, spread across the Gospels of Matthew, Mark, Luke, and John. For insights into the life of Jesus of Nazareth, these are our most ancient and valuable sources (apart from a few things in Paul's letters about Jesus). Here we have things written within the lifetime of people who met Jesus. The scenes we take in will include the supernatural incident of his transfiguration on a mountain; his momentous arrival in Jerusalem in the last week of his life; his words on the night before his death; and scenes after his resurrection.

As we advance along the trail, we will find out how much of the disciples' triune thinking was learned from Jesus, more even than those insights from Malachi and Isaiah. We will see that he taught about the ideal of God's presence in the temple, a temple not limited to a building, but something bigger—a temple built of many people. And he revealed himself to be the Name figure whom we know from Solomon's temple.

Already we have seen Jesus hailed as God coming to his temple, accompanied by fire. Already the Glory-fire and the Holy Spirit are linked, thanks to John the Baptist. Already, the three-in-one God of Solomon's temple is shaping up around Jesus and the Holy Spirit.

3. HIS TABERNACLE, HIS GLORY

The Story of Jesus' Ministry: the Middle of the Story

What did Jesus really think about the temple? The answer will come piece by piece. We will see that he was responsible for spreading visionary ideas that threatened the status quo of the Jerusalem temple's business. His followers revered the three-in-one God of the Old Testament, as the God of Solomon's temple. But at the same time, Jesus was priming his followers to think of the three-in-one God in the new way, the way that ultimately meant Christians being temples of the Holy Spirit.

---

4. Luke records them saying, "A great prophet has appeared among us. God has come to help his people." This calls Jesus both a prophet and God—both man and God.

"Destroy This Temple"

Just as we are getting used to the idea of Jesus being God returning to his temple, unexpectedly, a new idea appears in the story. It is this: Jesus was not only the temple's divine presence, but, at the same time, he was that temple, his body was that temple. So up to now we have thought about Jesus being the divine presence. Now we need to think about him being a temple.

We need to understand what kind of temple this could be. Jesus said, "Destroy this temple, and in three days I will raise it up" (John 2:19). And we are told: "But he was speaking about the temple of his body" (John 2:21).

This is groundbreaking stuff. Long before Christians were speaking of their bodies as "temples of the Holy Spirit," here was Jesus speaking of his body as a temple. It was he who was spreading these ideas. The disciples got the idea directly from him. He was getting them to understand that a new kind of temple would be needed, one not made of slabs of stone but of human flesh and blood.

A new kind of temple—our bodies and community—is his plan. He has planted the seeds of this idea in his disciples' minds by speaking of his own body as a temple. This is the second step, with Jesus sowing the idea of the temple of the body.

With what we have learned, if Jesus' body is a temple, we might expect this temple to be the home of the Name and the Glory: we will see that that is true. But that is getting ahead of ourselves.

Jesus' talk of being a temple lingered long with his audience, friends and foes alike. So much so that later at his trial (Mark 14:58, with more detail in Matt 26:61) we encounter accusers who had heard Jesus but not understood him. They come accusing him of saying, "I will destroy this man-made temple and in three days will build another not made by man."[5] The gospel accounts exonerate Jesus. He did not threaten to destroy Herod's temple. He spoke only of others destroying a temple, including the temple of his body.

The Temple and the Presence

What can it mean for Jesus to be both the temple and the divine presence at the same time? A big question. The answer is a unique biblical idea. It is an idea that we also find in St. John's book of Revelation. It forecasts a

---

5. After Jesus' resurrection, these ideas carried on being big news. The idea of the new-temple not being "man-made" and "not by human hands" is taken in all kinds of directions in Acts 7:48, 2 Cor 5:1, and Heb 9:11, 24. See Beale, *Temple and the Church's Mission*, 152. The idea goes back to Dan 2:34–45, which Jesus used in Luke 20:18 to speak of himself.

future where God is a temple: "And I saw no temple in the city, for its temple is the Lord God the Almighty and the Lamb" (Rev 21:22 ESV). God and the Lamb—the Lamb is a name for Jesus—are the temple in this visionary picture. At one and the same time, God and the Lamb are the temple, and they are the divine presence in it. Both are both.

It is something that could never be said of any disciple, apostle, or anyone else in God's kingdom. To be both the divine presence *and* the temple, only "God and his Lamb" fit the bill.

So Jesus' way of returning as God, coming to his own temple, has to do with his own body.

His Tabernacle, His Glory

Indeed, Jesus' very humanity was the temple of his divine nature. John's Gospel serves up one of the strongest impressions of this in its memorable first chapter. It says that Jesus "became flesh and tabernacled for a while among us" (John 1:14). And John adds, "we saw his glory." This is a momentous statement by John. Let's inspect the clues.

He puts the words "tabernacle" and "glory" together like a winning hand. His combination of the two words is a clue that this is temple thinking. We saw a little about it earlier. John intends us, as readers of his book, to call to mind the tabernacle tent built by Moses for God to dwell in. So picture this: the tabernacle was God's home on earth where his Glory rested.

There is a match here. To say that Jesus "became flesh and tabernacled" was a way of talking about his body and saying that it was a kind of tabernacle/temple. (The NIV reads here that Jesus "lived" among us—but this translates a Greek word that literally means "tabernacled" among us.)

So, come to the second part of the match and it becomes explosive. Because John meant Jesus' Glory when he said that it was *his* Glory.

Only the true God has a tabernacle with his own Glory there. The faithful did not dare to speak of anyone else in such terms. John has boldly laid his cards on the table: he is speaking of a tabernacle with Jesus' Glory.

John's Israelite friends would have known at once what a far-reaching statement he was making. He was using their way of thinking to make Jesus out to be the presence of the God of Israel.

His Glory, in his tabernacle.

Jesus' followers were sticking their necks out for Jesus by writing these things. Make no mistake. If—let's suppose—Jesus were not Israel's God, then John would be being blasphemous to put those words together in that way, guilty of promoting a temple for the glory of someone other than their one true God Yahweh. No one else's temple, no one else's glory, was valid.

It was Jesus' Glory with his tabernacle. And so he was John's God. He was Yahweh God.

This spicy combination of words also takes us back to the thought about God being both the divine presence and the temple at the same time. Jesus was both. It says something of both Jesus' humanity (seen in his flesh as a "tabernacle") and his divinity (seen in his Glory):

> Jesus "became flesh and tabernacled for a while among us . . . we saw his glory." (John 1:14)

Introducing Jesus in this way, John's Gospel has a three-in-one start every bit as strong as the start of Mark's Gospel with its ancient prophecies. It is an interesting fact that both Gospels begin by signposting to Jesus having a temple that is rightfully his, to call his own; and not only this, but also with his Glory.

Making their introductions like this is a measure of how vital the temple and the Glory were in their minds for understanding Jesus: not just the temple of the Pentecost church, but the temple of Jesus' body. It is all linked.

More of Jesus' Glory

John couldn't leave this alone. In his Gospel, he says even the prophet Isaiah had seen Jesus' Glory (John 12:41). And what is John referring to? He is recalling Isaiah's vision of the Lord seated high on a throne in the temple, being worshiped for his holiness and his Glory (Isa 6:1–10). It is daring for John to say, in this way, that this was the Lord Jesus, Lord of the temple.

And at what point in the gospel story does it come that Isaiah saw Jesus' Glory? Guess what? It's after reporting Jesus talking about himself as the "Name": "Father, glorify your name" (John 12:28). We will give more thought later to how Jesus referred to himself at the Name.

One thing is for sure. We are right on the map, on the trail of the three-in-one God of the temple.

Jesus actually prayed about his Glory. In John 17:24 he prays, "that they . . . see my glory." There was to be no secret about it. But when exactly had they ever seen his Glory? An answer to this question can be seen in one of the most extraordinary scenes in the Gospels—what is called Jesus' transfiguration.

4. JESUS AND THE TRANSFIGURATION

The unexpected idea of Jesus being the temple, as well as the divine presence, comes to the fore at the scene of his "transfiguration."

Famously, high up on a mountain, his three closest friends saw his appearance change into dazzling white light. Luke's Gospel says that Peter, James, and John "saw his glory"—Jesus' Glory (Luke 9:32).[6]

Witnessing Jesus' transfiguration will have spurred on their thinking. In Luke 9:29–36, we read of his face changing, his clothes becoming as bright as lightning.

Two Israelite prophets, Moses and Elijah, also appear on the mountain bathed in glorious splendor, but it is not written that it is their own glory.

Peter, not a man with an expensive religious education and who did not yet know what he was saying at this point (according to Luke) suggests putting up tabernacles (tents) for all three of them, Jesus and Moses and Elijah, as if they were all going to be staying around a while. But that was not to happen. Instead, they hear the Father's voice from within a cloud that enveloped them. The Father's voice singles out Jesus as the one to listen to. As it happens, it would have been needless to build Jesus a tabernacle, because his tabernacle was his own flesh: "the Word became flesh and tabernacled among us."

Handcrafting a tabernacle tent had had its place for meeting God. But Jesus' visionary thinking about the temple would have to be grasped. A new kind of temple was coming—a human community—a message he was soon to start putting across more forcefully. The disciples did eventually understand this, although it took them time.[7]

The Veil of His Flesh

A little more needs to be said about his Glory. The blinding light of the transfiguration, which had the disciples bowing their faces to the ground, reminds us of the Glory that the ancient priests saw hitting Solomon's temple, making them bow to the ground in awe too.

---

6. In 2 Pet 1:17–18, the author wrote that they heard God's voice—from heaven—coming out of the cloud—that is, the Glory. This seems to be God the Father's Glory, whereas alongside this Luke writes about Jesus' Glory, the Glory bestowed on him by his Father.

7. Paul taught that the church community will one day be bathed in the Glory that Elijah and Moses were bathed in at the transfiguration. As the body of Christ, they will all benefit from being in his Glory. Christians do not yet appear the way that Elijah and Moses appeared. But they shall ultimately be transformed into a new humanity, which glows like glory. This will be at the future resurrection, St. Paul wrote in 1 Cor 15.

But his transfiguration is also a bit of an enigma. The reason for this is that normally Jesus' Glory was hidden from view. Hidden, as it were, by the flesh of his body like a veil. The words of Heb 10:20 lead us to see Jesus this way. They call his body a veil. They recall the tabernacle where the Glory of God's presence in the holy of holies was hidden from view by a curtain, a veil of great size. The Glory was not normally in public view in Solomon's day because of this veil. And the Glory was not normally in view in Jesus because the flesh of his body hid it like a veil.

Hebrews gives us a lead: it is that Jesus' flesh did what the tabernacle's veil did—shielded human eyes from his Glory.[8] It is as if this veil was drawn aside at the transfiguration. And so, on the mountain, when Jesus' disciples saw his divine Glory, they did what the ancient priests did—they fell on their faces in awe.

What Peter, James and John Learned

Seeing Jesus' Glory was a life-changing experience for Peter, James, and John. They saw connections linking the transfiguration and the temple's God. John's Gospel shows us the connection they made with the words: Jesus "became flesh and tabernacled for a while among us . . . we saw his glory" (John 1:14).[9]

Their understanding of the three-in-one God had to do with how they thought about God's presence and Glory in the tabernacle/temple. It was not as if they came to appreciate the triune God without thinking about the temple.

"Gather in My Name"

Gradually, Jesus taught his followers about what his presence would mean to them in the future. He said, "Where two or three are gathered together in my name, there am I in the midst of them" (Matt 18:20 KJV).

This is a landmark claim by Jesus. He is speaking about his own spiritual presence. He is speaking as a voice of the three-in-one God of the temple.

---

8. St. Ambrose writing about the light shining through Jesus in the "transfiguration" recognized that the Glory was a sign of the presence of the Holy Spirit: "The apostles truly saw this glory, when the Lord Jesus on the mount shone with the light . . . Who is He, then, Who shined . . . Whom else do we think but the manifested Spirit?" Ambrose, *On the Holy Spirit*, III, 12, 87–88. The Glory is the Holy Spirit made visible, made "manifest," as he puts it.

9. For a similar connection between Jesus and his own Glory, we can turn to Peter's first letter. This speaks of Jesus and "his Glory" (1 Pet 4:13).

His words meant Jesus would be dwelling in any place where Christians met, with him as the spiritual divine presence, and them as the temple he's dwelling in. This is a big claim. And what a change it would mean! God's presence had dwelled especially in the Jerusalem temple, but Jesus' presence would be anywhere that his people gathered as a temple. Jewish teachers surely knew what such a claim meant. In later years, Jewish rabbis wrote their own version of this idea: "If two men sit together and occupy themselves with the words of the Torah [the Jewish law], the Shekinah is in their midst."[10] If we put the two sayings side by side, this counts Jesus and the Shekinah as equivalent, as God's presence:

Jesus said	Rabbis said
"Where two or three are gathered together	"If two men sit together
in my name	and occupy themselves with the words of the Torah
there am I	the Shekinah
in the midst of them."	is in their midst."

Jesus' disciples were being taught to treat Jesus' spiritual presence as God's presence, as the Shekinah. His presence would dwell in Christian hearts. This would be when the church community became a temple. We know of this as the moment when his presence was ushered in by the fire of the Holy Spirit—at Pentecost. Piece by piece, like pixels forming a picture, the clues to the three-in-one God are coming together.

The story now heads towards a crisis moment in Jesus' mission.

5. ON THE ROAD TO JERUSALEM

A little while after the transfiguration, Jesus led his disciples towards Jerusalem. He was sure that he would be killed there by the establishment. On the way, he taught about the kind of heart that anyone should have, to be truly one of his followers.

He said they should be so set on the kingdom of God that they should not worry about what they will wear and what they will eat: "For where your treasure is, there will your heart be also" (Luke 12:34).

The Bible has a rich heritage on the subject of the heart's problems, and how this could be put right. Its teaching can be summed up like this: what is needed is not only a different way of thinking, but a different heart to think with. The ancient promises of God—for example in Ezek 36:22

---

10. m. Avot 3:2.

through 37:14—were for a supernatural cure. God's Spirit would put new life and a new heart into people. That is, a new heart that the disciples would have when they were filled with the Holy Spirit—at Pentecost.

Hints of that moment keep turning up. Here now is one, with Jesus saying something that lines up with the prophecy about him baptizing people with the Holy Spirit and fire. We see just how animated Jesus was about this prospect, when he would breathe the Breath of God, the holy fire, upon the church:

> I have come to bring *fire* to the earth, and how I wish it were blazing already! (Luke 12:49–50 NJB)

He then describes how some will share this new kind of life, and others will face judgment instead, and in so saying he sets the stage for Pentecost, where Peter's message split people into those for and against.

This inner change in the human heart is needed. But when Jesus brings it by his inner fire, it would lead to painful division between friends and foes of his message. Jesus speaks of "father against son and son against father, mother against daughter and daughter against mother" (Luke 12:53). Even families would be divided over whether or not they respond well to the refining fire he brings: for some it was life and for others judgment. Jesus sees it as inevitable that such division will happen when he brings the fire of God, the Holy Spirit. He knew opposition all through his ministry. The Scriptures had said it would be this way: in Isa 30:27, both life and judgment are brought by the Name with tongues of fire.

As they approached Jerusalem, Jesus wasted no time spelling out the judgment that would come to its disreputable stone temple. He predicted, accurately, that their nation's enemies would destroy the temple (Luke 19:38–46). The enemies were Roman troops and they "will not leave one stone on another, because you did not recognize the time of God's coming to you." That prediction would come true a few decades after Jesus spoke. Jerusalem and its temple fell to the Roman army in a brutal war, and were destroyed.

But for Jesus, there was a crisis closer to hand. His life was heading to a swift and tragic end. God's return to his people was embodied in Jesus, but he was rejected.

6. THE LAST WEEK

In Luke chapter 19, we come to a turning point in the story. Jesus rode into Jerusalem. This was celebrated like he was already the King of the Jews. People came out to see, and they started acting out the words of Ps 118. This

Psalm is very much about temple worship, worship as in the temple of God's Name and Glory.

They shouted, "Blessed is the King who comes in the name of the Lord" (Luke 19:38). They were holding palm branches in their hands (John 12:13). These are the words they were acting out:

> Blessed is he who comes in the name of the LORD! From the house of the LORD we bless you... With boughs in hand, join in the festal procession up to the horns of the altar. (Ps 118:26–27 NIV)

We will shortly see Jesus quoting the same psalm. For now we need to hold on to Ps 118 as a clue that will become more meaningful when he quotes it.

Luke tells us that Jesus immediately entered the temple area. Like a refiner's fire, he begins to sift good things from bad. He had preached there often, but the religious authorities had not been inclined to follow him. It was the day for Jesus to demonstrate what he had been trying to tell them.

First, he had to show that he did not find all well at the Jerusalem temple. So Jesus put the temple's business temporarily out of action. This famous story is in Luke 19:45–46.

As he enters the temple area, he turns over tables of money changers, and he turns over tables of those selling doves for use in Israelite religious sacrifices. He speaks out against swindlers cheating ordinary Israelites who needed to exchange their cash currency to buy their sacrificial birds.

Jesus shouts out a quotation from the Old Testament. He accuses them of making God's house "a den of robbers." These words were sure to raise a storm, and we know exactly where he got them from: Jer 7:11, written hundreds of years earlier. By using these few words, Jesus was triggering their memory of the passage. They may have known it well.

In his distant day, Jeremiah was warning about danger of the Name vacating God's house, which had fallen into disrepute. History was repeating itself. The Name, Jeremiah said, had dwelled in a previous home called Shiloh. And God gave up on that home and destroyed it because of the sins of Israel. As in the time of Shiloh, so in Jeremiah's day. And as in Jeremiah's day, so in Jesus'. The temple was hardly fit for God's presence.

Let's recall Jeremiah's historic verses, so we can appreciate what use Jesus is making of them:

> This is the word that came to Jeremiah from the LORD:
> "Stand at the gate of the LORD'S house and there proclaim this message...

> "'Has this house, which bears my Name, become a den of robbers to you? But I have been watching! declares the LORD.
>
> "'Go now to the place in Shiloh, where I first made *a dwelling for my Name*, and see what I did to it because of the wickedness of my people Israel...
>
> "'Therefore, what I did to Shiloh I will now do to the house that bears my Name, the temple . . . I will thrust you from my presence . . .'"
>
> (Jer 7:1–15 NIV)

Visitors to Jerusalem were meant to find themselves near to the Name, not near to robbers. Those Israelites who knew the Scriptures should have got the point that Jesus was making.[11]

But it was to no avail. Some may not have understood that a stone temple was not the only place where God could be present. And within a generation, devastating events changed all that. Jerusalem's temple, which had once echoed to the sound of Jesus' footsteps, was reduced to rubble under the feet of Roman troops in a terrible defeat for the nation.

It was a sign. A temple without Jesus was worthless to God. A temple without the Name and the Glory isn't fit to stand.[12]

When Jesus was making his statements in the temple, the authorities dug in their heels and challenged what Jesus was doing and saying. For them, it was a crisis. The crisis only got deeper for them when they heard the sound of children shouting to Jesus, "Hosanna to the Son of David" (Matt 21:14–16).

Jesus justified the children praising him, and he did this in a way that was provocative. Again he borrowed Old Testament words that the Jewish leaders regarded as sacred, words that mention the Name. Jesus treated these words as applying to himself. They come from Ps 8:1–2 (NIV):

> O LORD, our Lord, how majestic is *your name* in all the earth!
> You have set your glory above the heavens. *From the lips of children and infants you have ordained praise*.

Jesus assumes that those words authorize the children to praise him. This is asking for trouble. He is equating himself either with God or with

---

11. Quoting a fragment of Scripture would stir up in their minds the Bible passage from which it came; just as hearing a line from a familiar song triggers the memory of more of the same song. People's memories in much of the West hold music; theirs held Scriptures in a similar way.

12. In Jeremiah, the tragic story tells us of the 3D God: in different ways God and his Name and his Glory all feature. We have already read Jeremiah's warning that the Name would depart. Jeremiah also pleaded with God: "For the sake of your name do not despise us, do not dishonor your glorious throne" (Jer 14:21). The throne was connected with the Glory—that is what made it glorious—as the Glory shone above the temple's throne.

God's majestic Name because that is who the psalm's praise is for. The authorities had to listen to Jesus justifying the children's praise on those terms, which was the last thing they wanted.

They must have thought he was arrogant, or mad, if they did not think he was God or God's Name. By now, some loved him, some hated him. Jesus was establishing that he was present with the authority of God's presence, worthy of praise that was rightfully his.

And his enemies hardened their hearts against him.

The Psalm

Let's take a moment to see the way that Jesus was using this psalm to influence people. Ps 8:1–2 starts with God's Name being praised as majestic all over the earth. Ps 8:5–6 gives us a picture that Christians take to be the enthronement of Jesus, in the heavenly sanctuary, on the throne, in the Glory, after his ascension.[13] It calls him the Son of Man, his famous title, and then describes him being made Lord and "crowned with glory and honor" (Ps 8:5). Ps 8:6–9 has "the Name" being praised all over the world and "the Son of Man" being Lord all over the world. Jesus takes both titles as describing himself. He takes the praise for God's majestic Name as praise for himself. And he calls himself the Son of Man too.

He is the Son of Man, and he is the Name, and as such he is crowned Lord of all. That is a message he keeps putting across, all through the most important week of his life.

Jesus and Heaven's Throne

As if that wasn't enough, Jesus boldly announced to a group of his opponents—the Pharisees—that he would be enthroned with God the Father (this would be in the heavenly sanctuary). He does this by quoting Ps 110, which refers to both Jesus and God the Father as "Lord":

> The Lord said to my Lord: "Sit at my right hand . . ." (Matt 22:44)[14]

---

13. Wesley, *Explanatory Notes*, 731.

14. It is also in Luke 20:41–44 and Mark 12:35–37. Jesus quotes the psalm, calling both himself and his Father "Lord." In the original Hebrew Psalm, two different Hebrew words make a distinction. There, the name Yahweh is given to the Father, and the title Adonai—meaning "Lord"—applies to the one seated with him. The Gospel quotes from a Greek translation of the Hebrew psalm where both *Yahweh* and *Adonai* are rendered as "Lord." In so doing, this gives us a parallel between "Lord" and "Lord" enthroned side by side.

This statement by Jesus made its mark and was widely remembered—indeed, Ps 110:1 is one of the most quoted parts of the Old Testament that we find in the New Testament. Famously, the apostle Peter said that these words were about Jesus being enthroned at the Father's right hand as Lord in heaven (Acts 2:32–36).

To check where this puts us on the treasure map, we can go straight to Rev 3:21 and here we get our bearings. It is where Jesus, after his resurrection and ascension to heaven, says, "I overcame and sat down with my Father on his throne." It is Jesus sharing the throne of God the Father. Of course, no one but God can rightfully be seated on God's throne. The Father and the Son are on their throne as the God of the heavenly sanctuary. It is a triune God moment.

The Ideal Temple

If some in Jerusalem had lost sight of what God's presence in the temple should mean, Jesus hadn't. He gets a chance to say more about it in a tense encounter with the Pharisees. He is making a stand against their religious practice of swearing oaths by "the gold of the temple" and "by the gifts on the temple's altar." What he says next is an education in how to think of God's presence. His words, as we saw earlier, are in Matt 23:21–22 (NIV):

> he who swears by *the temple* swears by it and by *the one who dwells in it*.
>
> And he who swears by *heaven* swears by God's throne and by *the one who sits on it*.

Two dwelling places for God—it's a familiar picture that Jesus is painting, an Old Testament way of speaking about the temple and heaven. We see it in Ps 11:4 (NIV):

> The LORD is in his holy temple;
> The LORD is on his heavenly throne.

One God, two dwelling places. Jesus' words and the Psalm match up well:

Jesus speaking: Matt 23:21–22	*Ps 11:4*
he who swears by *the temple* swears by it and	
by *the one who dwells in it*.	The LORD is *in his holy temple*;
And he who swears by *heaven* swears by	
God's *throne* and by the one who sits *on it*.	The LORD is *on his heavenly throne*.

In the Old Testament, this was about God having a presence in the earthly temple, distinct from his presence in heaven, so that he could be amongst his people as well as in heaven at the same time.[15] And Jesus knew exactly that meaning.

It is vital to remind ourselves again of how Solomon spoke about the three-in-one God and the temple, when he prayed at its dedication. He said:

> . . . praying in your presence. May your eyes be open towards this temple day and night, this place of which you have said you would put *your Name there*. May you hear the prayer your servant prays towards this place . . . *Hear from heaven* your dwelling place . . . (2 Chr 6:19–21 NIV)

The two passages line up next to each other like this:

Jesus speaking: Matt 23:21–22	Solomon praying: 2 Chr 6:19–21
"he who swears	"May your eyes be open towards
by *the temple*	*this temple*
swears by it and	day and night, this place of which you have said
by *the one who dwells in it*.	you would put *your Name there* . . .
And he who swears by *heaven*	Hear from *heaven*
Swears by God's throne	*your dwelling place*."
and by the one who sits on it."	

Solomon's prayer shows Solomon and Jesus thinking on similar lines: even after God's presence came to its resting place in Solomon's temple, God would still be in heaven hearing prayers. It is an unmovable feature of the Bible: the distinct presences of God—above in heaven and below with his people. This was the understanding of the temple that Jesus had, and that he expected others to understand.

So, a familiar question arises: if God the Father was still in heaven, who or what is the presence dwelling in the temple on earth? Where did the double presence—the Name and the Glory—fit in now? We know how it looks in the church with hindsight: one in heaven, two in the church, known by the early Christians as the heavenly Father, plus Christ and the Holy Spirit. But did Jesus at this time see himself as somehow playing such a part? How much did the disciples learn about this from Jesus?

We have already seen that earlier in the same Gospel, Jesus said, "where two or three are gathered together in my name, there am I in the midst of

---

15. Wilson, *Out of the Midst of the Fire*, 68–70.

them" (Matt 18:20 KJV). This counts Jesus and the Shekinah presence as equivalent, as God's presence. This is his promise of how his spiritual presence would dwell in the church community, like the Shekinah in the temple.

That is not all, as we have seen. Jesus had already been pitched as Yahweh God returning to his temple with the Holy Spirit and fire, and received the children's praise as due to God's majestic Name, and predicted that he would be enthroned with his Father as Lord in the heavenly sanctuary. So we need to be alert to anything Jesus says that could be about his presence in the temple, and see where the evidence takes us.

Although Jesus equated himself with God's presence in the temple, we can be sure that it would not be in Herod's temple now, given his clear prediction of its violent destruction.

That leaves the prospect of Jesus' presence having a place in the new temple, the church community.

There are hints of the coming Pentecost, for which the disciples were being prepared, for Jesus' spiritual presence to extend from heaven's throne to the church community through the Holy Spirit.

Rejection

Having challenged much of what he has seen and heard, Jesus leaves the area of Herod's stone temple, and on the way out he confirms judgment will fall on it with these words: "Not one stone here will be left on another; every one will be thrown down" (Mark 13:2 NIV). As the Bible says at this point, "Jesus left the temple." It has the feeling of judgment. And we are reminded of how the temple ceased to be a home for the Name once before in the days of Jeremiah.

The promised destruction of the temple—though it was radical and unsettling for the disciples—was a sign: change was coming. Jesus signaled that the temple ideal could still be a reality, but was not just limited to a stone building.

Jesus Predicts His Own Death

Jesus said his death would be like a seed dying in the ground. That he predicted his death is striking enough in itself. But what makes it more so is some of the language he used in his prediction—the language of the Name and the Glory.

Jesus reveals his thoughts and uses a group of titles for himself: "The hour has come for *the Son of Man to be glorified* . . . for this purpose I have come to this hour. Father, *glorify Your name*" (John 12:23-28 ESV); "*glorify your Son*" (17:1).[16]

It hints at Jesus' awareness of a few things: that he embodied the Name; that his death and his Glory would be connected. We will hear him reveal more at what Christians call, in religious language, the Last Supper.

As tensions increased over what Jesus was saying and doing in Jerusalem, his enemies moved in for the kill. With thirty pieces of silver, they bribed his disciple Judas to betray him, to gain a chance to arrest, convict, and pass sentence on him. That day was getting closer.

7. THE LAST SUPPER

The Story of Jesus' Ministry—Endings

When Jesus spoke judgment upon Herod's stone temple, he went straight on to make some astonishing revelations about what the Holy Spirit would do for the disciples. Now, Jesus' relationship with the Holy Spirit was a very close one. Not only does he have the authority to baptize his followers with the Holy Spirit (Mark 1:8). (That's amazing enough because God's Holy Spirit is unique to God, and only God has the right to give it. Jesus will do that. It's evidence that Jesus is included in God's identity.) Now, Jesus says something extraordinary.

He makes a promise on the part of the Holy Spirit that the Holy Spirit will one day give words to his followers when in trouble: "Whenever you are arrested and brought to trial, do not worry beforehand about what to say. Just say whatever is given you at the time, *for it is not you speaking but the Holy Spirit*" (Mark 13:11 NIV). So, Jesus has inside knowledge about when the Spirit would speak in the future, and he has an eyebrow-raising right to pledge it as only God should! This is the Trinity doing what only the Trinity can do together. And Luke 21:15 adds a telling little detail to that: these sacred words of the Holy Spirit will come from Jesus. So, the Spirit will be speaking through them with words from Jesus.[17]

A day or so afterwards, Jesus has his famous Last Supper with his disciples. There, he again claims the divine right to make a promise on the part of the Holy Spirit! "But when he, the Spirit of truth comes, he will guide you into all truth. He will not speak on his own; *he will speak* only what he hears, *and he will tell you* what is to come" (John 16:13-14 NIV). The Gospels of Mark and John reveal that the Holy Spirit will speak in aid of the disciples,

---

16. Hurtado, *Lord Jesus Christ*, 386.
17. Johansson, "Trinity Mark," 56. Thompson, "Trinity Luke-Acts," 74.

a point made by Jesus to them twice in a couple of days or so. It matters that they be prepared for listening to the Holy Spirit.

A lot of the things we have learned about the temple and God's three-in-one presence now come out into the open as Jesus speaks. On one issue, he lays his cards on the table for his disciples. He says the Holy Spirit "will be in you" (John 14:16–17). He has already said the old temple would be destroyed. Now he is becoming more explicit about what the new temple will be. It will be their own bodies. The dwelling place of God would be in them.

Jesus says they will be part of a new fellowship with the three-in-one God. It will not only be the Holy Spirit in them. Jesus and his Father will also be spiritually present and make their home with them. Jesus' impressive promise: "If anyone love me, he will keep my word, and my Father will love him, and we will come to him and make our abode with him" (John 14:23, Darby translation). Now, although "our Father in heaven" would hear prayers in heaven, he would also be with Jesus' church. Jesus is making a specific pledge on the part of God the Father, as well as making promises on the part of the Holy Spirit! No one lower than God could do that. Jesus is speaking as one of the three-in-one God.

As Jesus teaches them this, his followers are now primed to become the true temple of the triune God; ready for the Trinity—Father, Son, and the Holy Spirit—to dwell in the church community spiritually. This is the third step.

On this, the night of his arrest, he was ensuring everything was prepared for. He has been explicit that the Holy Spirit will dwell in the disciples, and his own spiritual presence with the Father. When the church is a temple, it's a temple of the three-in-one God.

At the end of the Last Supper, Jesus prayed a memorable prayer, his longest recorded prayer (John 17). It reveals more of his own thoughts about the three-in-one God of the temple. It's an extraordinary glimpse into the heart of the Trinity. In it, Jesus does new things with the language of the Name and the Glory for a new kind of temple—the fourth step.

8. THE LAST SUPPER PRAYER

Bible scholars have long recognized that Jesus' Last Supper prayer bears more than a passing resemblance to Solomon's dedication prayer for his temple. We saw Solomon's prayer in 2 Chr 6, while we find Jesus' prayer in John 17. Side by side, they confirm they had a similar understanding of God's presence:

2 Chr 6 (NIV)—Solomon:	John 17 (NIV)—Jesus:
"all the work Solomon had done for the temple of the LORD was finished" (5:1)	"finishing the work you gave me to do" (17:4)
God says: "I have chosen Jerusalem for my Name to be there" (6:6)	"I [Jesus] came from you . . . you sent me" (17:8)
Solomon prays: "so that all the peoples of the earth may know your Name" (6:33)	"so that the world may believe that you have sent me" (17:21)
"there is no God like you" (6:14)	"you, the only true God . . ." (17:3)
"those who continue wholeheartedly in your way" (6:14)	"they have obeyed your word" (17:6)
"Hear the supplications of your servant" (6:21)	"I pray for them" (17:9)
"you said you would put your Name there" (6:20)	"the name you gave me" (17:11)
"the glory of the Lord filled the temple" (7:1)	"the glory that you gave me" (17:22)
"When your people go to war against their enemies. . . then hear from heaven their prayer and their plea, and uphold their cause" (6:34–35)	"My prayer is not that you take them out of the world but that you protect them from the evil one" (17:15)
"come to your resting place" (6:41)	"that I myself may be in them" (17:26)
God's answer: "I have chosen and consecrate this temple" (7:16)	"I sanctify myself, that they too may be sanctified" (17:19)

Two prayers, two differences

There are some standout clues in the similar details in that table. Jesus speaks to his heavenly Father about "the Name you gave me" and "the Glory you gave me" (17:11 and 17:22).[18] This is temple talk, ideas that go all the way back to Solomon, even earlier. It announces to us that Jesus is a temple of the Name and the Glory.

Both prayers were said in Jerusalem, and each was marking a similar occasion—it was time for a new temple for God's people. But Jesus' prayer was different from Solomon's for two main reasons which we gathered clues about earlier.

One is that Jesus was preparing for a different kind of temple, one of living stones—people—not hand-carved stones.

---

18. Hurtado, *Lord Jesus Christ*, 389.

Also, the person praying the prayer was very different from Solomon. Solomon only built a temple. Jesus on the other hand *is* the temple and the presence in it!

Becoming Temples

Jesus' prayer is for his disciples to become temples of the eternal God. This way, they have eternal life in them. The words he uses in this prayer take us right back to Solomon's temple.

For this, Jesus must go from tabernacling amongst them to tabernacling *in* them. So he prays "that I may be in them" (John 17:26 NIV). He is talking about his spiritual presence in his followers. Like the tabernacle, like the temple, they would become the home of God's presence.

When they have Jesus to dwell in them, they have God's life in them, eternal life.[19] This is how he prays for it.

> Glorify your Son, that your Son may glorify you. For you granted him authority over all people that he might give eternal life to all those you have given him. Now this is eternal life; that they may know you, the only true God, and Jesus Christ whom you have sent. (John 17:1–3 NIV)

This is an amazing message. When they know God's heavenly presence, and Jesus' earthly presence that is sent to dwell in them, eternal life is in them. For a check on what this says about Jesus, we can turn from John's Gospel to his first letter, where he wrote:

> Whoever has the Son has life; whoever does not have the Son of God does not have life. (1 John 5:12)

Without having the Son who was sent to dwell among them and in them, people are without eternal life. It is something vital that Jesus is praying into existence.

Eternal life is nothing less than having this fellowship with the Father and the Son. Simple knowledge or information about the Father and the Son would not be eternal life. It would just be knowledge. Jesus is talking about much more than that: meeting God in his Son. It is to join in with the fellowship that already exists between Jesus and his Father: Jesus speaks of himself dwelling in the Father, and the Father dwelling in him.[20] This is the kind of life

---

19. See Turner, "Approaching 'personhood' in the New Testament," 221.

20. Scholars have a term—"mutual indwelling"—for describing how the Father, the Son, and the Spirit interact with each other.

the believers are to join. Jesus puts it in a memorable way: "just as you are in me and I am in you. May they also be one in us" (John 17:21 NIV).[21]

When Christ prays "that I may be in them," this is so as to open up access to this kind of life for them.[22] When Christ is in them, they are also "in Christ."

Jesus has blazed the trail, describing himself as a temple, speaking of "the Name you gave me" (17:11) and "the Glory you gave me" (17:22). By becoming one with him, the double presence of the Name and the Glory is passed into the church community.

Jesus' prayer is about the three-in-one God of the temple: God, his Name, and his Glory.

To be clear, for a Christian, being a temple is not just an added extra. It is a keystone of being a Christian. Becoming a temple is the point where eternal life begins.

Sent as Temples

Jesus was sending his disciples, spiritually reborn, into the world. He makes it sound like they were coming from heaven into the world for the first time as newborns, just as he had come from heaven to earth (16:28). Jesus says, "no-one can see the Kingdom of God without being born from above"[23] (John 3:3, NRSV). As Jesus was from heaven, in a sense they are now from heaven too.

He was born as a temple. In his case, he was sent into the world, born in human form, "tabernacling" amongst them in the temple of his body. In their case, it was spiritual rebirth as temples. He puts his plan into action after his resurrection:

> Jesus said to them again, "Peace be with you. As the Father has sent me, even so I am sending you." And when he had said this, he breathed on them and said to them, "Receive the Holy Spirit." (John 20:21–22 ESV)

And this makes them temples of the Holy Spirit, a community in which the breath of Christ lives. This is the fifth step. Jesus has inducted his disciples into the ideas of the three-in-one God of the temple.

---

21. Some ancient manuscripts say "one in us" in this verse.
22. It is then they are said to be "in Christ," as St. Paul would put it.
23. Some translations go with an alternative reading, "born again," but with much the same meaning as "born from above."

Jesus Was Sent as God's Presence, the Name

When reading that Jesus speaks to "the one true God" and about himself as "Jesus Christ whom you have sent" (17:3), don't be confused. This is not splitting off the one true God from Jesus, as if they are two gods. Not at all. In this Gospel, speaking about "God and Jesus" is equivalent to speaking about "God and his Name." Jesus talks all about coming from heaven as God's *temple presence*. Jesus is the living embodiment of "the Name" (17:8). Just as the one true God put his Name in Solomon's temple, so the one true God put Jesus as his Name among his people. So, as John keeps showing us, here is Jesus as God's Name with his own Glory in the temple of his body (his tabernacle, with his Glory). Jesus is John's God. The words "the one true God" and "Jesus Christ whom you have sent" needn't be taken any other way.

It is no different really from the fact that the Holy Spirit is God, where we see that the Holy Spirit has God's privilege of dwelling in God's temple. The perfect verse to see this—1 Cor 16:9:

> do you not know that your body is a temple of the Holy Spirit
> within you, whom you have from God?

So, it is right to say that the Holy Spirit is *from* God, with a distinction between the Holy Spirit and God. But at the same time the Holy Spirit is what God is, dwelling in God's temple. It's just the same with Christ, sent *from* God, and dwelling in God's temple *as* God. The one and only thing that makes proper sense of the Bible here is the Trinity, the three-in-one God of the temple.

The model for this is God, his Name, and his Glory in the Jerusalem temple. The Name is from God, placed in the temple as his dwelling place.

The disciples hear the point of Jesus' prayer. Jesus is ready for the next stage of *his* journey, which makes possible *their* journey. He goes from "tabernacling" amongst his people—such that they see him and his Glory—to tabernacling in them, so that they know his presence within them.

Solomon's prayer was for the world to know God's presence, the Name. Jesus' prayer was for the world to know Jesus, the Name. The world needs something special, so God sent the Name, he sent Jesus.

Sent as "the Name": What This Says About the Three-In-One God

When talking about Jesus being sent by the Father, scholars have an apt phrase: they say the Father is "higher in office" than the Son. The one is in a position to send the other. This is what happens in the Trinity. John's

Gospel is clear that the Son did nothing of his own accord, but only what his Father's will was.

An obvious example to hand is that God is "higher in office" than his Name, as shown by putting his Name in Solomon's temple as he chooses (2 Chr 6:6). This is how we could tell apart God's presence in heaven and God's presence in the temple of Solomon: one sends the other; it is God in heaven who decides where his Name will dwell.

Like a mirror, this is a picture of Jesus being sent. He fulfills a role that is always a role of the Name—to dwell in the temple chosen by God.

It shows the Son's relationship to the Father in a perspective true to the triune God of the temple. The Father takes a leading role in the Trinity. The Son's service and obedience is represented in his being sent, his becoming human, and in how he receives his role from the Father. It is not only to do with him becoming human; it is in harmony with something that is *always true* about "the Name" and God.

Two Strange Sayings About the Name and the Glory

The words Name and Glory are prominent in Jesus' prayer. We find them in two eyebrow-raising phrases: "I have manifested your name" (John 17:6 ESV); and "glorify your Son" (17:1). That is how some translations put it.

The words "glorify your Son" may sound strange on Jesus' lips because he was never a "glory-seeker" as we would call it. We began to touch on this earlier.

The words "I have manifested your Name" make a very strange saying altogether and we should look at this first. Its meaning is found when we detect Solomon's temple as the background of the prayer. Here we are digging deeper into Jesus' understanding of the Name and the Glory. And we will see deeper into the understanding of the three-in-one God of the temple that was taking shape in the disciples' minds.

1. The Name Made Visible

As some translations put it, Jesus said to his Father, "I have manifested your name" (John 17:6).[24] So how does someone "manifest" a name?[25] Does this translation make sense?

---

24. The NIV translates this as "I have revealed you" but this unnecessarily adds the word "you" and leaves out the word "Name," the word Jesus actually used.

25. Hurtado, *Lord Jesus Christ*, 382–85.

The word "manifest" needs to go under the detective's microscope first. "Manifest" is one way of translating the Greek word: *phanero-o*. It means making something visible. It can be translated straightforwardly into English as such. So verse 6 can read: "I have made your Name visible." This is plainer English. It signals a big development in the story of Israel. The Name—God's presence—had been invisible in Solomon's temple, but the Name was now made visible in the form of Jesus Christ. Jesus has made God's presence visible. He has manifested the Name. He is the Name made visible.

For a health-check for our translation "made visible," we can turn from John's Gospel to John's first letter to see how exactly the same word gets translated there. And we see *phanero-o* translated as "made visible":

> Something which has existed since the beginning, which we have heard, which we have seen with our own eyes, which we have watched and touched with our own hands, the Word of life—this is our theme. That life was *made visible*; we saw it. (1 John 1:1–2 NJB)

This life is Jesus. Invisible before, but visible now as the disciples could see. So, 1 John 1:2 emphatically calls Jesus "the Life made visible." So, translating consistently, John 17:6 has Jesus saying, "I have made your Name visible" (author's translation). He has made *the temple presence* visible: it is himself.

These words stand well next to John 1:14: "And the Word became flesh and he tabernacled among us, and we saw his Glory." Jesus is "the Life" made visible. He is "the Name" made visible. He is "the Word made flesh." He is the Name made flesh.[26]

Side by side, these words line up like this:

John 17:6 (author's translation)	1 John 1:1–2 NJB	John 1:14 NIV
"I have made your Name	"the Word of life—this is our theme. That life was	"The Word
visible	made visible	became flesh
to those whom you gave me"		and lived for a while among us.
	we saw it"	We have seen his glory"

---

26. Hurtado, *Lord Jesus Christ*, 384, sees that such talk of the Word dwelling among us is a carryover from talk of the Name dwelling among us.

To avoid misunderstanding, this means that being made visible, it was Jesus' humanity that was seen, his body which they could see and touch, as 1 John 1:1–2 says. It took spiritual insight to discern his Glory unseen beneath his skin (except on the day of his transfiguration, one day when it was visible to his closest disciples, and except after his resurrection).[27]

The Temple of the Name and the Glory

A temple just isn't a true temple without the Name and the Glory, so the church community is going to need both. Jesus' prayer for them is that the Name will continue to be known, and the Glory (a sign of the Holy Spirit) among them (John 17:26 and 17:24 respectively). He will kick-start their new life as a temple by dwelling spiritually in their community. So he makes a request in his prayer "that I myself may be in them" (17:26).

People ever since should be able to detect the presence of Jesus and the Holy Spirit in the church community, as that is what he has prayed for. As such, Jesus' ministry can carry on in the church community. We see it in the book of Acts, where the disciples make Jesus and the Holy Spirit known through their lives and words. This is the task of the true temple, the church, the home of the three-in-one God.

The Inherited Name

A question we might want answered is this: what more could Jesus mean in speaking of "the Name you gave me"? It was given to Jesus to embody the divine Name, the temple presence. But in what other manner did God give the Name to Jesus? It is as a personal name. We have already seen in Philippians and Hebrews that Jesus was given the Name: but Jesus said it too. Behind the title "the Name" a personal name lies—the name Yahweh. The one to whom the name "Yahweh" is given *is* Yahweh (a point made earlier). This is not only before Jesus' death but also afterwards (Phil 2:9).[28] As the Son and heir of the Father, he inherits the Father's name Yahweh (Heb 1:2–4).[29]

---

27. Elsewhere, the New Testament makes quite a point about this. 1 Tim 3:16 NIV says simply, "he appeared in a body." 1 John 4:2 ESV speaks of him having "come in the flesh."

28. Kostenberger and Swain, *Father, Son and Spirit*, 384.

29. We will see him speaking of himself in the third person (instead of saying "I" or "me," where he says "the Name" or "the Son of Man"). It is characteristic of Jesus. Many writers in the ancient world did the same.

2. "Glorify Your Son"

We come to the other phrase that might sound strange. Jesus prays: "Father, the time has come. *Glorify* your Son, that your Son may glorify you" (John 17:1 NIV).

The keys to understanding this Glory are in the story of Solomon's temple, and also in Pentecost. Pentecost reveals that the Glory is a sign of the presence of the Holy Spirit. See the ways that the Holy Spirit figures in Jesus' prayer:

- When Jesus talks about the gift of the Glory to his followers (17:22), this is the gift of the presence of the Holy Spirit. They become one in the Holy Spirit. That is why this gift makes them one.
- When he says, "Glorify your Son, that your Son may glorify you," this has a lot to do with the interaction between the Father and the Son in the Spirit of the Glory, the Holy Spirit. It does not happen without the Holy Spirit.

It also has a lot to do with what happens when the Glory enters the true temple. The Glory would usher Christ into his followers' hearts at Pentecost—just as the Glory ushered the Name into Solomon's temple.[30]

It is not the first time Jesus has spoken this way. As we saw in an earlier scene, Jesus said:

> The hour has come for *the Son of Man to be glorified* . . . for this very reason I came to this hour. Father, *glorify Your name*! (John 12:23–28 NIV)

The timing of this, at this tense point in Jesus' life, makes his words jar a bit. He was about to suffer a humiliating death and there is not much glorious for him in that, or so it may seem. But for Jesus, God's Glory needed to be present in this part of his journey more than ever. His death at Calvary was a stepping-stone towards humanity becoming a temple.

The Glory was not just to be found in Jerusalem's temple anymore. The Glory was going with Jesus. He is the Name. And the Name and the Glory belong together.[31]

Much of what Jesus speaks of in his prayer comes through his knowing the Spirit of the Glory, the Holy Spirit. Jesus prays that the Father's love will

---

30. Jesus entered the hearts of his people by becoming sin for them on the cross, and later pouring the Spirit upon them at Pentecost. Paul has an interesting way of putting this in Rom 6:2–6; 8:9–11.

31. Hurtado. *Lord Jesus Christ*, 389.

be in the disciples, and that he himself will be in them (17:26)—it is through the Spirit that he comes to be in them.

To verify this, we can turn again from John's Gospel to John's first letter, where he wrote this:

> ... God lives in us and his love is made complete in us. We know that we live in him and he in us, because he has given us of his Spirit. (1 John 4:12–13)

So, it is when the disciples become temples of the Holy Spirit that Jesus' prayer is answered.

Jesus' words—"glorify your Son"—are not like the words of a vain selfish person such as one whom we might call a "glory-seeker." If anyone thought that, such is not the case here. What Jesus is saying has everything to do with being in the life and power of the Spirit of Glory.

Everything Jesus had prepared was taking shape. When his prayer was finished, Jesus and the disciples headed into the night, and before long his arrest took place.

The Sign of the Veil

But at Jesus' death, the message that all was coming true was put across in the most dramatic fashion. At the holy of holies in Jerusalem's temple—where the Glory was traditionally supposed to be—there was a bizarre and unexpected turn of events. At the very moment of his death, the large veil that shielded the holy of holies was suddenly torn in two (Luke 23:45).

It was to be taken as a sign from God. It meant radical change to do with the temple. With the veil torn, the Glory was not limited to being in a hidden place in the holy of holies. The Glory was going with Jesus into the church community. On his death, we will need to say more.

9. PUTTING ALL THE CLUES ON THE TABLE

The themes of Solomon's temple run like a golden thread through the Gospels. They reveal the way that the triune God of the temple was talked about in the days of Jesus' ministry. Before we come to the dramatic moments of his death and resurrection, it will be good to pause and reflect on what Jesus prepared his disciples to understand.

His disciples saw him accepting children's praise as rightfully his, as praise due to God's majestic Name, and in other ways showed himself as embodying the Name.

He used the words of Jeremiah to put paid to any ideas that Herod's temple was ever guaranteed to be the dwelling place of the Name. It wasn't. He used well-known Scriptures that describe the Name vacating Jerusalem's discredited temple. He predicted its destruction. A new temple would be needed, but not a stone one. His body was the new temple that he spoke about, the true temple of the Name and the Glory. And it would lead to his disciples' bodies being temples too, for the Holy Spirit and himself to dwell within spiritually.

He talked the language of Solomon's temple, and endorsed the belief that God had a presence in heaven and at the same time a presence dwelling in the earthly temple.

He put his seal of approval on John the Baptist's use of the Malachi prophecy. That is to say that Jesus embodied Yahweh God returning to his temple with Glory fire, to baptize people with the Holy Spirit, as only God can do. It would be a kind of return of Israel's glory days, harking back to Solomon's temple.

The disciples came to recognize that Jesus was the divine presence among them, the one who "tabernacled" with his Glory. He was going from tabernacling amongst them to tabernacling in them. He saw himself, along with the Holy Spirit fulfilling their role of dwelling in the church community, the new temple. We find his prayer "that I may be in them" and his promise that he would be spiritually present in the midst of the church community, wherever two or three are gathered in his name.

He predicted his death, but also predicted what would happen after he rose from the dead, that he was the one to be enthroned with his Father in heaven; the one to pour out the Holy Spirit. The disciples were being prepared, made ready to become temples of the triune God.

10. JESUS' DEATH AND RESURRECTION

We come to the end of a momentous week, and to Jesus' death at Calvary, just outside the walls of the city of Jerusalem. We recall how he predicted this. It was time for his enemies to "destroy this temple," as he said, talking about his body. But his accusers had little or no understanding that the future would bring a new thing. Even when the veil of the temple was torn in two from top to bottom, many would not understand. Jesus' death and resurrection were beginning a new era, the age of the temple of the church community.

Jesus After the Resurrection

On the third day, he rose again. John gives us a now-familiar picture of the risen Jesus and the Holy Spirit. It describes Jesus breathing the Spirit upon his disciples. It makes into reality what is pictured in Isa 30:27, which showed breath coming from the mouth of the Name. It was a foretaste of the Pentecost experience:

> Jesus said to them again, "Peace be with you. As the Father has sent me, even so I am sending you." And when he had said this, he breathed on them and said to them, "Receive the Holy Spirit." (John 20:21–22 ESV)

God's Name breathes out the Holy Spirit. No one less than God's Name ever does so or can do so. Only God's Name breathes out the Spirit upon the church community. The three-in-God is here.

Jesus' is affirmed again as God's presence when the story reaches its climax: one disciple had been absent when Jesus breathed the Holy Spirit upon them. It was Thomas. After the others have explained to him what happened, and after he has seen Jesus for himself, Thomas says to Jesus, "My Lord and my God!" (John 20:28). It's quite a climax to the Gospel.

Having read the story, we can see how Malachi's prophecy has dramatically been fulfilled:

> See, I will send my messenger [John], who will prepare the way before me [Jesus]. Then suddenly the Lord you are seeking will come to his temple . . . he will be like a refiner's fire . . . (Mal 3:1–2 NIV)

Malachi's words launched our search through the Gospels. They have taken us on a journey to see how the early Christians were primed by the ancient temple stories, and prepared by Jesus, to appreciate the three-in-one God. The lesson is this: if we've got sight of God, his Name, and his Glory, we've got sight of the Trinity of the Father, the Son, and the Spirit.

It is not so surprising, then, that the Glory of the Lord—perhaps unseen for hundreds of years—appeared at Jesus' birth, alerting shepherds to go and see for themselves that Emmanuel—God with us—was born (Luke 2:9–11; Matt 1:23).

Reflection and Application

- When did Jesus teach that God is present both in heaven and in the temple?
- Jesus promised to be present wherever two or three are gathered in his name. What connects this to the Shekinah?
- What clues are there that Jesus is both a temple and at the same time the divine presence in the temple?
- How were the disciples primed by the Old Testament to learn from Jesus that they would be the temple of the three-in-one God?
- How should Christians today teach about the three-in-one God of the temple?

Chapter 6

Links in the 3D Chain

1. EARLY CHRISTIAN AUTHORS

One trail of clues ends, another begins. We have uncovered clear trails of evidence of the three-in-one God in the Bible. But the adventure doesn't end there. Others found the trail before us, not least Jesus' disciples and the people they taught, the early church. So what did these Christians do with this knowledge after all the books of the Bible were written?

Did they talk about it? Did they teach it? Did people still believe in God, his Name, and his Glory?

In search of answers, the trail takes us to other lands where Christians traveled with the gospel. We want to catch up with them and find out what they did with this valuable knowledge. Records will show that the Trinity was known to early Christians, as the three-in-one God of the temple.

By the end of the first century, the twelve disciples had died, but the churches they started lived on and were spreading the word. An exciting new era was opening up. They traveled to Africa, Europe, and Asia. A new wave of Christian writers was writing and being read, including some who knew the churches where the apostles had taught. They wrote powerful books, showing a deep knowledge of Christian belief and the Bible. Many of the books they authored are still available to be read, nearly two thousand years later. They are often found in collections with titles like "the church fathers."

Their way of thinking about the Father, the Son, and the Holy Spirit—and the church community—was still shaped by the ideas we have encountered on our journey: the ancient Israelite way of understanding the three-in-one God of the temple. We will see this in some gems from the first two hundred years after Jesus' earthly life.

After that, we will move on to the next two centuries—we won't need to travel any further than that—the years when talking about the triune God of the temple took a turn in another direction.

Let's get a taste of how good the evidence is. So, for example, the famous writer St. Augustine wrote this way:

> God, then, dwells in His temple: not the Holy Spirit only, but the Father also, and the Son . . . The temple of God, then—that is, of the Supreme Trinity as a whole—is the Holy Church . . .[1]

But we will start with the first two hundred years after Christ, with writers who knew about "the Name" dwelling in the temple.

The Didache, Hermas, and Barnabas

Our first three Christian letters and books are the so-called Didache,[2] *The Shepherd* by Hermas,[3] and the letter of Barnabas.[4]

The Didache (which just means "the teaching") includes a prayer for use in church services for taking the bread and wine. Here, you can tell apart the Father and the Name, where the prayer to the Father talks about the "Name." It is the Name who dwells in the temple of their hearts:

> And when you have had enough to eat, you should give thanks as follows:
>
> "We give you thanks Holy Father, for your holy *name* which you have made *reside* in our hearts . . . To you be the glory forever."
> (Did. 10:2)

Look at the words used. When "the Name" is talked of as dwelling, the word "Glory" is often close by too.

What's more, the word translated into English as "reside" is the Greek word *kateskenosas*, which really means "to tabernacle."[5] The Name "taber-

---

1. Augustine, *Enchiridion*, 56.

2. Ehrman, *Apostolic Fathers, Vol. 1*.

3. Ehrman, *Apostolic Fathers Vol. II*. See 197, 453–54, 201, 241, 335 for Hermas verses 10:1–2; 105:2, 5–6; 11:3–5; 28:1; 59:5–7.

4. Ehrman, *Apostolic Fathers Vol. II*.

5 Gieschen, "Divine Name," 146.

nacles" in their hearts. That puts us right back on the map of the three-in-one God. The Name who dwelled in Solomon's temple dwells here in the church community.

Did. 14:3 goes even further. It tells how a prophecy of Malachi is fulfilled in the bread and wine service. It uses Malachi's warning that God was displeased with sacrifice rituals at the Jerusalem temple. It uses Malachi's encouragement that acceptable sacrifices could be presented to God's Name in every place (Mal 1:10–11). The church community's way of giving thanks and praise in its bread and wine service is an acceptable sacrifice to God. The church community is a temple, where this sacrifice is made to God's Name. That is the Didache's message here.

In a second-century book called *The Shepherd*, written by a Christian called Hermas, we hear about suffering for "the Name." In an echo of Acts 5:41, where Jesus is the "Name," Hermas wrote:

> [They have endured suffering] for the sake of *the name*. For this reason, the right side of holiness belongs to them, and to anyone who suffers on account of *the name* . . . they alone sit on the right and have a certain glory. (10:1–2)

When Hermas talks about the Name for whom they suffer, he means Jesus (105:2, 5–6). Hermas also describes a vision of the church as a tower:

> the tower is founded on the word of the *almighty and glorious name* and it is strengthened by the invisible power of the Master. (11:3–5)

The church is founded on the Name's teaching, and strengthened by a power. This power we could take to be connected with the Holy Spirit.

Hermas had a real appreciation of the triune God of the temple. The way he can tell apart God from the Lord Jesus and the Holy Spirit is clear when he says it is God who causes the Holy Spirit and the Lord to dwell in believers. And so he sees Christians as the dwelling place of both the Lord and the Spirit:

> As for the Spirit: "God made the *Holy Spirit dwell in the flesh* that he desired . . ." (59:5–7)

> As for the Lord: "so that the spirit that God made to live in the flesh may be recognized as true by everyone; in this way *the Lord who dwells in you* will be *glorified*." (28:1)

These writers had the temple as the starting point for appreciating the three-in-one God.

"The Name" features in Barnabas. He wrote of those who have hoped in "the Name" and who are themselves God's dwelling place:

> . . . a temple of God will be gloriously built in the name of the Lord. (Barn. 16:6)

> . . . we have received the forgiveness of sins and have hoped in *the name*. Therefore *God truly resides within our place of dwelling—within us* . . . (Barn. 16:8)

It can be understood that the temple is built in glory because it is filled with the Glory, and hope in the Name is a way of welcoming God's presence into the church.[6]

Ignatius and Second Clement

We come to a famous Christian writer, a church leader called Ignatius. Born in the first century AD and writing early in the second century, Ignatius is one of the important links for the church in those centuries. He was familiar with St. Paul's letters.

What is so helpful to us is that he completely understood the idea of God dwelling in a true temple, and that Jesus was the God dwelling in the new temple (that is, the church community). He wrote in a letter to the church in Ephesus:

> Nothing escapes the notice of the Lord [Jesus], but even what we have kept hidden is near to him. And so, we should do everything knowing that *he is dwelling within us, that we may be his temples, and he our God in us*, as in fact he is. (Ign. *Eph.* 15:3)[7]

When he says "the Lord" there, he means Jesus. A few lines later, he says it is "the Lord" who received the ointment on his head—a famous story about Jesus (17:1)—and even goes on to speak of "our God, Jesus Christ" (18:2). Ignatius is clear that Christians are temples in whom Jesus dwells as their God.

Ignatius would speak of the Name in eye-catching ways. In the same letter, written when he was in prison simply for being a Christian leader, he said "I have been bound in the name," and that those he was writing to were "worthy of the name" (3:1, 4:1). Writing in a letter to the church in

---

6. Cf. Beale, *Temple and the Church's Mission*, 252.
7. Ehrman, *Apostolic Fathers, Vol. I*, 235.

Philadelphia, he said to "give glory to the name," and spoke of ministry "on behalf of the name of God" (10:1–2).

In the same century, a writer we speak of as Clement was thinking and writing in familiar ways. In the style of Paul's teaching about being temples, he wrote: "we must guard the flesh like the temple of God" (2 Clem 9:3).[8]

Of even more interest is that Clement shows he could refer to Christ simply as the Name. This comes in his account of Jesus speaking through Scripture. Anyone who ignores Jesus' command to "love your enemies and those who hate you," by ignoring him, "causes my name to be blasphemed." So he comments simply, referring to Jesus, "the name is blasphemed" (2 Clem. 13:1–4).[9]

Justin Martyr

Justin Martyr was a major influence on Christian thinking in the second century (and so-named because he was a Christian martyr). He saw how the Bible shows Jesus glorified as "the Name." One time, he focused on Isa 42:8 which says:

> I am the LORD, that is My name; I will not give My glory to another.

What Justin does with this is startling. From Isaiah's verse, Justin was able to pick out three things: the Lord, the Name, and the Glory, as if to say, "Here is the Lord," and, "There is the Name," and, "That is the Glory."[10] Justin could tell "the Lord" and "the Name" apart from each other. He could say that the "Glory" is given to the "Name," and this is done by "the Lord." Without doubt, the "Name" who receives the Glory, according to Justin, is Jesus. No one else but the Name could receive God's Glory.[11]

---

8. Ehrman, *Apostolic Fathers, Vol. I*, 179.

9. Ehrman, *Apostolic Fathers, Vol. I*, 187. What is more, Clement says that it was God who said, "love your enemies and those who hate you," making Christ to be God.

10. Justin Martyr, *Dialogue with Trypho*, 65:1–7.

11. Reading this, we might have a question of why God cannot share this Glory with anyone other than "the Name." After all, we might ask, wasn't Moses' face seen to shine after he witnessed the Glory? And aren't Christians too changing from glory to glory? (2 Cor 3:13—4:6) A difference in Scripture is that only a reflection of the Glory shines in the faces of Moses and Christians. On the other hand, Christ himself is the radiance of the Glory, not just a reflection of it, and this describes the unique way in which Jesus shares in his Father's Glory. This is clear from Justin because he says the Father will not give his Glory to another apart from his Name.

Justin adds, "you may recognize even from this very [passage] that God gives glory to His Christ alone." That, he says, is because Jesus is "the Name."[12]

According to Justin, he was discussing this with Jewish thinkers. They were able to tell God and the Name apart as he did, and could understand exactly the point he was making. Christians were still in touch with the Israelite roots of their belief in God and his Name. We come now to more Christian writers, starting with Irenaeus and Tertullian who were born in the second century. In the grand scheme of things, that's still not much later than the first century and the early church of the apostles.

Irenaeus

In his young days, Irenaeus had listened to a Christian leader called Polycarp who knew the apostle John.[13] A contemporary of Justin, Irenaeus showed his knowledge of the triune God of the temple in a different way, with comments like these, calling the church community "the temple of Christ," and "the temple of God, in which the Spirit of the Father dwells."[14]

Those words of Irenaeus more than hint at the pattern for how later Christian writers would speak of the three-in-one God of the temple. With little mention of the Name and the Glory, he focused on the church community being a temple.

Tertullian

We are halfway through a whistle-stop tour of four hundred years of early Christian thought. If we step forward in time to the next century, we can meet some of the most prolific Christian writers, Tertullian and Origen, and Cyprian too.

Born in the second century, Tertullian was a younger contemporary of Irenaeus. He wrote his most famous works after AD 200. The idea of the church as a temple of the Trinity is unmistakable where he wrote that the people of the church community are the ones

> in whom is the Trinity of the One Divinity—Father, Son, and Holy Spirit.[15]

12. Hurtado, *Lord Jesus Christ*, 387.
13. Irenaeus, *Against Heresies*, III.3.4.
14. Irenaeus, *Against Heresies*, V.6.2.
15. Tertullian, *On Modesty*, VII. XXI.

Apart from that obvious trinitarian temple message, the striking thing is the appearance of the word "Trinity" in that quote. It is in Tertullian that we find the word Trinity in written use for the first time on record. It was coined by combining two bits of Latin—*tri* and *unitas*—meaning "three" and "unity." Put together, this made the Latin word *Trinitas*; and we know it translated into English as Trinity. It also gives rise to the phrase "triune God." The word Trinity was coined too late to find its way into the Bible.

The Bible is of course very old and no one would expect to find in it every kind of word that we have today. Trinity is a useful word. It came into use as a shorthand word because it saves being repetitive when referring to the Father, the Son, and the Holy Spirit as one. New words can save using many more words! In Jesus' century, the words "Tri" and "unitas" had no more been joined together than the words "three-piece suite." But, as for us "three-piece suite" is a lot handier than saying "two chairs and a sofa," so using a shorthand word like Trinity is handier than saying "three-in-one God" all the time. So, once it began to be used, the word Trinity stuck in the language.

Cyprian

Cyprian was another who was writing in the first half of the third century. In one of his letters, he talks about whether it is any good for heretics that they have been baptized. What is of interest here is that his argument shows he knows about the Trinity being the God of the true temple:

> If [the heretic] was sanctified, he also was made *the temple of God*.
> I ask, of what God?
> *If of the Creator*; he could not be, because he has not believed in Him.
> *If of Christ*; he could not become His temple, since he denies that Christ is God.
> *If of the Holy Spirit*; since the three are one, how can the Holy Spirit be at peace with him who is the enemy either of the Son or of the Father?[16]

So the temple of what God, asks Cyprian? Of God the creator? Of Christ? Of the Holy Spirit? Cyprian knew that a Christian was truly the temple of the Trinity: "the three are one," as he says—God and Christ and Holy Spirit. A heretic, he argued, was not the temple of any member of the Trinity.

---

16. Cyprian, "Epistle 72, to Jubaianus."

Cyprian expected this rhetoric to work because he expected that his readers already knew that the Father, Son, and Spirit dwell in God's temple as one God. So this idea was around before Cyprian wrote about it.

Origen

In the same century, we come to Origen. He saw a key connection: on the one hand Jerusalem's temple which contained God's presence; and on the other, Christ's body which also contained God's presence. He wrote: "... as the temple had the glory of God dwelling in it, so He *[Christ] who was the image* and glory[17] of God could rightly be called . . . *the temple containing the image.*"[18]

Origen is saying that Christ dwells in the temple as God's glory and image. And because Jesus' body is a temple, he is both the temple and the divine presence in it at the same time (a belief we saw already).[19]

To that, he added a little about the church community being a temple too: "The body is the Church, and we learn from Peter that it is a house of God, built of living stones, a spiritual house . . ." The familiar link between the Spirit and the temple shows.

Ambrose

Let's step forward in time to the 300s. This was a landmark century for Christianity. It is when the Nicene Creed was written, the Creed read in

---

17. In his perspective, Origen calls Christ the "glory," rather than attaching "glory" to the Spirit here.

18. Origen, *Commentary on the Gospel of John,* X.23. In full: "the body (in either of these senses) is called the temple, because as the temple had the glory of God dwelling in it, so He who was the image and glory of God, the first-born of every creature, could rightly be called, in respect of His body or the Church, the temple containing the image." So the church is a temple containing Christ.

19. Origen was making a point that is rather clever. He calls Christ the image in the temple. Origen will have known full well just what that would have meant to his readers. It is a challenge to pagan temples. Pagan temples contained a man-made idol, meant to be the image of their pagan god. Pagans thought that worshiping this man-made image was a proxy way for their supernatural god to receive their worship. They would bring food and drink to the image, as if their supernatural god was getting fed that way. That was the kind of thing going on in pagan temples. When Origen calls Christ the image in the temple, he is taking up the pattern. This would mean that worship towards Christ as God in the temple will be received as true worship to God in heaven. This also echoes how it was in Solomon's temple, with the Name dwelling there instead of an idol; so Christ dwells instead of an idol.

many churches today. In this century, St. Ambrose summed up the three-in-one God of the temple simply:

> the Spirit dwells in His holy temple, as the Father dwells and as the Son dwells.

Beautifully put by Ambrose: the Father and his Son and his Spirit are the God of the temple, dwelling as one there. Here is the eye-catching passage in which he wrote it, worthy of a full hearing:

> . . . the Holy Spirit has a temple. For it is written: 'You are the temple of God, and the Holy Spirit dwells in you.' Now God has a temple, a creature has no true temple. But the Spirit, Who dwells in us, has a temple. For it is written: 'Your members are temples of the Holy Spirit.' But He does not dwell in the temple as a priest, nor as a minister, but as God, since the Lord Jesus Himself said: 'I will dwell in them, and will walk among them, and will be their God, and they shall be My people.' And David says: 'The Lord is in His holy temple.' Therefore *the Spirit dwells in His holy temple, as the Father dwells and as the Son dwells*, Who says: 'I and the Father will come, and will make Our abode with him.
>
> We observe, then, that *the Father, the Son, and the Holy Spirit abide in one and the same*, through the oneness of the same nature. Therefore, He Who dwells in the temple has divine power, *for as of the Father and of the Son, so are we also the temple of the Holy Spirit*; not many temples, but one temple, for it is the temple of one Power.[20]

The influence of St. Paul's letters and John's Gospel is there to be seen.

We can add that St. Ambrose knew of the link between the Holy Spirit and the Glory. He wrote this, about the light shining through Jesus in the "transfiguration." It was the Glory and a sign of the presence of the Spirit:

> The apostles truly saw this glory, when the Lord Jesus on the mount shone with the light . . . Who is He, then, Who shined . . . Whom else do we think but the manifested Spirit?[21]

The Glory is the Holy Spirit made visible here, made "manifest" as this translation puts it. Gems of the triune treasure light our path.

---

20. Ambrose, *On the Holy Spirit*, III.12.91–93.
21. Ambrose, *On the Holy Spirit*, III.12.87–88.

Augustine and Jerome

In the next generation of Christians after Ambrose, two of the most influential were Augustine and Jerome. Here again are Augustine's noteworthy words on the three-in-one God of the temple:

> God, then, dwells in His temple: not the Holy Spirit only, but the Father also, and the Son ... The temple of God, then—that is, of the Supreme Trinity as a whole—is the Holy Church ...

And Augustine repeats Ambrose's point:

> the Holy Spirit, if a creature ... would not have a temple.[22]

His point is that the true God is, by definition, the rightful dweller of the true temple. So, the Holy Spirit rightfully is the God of the temple, as also are the Father and the Son.

Similar thoughts are in Jerome's writing:

> ... a man, baptized in the name of the Father and the Son and the Holy Ghost, becomes a temple of the Lord, and that while the old abode is destroyed a new shrine is built for the Trinity ...[23]

Eusebius

In the fourth century, church historian Eusebius celebrated new Christian freedoms, writing that God

> looks at the live temple consisting of us all, and views the house of living and immovable stones, well and securely based on the foundation of the apostles and prophets, Jesus Christ Himself being the chief cornerstone ... This temple built of you yourselves, a living temple of a living God ... are in truth a Holy Place and a Holy of Holies.[24]

Celebrating this, Eusebius quotes from verses we have seen often in this book, "Lord, I have loved the beauty of Thy house, and *the dwelling place of Thy glory.*" And he remembers when enemies of God "set on fire the sanctuary of God; they profaned to the ground *the dwelling place of his name* ... "[25]

---

22. Augustine, *Enchiridion*, 56.
23. Jerome, *Dialogue Against the Luciferians*, 6.
24. Eusebius, *History of the Church*, 10.4–72.
25. Eusebius, *History of the Church*, 10.4–72.

These verses had not completely fallen out of the view of Christians who saw the church community as a living temple, but sadly Eusebius does not tell us more about it.

Cyril of Alexandria

In the next century, Cyril of Alexandria put it very briefly. To say that the church community is God's temple, with the Trinity dwelling in it—Father, Son, and Spirit—Cyril put it this way:

> for the fulness of the Holy and Consubstantial *Trinity dwells in us* through the Spirit. And truly Paul says, Do you not know that *you are God's Temple and the Spirit of God dwells in you,* yes, *and Christ* Himself, If a man love Me he will keep My word, and *My Father will love him and* we will *come to him and make Our Abode with him.*[26]

Cyril of course is citing 1 Cor 3:16 and John 14:23. We have seen the same quotes over and again to make the same point that the Trinity dwells in the true temple, the church community.

Whether or not we use the original language of God and his Name and his Glory is not the whole thing. The point is that we appreciate how the true temple is rightfully the temple of the Trinity. The church fathers effortlessly displayed that they knew the Trinity this way. Records really do show that the triune God, as known to early Christians, was the Trinity of the temple. The evidence for that is overwhelming.

The vocabulary of the Name and the Glory can be found in the earlier writings, but, despite everything, that part of the message passed virtually into disuse in the church around the third century. We want to find out why this happened. The following pages look into this strange development.

2. NEW WAYS OF TALKING ABOUT GOD: LINKS IN THE 3D CHAIN

Even when the earliest disciples had died in the first century, what they had learned about the three-in-one God lived on. Their belief was that you could understand God by understanding his presence in the temple, and that belief was never lost.

---

26. Cyril, *That Christ is One*, 282–83. Language updated by this author.

For first-century Christians thinking about the triune God, their priority was becoming a people who knew God's presence among them, who thought of themselves as God's temple. That was their business, and it was life changing. They had no concern to put together arguments or proofs for creeds and doctrines about it. There was no need.

The way that Luke wrote his book of Acts shows this. It includes God, his Name, and his Glory in such a way as to reveal the Father, his Son, and his Spirit. But it is not as if it were written under pressure to prove something. Luke was not expected to come up with proofs for it. He simply weaved his reflections on the temple and on God, his Name, and his Glory into his writing beautifully, as if no one would care to challenge him. His readers could simply appreciate what he wrote.

That fits with the fact that the New Testament authors had lived in an era when Jerusalem's temple was a familiar sight, easy to relate to, a language people understood. They still had their traditional and treasured ways of talking about God's presence in the temple. As part of the Jewish community, a historic way for them to appreciate God's presence was to appreciate the Name and the Glory. It was just understood.

It was the same in Old Testament times. Writing creeds was not really the way religion was done back then. That's why you wouldn't expect the Bible to contain a long complicated creed or doctrine about the Trinity, or about any topic for that matter. Religion was the things people did in practice. Worship taking place at the temple of the Name and the Glory is a good example. We get the story rather than a creed.

Philosophers

People who began to put together Christian creeds lived in the centuries that followed, when the church was challenged to produce arguments to prove the triune God.

Who would have foreseen this task? It more or less began when the church began debating the gospel with pagan philosophers. Christians were faced with intellectuals who would not accept that God could come into the world as a man. A God who became man? That fell short of their pagan philosophical ideals about deities—it seemed to them that this imperfect world would be far too defiling and dirty for a perfect God to enter it. Suddenly, the acceptance of Christ as God's presence was facing a new challenge.

Dealing with this, Christian authors became more interested in Paul and John's way of talking about the Trinity rather than Luke's way of doing it. Authors such as Ambrose and Augustine quoted Paul and John to demonstrate the Trinity as a temple-dwelling God. They made their point the way we have seen, showing that God and his Son and Spirit dwell as one in the true temple. But the Name and the Glory were hardly the words they used for saying so.

The later Christian authors also argued against pagan philosophers by turning their own philosophical ideas back against them (as we shall see in the next part when looking at the creeds). In fact they found they were not just arguing with pagans, but with Christians who were influenced by pagan ideas.

In their arguments, these thinkers had a preference for other Bible words, Greek words, such as *logos* (meaning *word*) and *sophia* (*wisdom*). These words better enable Christian dialogue with Greek philosophy. This was because they were words used by people on both sides of their debates. This helped for understanding each other, but caused quite a bit of misunderstanding too! "Word" and "Wisdom" began to dominate debates about Jesus and the Trinity. Jesus was "the Word of God" and "the Wisdom of God" in these debates.

More understanding of the temple's language—of God, his Name, and his Glory—could have been of some help in those days. It was the seed that the church's appreciation of the Trinity had grown from. Forgetting about it was no help to anyone. Christians could have found ways to agree more quickly.

So the temple vocabulary of the Name and the Glory took a back seat. Greek philosophy was the new road for understanding the Trinity. But what other reasons were there for the Name and the Glory being virtually forgotten?

Romans

One thing stands out like a "skull and crossbones" on our trail. It is the devastation caused by the Roman troops who destroyed Jerusalem's temple nearly two thousand years ago, in AD 70. Predicted by Jesus, this event sent out shockwaves that are still felt to this day. For Jewish people, that fateful battle marked the end of the era of Old Testament-style animal sacrifices at the temple. With no temple, there has been nowhere for the high priest's sacrificial rituals to take place for nearly two thousand years now. Their religion was redesigned so that they could carry on without the temple. This redesigned religion is seen in the Judaism of today.

Time passed and the old ways of worship in Jerusalem's temple were fading from living memory in the second century. As the temple would never again be a familiar sight, this will have weakened the influence that it had on Christian ways of thinking.

Some of the Christians writers, or their parents or grandparents, would have remembered the grand sight of Jerusalem's temple. However, it would perhaps be understandable that, for following generations, the memory became less personal, and they no longer thought about the temple as people had once done.

Gentiles

Something else was changing how the church talked about things. The church community was becoming more gentile—that is, non-Jewish. Gentile Christians became dominant and had less and less contact with Jewish Christians. The gentile church began to grow apart from its roots in the Jewish church, and it could not claim to match the Jews' understanding of the culture of the temple of old.[27]

Jewish Writings

Evidence that Jewish understanding of the old ways did not just disappear comes in a book written in the decades after the Romans destroyed the Jewish temple, in 2 Baruch. In this book, the Jewish writer looks back on the fall of Solomon's temple. He writes, "your enemies will come to this place and pollute your sanctuary . . . And the Lord said unto me, 'My name and my glory are unto all eternity'" (2 Baruch 5:1–2). The message was that God would always have a holy place for his Name and Glory because of his own good character.[28]

The Jewish community who had lived at Qumran and wrote the Dead Sea Scrolls had had something to say too. Their writings were rediscovered in the twentieth century after being hidden around the time that the Romans destroyed Jerusalem and its temple. In their temple scroll, this community wrote that God said this: "I will dwell with them for ever and ever and will sanctify my sanctuary by my glory. I will cause my glory to rest on it . . ." And God speaks of "the city of the sanctuary where I cause my name to abide . . ." As in Deuteronomy, there are many references to God's Name abiding in the place which God chooses, and his Glory being there.[29]

27. Gieschen, "Divine Name," 156.
28. Stevenson, *Power and Place*, 203.
29. 11Q19 29:3–9; 45:11–18; 46:11–21.

Sadly, the growing apart of Jews and gentile Christians happened in an era when more contact with such Jewish ideas would have been helpful. Christians were missing out. In these same centuries, Jewish communities were developing exciting ways of reading the Bible that were recorded in writings called Targums. These were in some ways like paraphrases of Bible books, with very interesting changes. In how the Targums deal with the "Name," we can trace a legacy of the idea of it being a word for God's presence. They re-named the Name as "the Shekinah" in some places.

Look for instance at this Targum reading of 2 Chr 6:1, the scene of the dedication of Solomon's temple:

> Then Solomon said: "The Lord has chosen to cause his Shekinah to dwell in the city of Jerusalem, in the sanctuary house which I have built for the Name of the Memra, but a thick black cloud has concealed before him."[30]

This takes material freely from 2 Chr 6. The Targum swaps the word Shekinah for the word Name. The Shekinah is a celebrated Israelite word for God's presence dwelling in the temple. This way of swapping the word Shekinah for Name tells us that the rabbis had carried on thinking about the Name being God's presence, dwelling in the temple. Long after Christ, rabbis were still thinking like this. That Targum continues: "the sanctuary house which I have built for the Name of the Memra." Now there's an interesting phrase! "The Name of the Memra" means "the Name of the Word." (*Memra* is a Hebrew word that means "Word.") So here's a question about this strange phrase: who or what was "*the Name of the Word*"? The answer that will leap to the mind of many a Christian hearing "Name" and "Word" will be this: it is Jesus. The Jewish author of the Targum might not have seen it that way, as far as we can guess. But for a Christian, it is difficult to resist the message that this gives: the presence in the temple called the Name is the same presence known to Christians as the Word, and that is Jesus himself.

The Targum says the same thing over and over. It takes a phrase, "I have chosen Jerusalem for my Name to be there" (2 Chr 6:6) and turns it into "I have chosen Jerusalem in which to cause my Shekinah to dwell." It swaps Shekinah for Name, as it also does where it says the temple is "the place where you promised to cause your Shekinah to dwell"; it says "and the glory of the Shekinah filled the house" (2 Chr 6:6; 6:20; 7:1).[31]

Let's take another important example from the Targum. You may recall reading from Jer 7 where God says that Shiloh had once been the dwelling

---

30. *Targum of Chronicles*, 153–58.
31. *Targum of Chronicles*, 153–58.

place of "the Name." Here is what the Targum does with that. In it, God says, "But go now to the place of the house of my sanctuary which was in Shiloh, where I made my Shekinah dwell formerly, and see what I did to it because of the wickedness of my people Israel" (Jer 7:12).[32] It swaps Name and Shekinah again.

We see the same again and again. Where Deuteronomy talks about a place where the Name will dwell, the Targum swaps in Shekinah, and again it talks about the Memra too. So it says this: "And it is to the place in which the Memra of the Lord has chosen to cause his Shekinah to dwell that you shall bring there all your sacrifices" (Deut 12:11).[33]

To take another example, the Targum version of Ps 122:4 reads this way: "his Shekinah dwells among them, when they go to give thanks to the name of the Lord."[34]

It's a shame that the Christians of the fourth century were not taking more notice of what the rabbis were thinking about, how the Name dwelled in the temple, as the rabbis stirred together all these words—the Name, the Name of the Word, the Shekinah, the Glory. Those fourth-century Christians could have held on to how the Trinity had to do with "the Name" who dwelled in the temple. The tools for a Jewish understanding of the Trinity were to hand, but concealed from Christian view by neglect.

.

Gnostics

In the meantime, a threat to the unity of the church had come over the horizon. There were groups of religious people who became known as gnostics. These groups took an interest in "the Name" but they did it in a way that took it away from the Old Testament and the temple, like a boat losing its moorings and drifting out to sea. In the second century, the famous Christian Irenaeus examined the beliefs of the gnostics.

Irenaeus had a good pedigree in Christian matters. As mentioned, he had begun learning under Bishop Polycarp who had learned first from the apostle John. So Irenaeus had good access to the roots of Christianity and the churches where the apostles had taught, and he saw the gnostics as a group that was throwing that heritage away.

Part of the background to the problem was that the gnostics tended to teach that the human body was basically an unwanted hindrance to true

---

32. *Targum of Jeremiah*, 71.
33. *Targum Pseudo-Jonathan: Deuteronomy*, 39.
34. *Targum of Psalms*.

spirituality. The gnostics were increasingly of the view that the flesh-and-blood body was an evil design altogether. They believed there was a higher power than the Old Testament creator God, a power that would never want to touch the imperfect physical world. They wanted a purely intellectual or spiritual-sounding religion. That, they thought, was the way for them to become perfect beings.

This set the gnostics against the Old Testament where God originally looked at the world he had created—including flesh and blood—and thought it was good. So, the gnostic tendency was to reject the Old Testament and to call this physical world evil, rejecting that it is the place where God wants to dwell with humanity. But the gnostics borrowed ideas. It is as if they had met Jewish followers of Jesus, but taken off the Jewishness like a wrapper and thrown it away.

The gnostics were hostile to what the God of the Bible loved. Created for good, the human body was truly meant to become the temple of the Holy Spirit. Irenaeus endorsed our flesh and blood bodies as such. Thinking of "the Name" as spiritual appealed to them, but not thinking much about an earthly temple for the Name.

Irenaeus came across a secret name rite for gnostic baptism. He describes it in his summary of contradictory gnostic beliefs.[35] Some gnostics claimed to be Christians, but the baptism rites they invented were different to the churches' form of baptism. They were very much into the idea that some words were secret and only for their sect's elite religious figures to pass on, in exchange for a sum of money.

Churches tried to distance themselves from gnostic groups and the ideas they were spreading.[36] But a situation was left in which, over time, the gnostics were talking about the Name more than the Christians were. This was a loss to the church.

For my purposes here, I need only quote teachings that are closer to mainstream Christianity. These are the sorts of more orthodox things that were being said by the gnostics in the second century about Jesus:

> The visible part of Jesus . . . he put it on through the flesh . . . but the invisible part is the Name, which is the Only-Begotten Son.[37]

And when making a point that God the Father has his Son, some gnostics put it this way:

---

35. Irenaeus, *Against Heresies*, I.21.3.
36. Gieschen, "Divine Name," 157.
37. Casey, *Excerpta Ex Theodoto*, 26.

> His [God's] is the name; his is the Son. It is possible for him [the Son] to be seen. The name, however, is invisible. . . it pleased him that his name, which is loved, should be his Son.[38]

It could hardly be clearer that Jesus was known far and wide as the Name figure that we know from the Bible.

Their mention of invisibility sounds like a strange expression but it is not unorthodox. Those who saw Jesus with their own eyes saw his body, his human flesh and blood, not his inner divine nature, which remained unseen.[39]

We can tell that older Christian ideas were still getting passed around in the second century, just by hearing these few words from the gnostics.

Suffering for the Name

Irenaeus did speak of the Name. This was when he talked about his fellow Christians being persecuted. He talked about them suffering for "the Name." As we saw in Acts 5:41 this meant suffering for Jesus.

Irenaeus wanted his fellow Christians to see a key difference between themselves and gnostics. He was a pastor in the south of France (or Gaul as it was called in those days) where the state disapproved of Christians, and large numbers had suffered and died for their faith. But the gnostics who claimed to be Christians were less willing to endure such a fate for their beliefs. Irenaeus wrote about them: "such people are ready to deny and indeed cannot suffer for the Name."[40] And: "in the whole time since the Lord appeared on the earth, hardly one or two of them, as if obtaining mercy, has borne the disgrace of the Name with our martyrs . . . "[41]

But times were changing. After the Roman troops' destructive work in Jerusalem in AD 70, and with the growing second-century influence of gentiles, philosophers, and gnostics, the church was always responding to change around it. It did remarkably well under the circumstances. In fact it did well to flourish as it did with the occasional waves of persecution it also suffered in its first three hundred years.

But it seems poignant that the temple vocabulary of "the Name" and "the Glory" fell quieter. It had been a foundation for the first Christians'

---

38. *The Gospel of Truth*, 49–50.

39. In keeping with this, we note that 1 Tim 1:17 says God is "unseen." The NIV says "invisible" meaning "unseen." It is not that God could not be visible. It is that God remains unseen. If God chooses to be visible, then God is.

40. Irenaeus, *Against Heresies*, I.24.6.

41. Irenaeus, *Against Heresies*, IV.33.9.

faith. But now it was virtually consigned to history, fading into echoes in changing times. It tells us that Jewish Christianity—for the first Christians were all Jews—was getting sidelined. The church did little to keep alive the old ways of talking about the three-in-one God of the temple.

To cope with new challenges, churches started to talk about their belief in the Trinity in a different way. The way of understanding God's presence as the Name and the Glory in the temple gave way to thinking about words such as "person" and "being." We will see about that when we turn to look at the church's creeds later.

Reflection and Application

- As Jewish Christianity got sidelined in the church, the language of the temple and the Name and the Glory was disappearing. What advantages did the church lose because of that?
- Why is it such a powerful argument for believing in the Trinity, to say that the church is a temple that is indwelled by three persons, when it has to be indwelled by a single God?
- Which of the quotes from the church fathers do you find most helpful? Augustine? Ambrose? Another?

Chapter 7

3D Discipleship

1. GRACE, LOVE, AND FELLOWSHIP

Jesus' first followers came to think of themselves as temples, as homes for God's presence. In the writings they left behind, we find encouragement to experience more of God's presence, and to be filled with his presence as befits temples. And now, this part of the book will draw open the curtains to find truths behind Christian experience of God's presence, with some practical suggestions.

Understanding the Trinity is an important way of resolving questions and longings that people have to know God better. This is about the reality of God just as Christians know him for themselves, experienced in the Bible they read, known personally, especially in their times of worship and prayer, and in Christian community.

Once when I was explaining the Trinity to a young audience, I put it something like this—someone had said something similar before me. We thought in turn about the Father, then the Son, and then the Spirit.

The Father looks from heaven and loves his people. He watches the progress Christians make in their lives, like a doting Father watching his child's steps, and his heart delights in them. When they do something good, he is like one of those fathers who proudly says, "That's my boy!" or "That's my daughter!" He is a Father who encourages them to be the best they can be.

The Son, Jesus, sees and loves people. So much so that he can say, "I am even willing to die for you." He showed how valued people are to him by the personal price he was willing to pay for them—giving his own life, so that people could have a fresh start in life.

The Holy Spirit sees and loves people, so as to say, "I want to be with you, living inside you." The Holy Spirit, as he lives inside Christians, is always there, fulfilling this promise.

This is the God of Christians, who they know in three persons: the Father who says, "That's my boy!" or "That's my daughter!"; the Son who says, "I would die for you!"; and the Holy Spirit who says, "I want to stay with you." That is an echo of one of the Bible's most celebrated verses which speaks of:

> the grace of the Lord Jesus Christ and the love of God and the fellowship of the Holy Spirit. (2 Cor 13:14)

It is the grace of Jesus to save humanity; the love of God with fatherly kindness; the fellowship of the Holy Spirit in people. To be a friend of God means to be a friend of the Father, the Son, and the Holy Spirit.

This verse has Greek words known to many Christians. God is love, and this is called *agape* love. Jesus' grace is called *charis*. The Holy Spirit's fellowship, and church fellowship, is called *koinonia*. These words are learned in many churches today, along with an Aramaic one, *Maranatha*, meaning "Come, Lord!"

2. THE INNER LIFE OF GOD

In the Bible, the Father, the Son, and the Holy Spirit are alive to each other in dramatic scenes. Here is a scene I have used when speaking to groups to illustrate that Father, Son, and Spirit are three distinct persons, that the Father is not the Son, and neither of them is the Holy Spirit.

Jesus' Baptism

In the way Luke describes Jesus' baptism (Luke 3:21–22), Jesus is in the water, God the Father is in heaven, and the Holy Spirit is coming from heaven to earth. It is only the Father who speaks from heaven, saying, "You are my beloved Son; with you I am well pleased." It is only Jesus who is praying and coming up out of the water. And it is only the Holy Spirit who comes down to earth in the form of a dove.

Telling them apart, obvious though it is, matters for understanding what happens between them. There are some sects who mistakenly teach that the Father is the Son; that they are merely one and the same person; as if it is one person speaking to himself when Jesus prays! This is silly. This mistake sadly destroys the picture of mutual love between them, as well as denying the three-in-one God. We can tell them apart, Father and Son. They are two distinct persons, as is the Spirit. The very picture of the Trinity.

Luke's description of the scene speaks volumes about their mutual relationship of love. The Holy Spirit comes as a dove—a sign of peace, a sign of the harmony in the relationship of the Father to the Son, and the Son to the Father.

This is echoed in the Father's words to Jesus, "You are my beloved Son; with you I am well pleased." And Jesus is praying to the Father in the scene. Each of the three is interacting with the others, and it gives us an insight into the inner life of God. (This is not meant to "prove" the Trinity. We have demonstrated that God is a Trinity already. Here, we are getting insight into the inner life of the Trinity.)

Communication

The Son and the Spirit communicate back to God the Father. The New Testament gives us this inside look into the three-in-one God. And it is an encouragement to Christians to have a lively prayer life. This means speaking to, and listening to, God. The first encouragement is that the Holy Spirit brings communication to believers from the Father and Jesus. Jesus said:

> when he, the Spirit of truth comes, he will guide you into all truth. He will not speak on his own; he will speak only what he hears, and he will tell you what is to come. (John 16:13–14 NIV)

He speaks what he hears. That is, the Holy Spirit takes his words from heaven, from God's presence there. And Christians will hear him. That is an encouragement to the Christian listening to God in times of prayer.

The second encouragement is that the Holy Spirit prays *for* Christians. The Spirit, on behalf of believers, communicates to God the Father, knowing what they ought to be praying. St. Paul says:

> We do not know what we ought to pray, but the Spirit himself intercedes for us with groans that words cannot express. (Rom 8:26)

The Spirit is speaking to the Father on our behalf, to support Christians and their struggle in prayer. Further evidence, if needed, that the Spirit is no less personal than you or I are.

Jesus is speaking to the Father on our behalf too (Rom 8:34). Two-way communication between Jesus and the Father is seen aplenty, and Jesus spoke of this sometimes being for the benefit of all who listened in. Jesus said:

"Father, glorify your name!"

Then a voice came from heaven, "I have glorified and will glorify[1] again."

Jesus said, "This voice was for your benefit, not mine." (John 12:28–30 NIV, amended)

This mutual exchange was theirs to hear, to strengthen and encourage their faith. And as Jesus and the Spirit intercede for us, it encourages us to join in with them.

God is Love

These examples of the relationships between the Father, the Son, and the Spirit are a good place to start if we want to know what God's love looks like. It is a bit like the loyal love of the parent for the child. Such moments are happening in the heart of God all the time. That is what it means to say "God is love" (1 John 4:16).[2] Love always has someone to look to—the Father looks to the Son, and the Son to the Father, joined together in the Spirit's love. The Father, Son, and Spirit are forever and always in this union.

The message "God is love" would have sounded a bit hollow if there were ever a time before creation when God had no one to love, as if God the Father was alone and lonely. I once heard a preacher read a poem out to a congregation about how God was once lonely and made humanity to have someone to love. I wondered if I should tease him and ask which of the Trinity was lonely: was it the Father who was lonely, or the Son or the Spirit? Of course in such a union of love between them, there was no loneliness in the Trinity. God was never a needy soul. On the triune trail, we learned that they are as one, eternally in relationship with each other.

It was to share in their love that humanity was made. The purpose of life, though it might sound strange to say it at first, is to glorify God, and joining in with the love that is shared in the Trinity glorifies God. That is why the way of God's love is to be followed by church communities.

---

1. Translations often add the word "it" twice here, where there is no word in the Greek at all. They could have added "him" instead if they thought it appropriate. I have excluded "it."

2. This translates a Greek word for love: *agape*. It's different from the kind of love that lovers can have for each other (conveyed by the Greek word *eros* that gives us the English word "erotic").

3. WHERE DOES GOD LIVE?

"Where does God live?" is a child's question that deserves a considered answer. As touched upon earlier, Christians can be heard offering not one but three different answers to it: "God is in heaven," or "God is everywhere," or "The Holy Spirit lives in us." A child—or an adult for that matter—could be confused, wondering if one answer is right and the others wrong. But each of the three answers reveals something about where God lives, as the Bible describes it. With help from what we have learned about the three-in-one God of the temple, we can look deeper at these three answers.

How do they make sense when taken together? The Bible does not treat them as if they are at odds with each other. It maintains that God is in heaven, without losing sight of God dwelling inside Christians, and God being everywhere. Solomon's temple has given us a ready picture that explains this: God is in heaven hearing prayers—the first answer. God is also too great to be contained by a mere temple—the second answer. At the same time, his Name and Glory reach down to earth and dwell within the temple—the third answer. God can be in heaven and earth at the same time, and inside and outside the temple in a different way.

Earlier, Jer 23:23–24 told us that God's presence can be found everywhere that someone might choose to go, present in the form of the Spirit. But we could also consider these words:

> Where can I go from your Spirit? Where can I flee from your presence? If I go up to the heavens you are there; if I make my bed in the depths, you are there. If I rise on the wings of the dawn, if I settle on the far side of the sea, even there your hand will guide me, your right hand will hold me fast. (Ps 139:7–10 NIV)

> the earth shall be filled with the glory of the LORD. (Num 14:21)

So whereas we generally say that the Father lives in heaven, we say that the Holy Spirit can be found everywhere in earth and heaven. It's a matter of emphasis. Worldwide, the Holy Spirit is at work. A famous example of this is in the work of creation, where it is said that "the Spirit of God was hovering over the face of the waters" (Gen 1:1). The Holy Spirit can even be said to be in heaven and on earth at the same time—as the Spirit is endlessly being poured out from heaven to earth. We have identified two roles of the Holy Spirit. One is in the Spirit's work everywhere, worldwide. And the other we especially have in mind is in Christians as "temples of the Holy Spirit."

Churches can recognize differences between the Spirit's work inside and outside the church community, inside and outside Christians. All who call themselves temples of the Holy Spirit should believe that the Holy Spirit is at work inside them but also in another way in the wider world. But as much as Christians believe the Spirit's presence is found across the whole world, they nevertheless ask now and then, sometimes daily, for the inner experience of being filled again with the Holy Spirit.

For each Christian who is a temple of the Holy Spirit, this is precious. It is understood as key to inner personal renewal in the lives of Christians. Something needs to happen for it to be an inner experience. Asking for it in prayer is what Jesus recommends (Luke 11:13). St. Paul backs Christians up in expressing this personal desire. He expects Christians to be responsive when he says: "be filled with the Spirit" (Eph 5:18).

That leads nicely into the question: where is Jesus? To understand that, let's delve deeper into the third answer Christians give about where God lives, about God being found in a particular place.

God in the Neighborhood

In the Bible, we sometimes see God "in the neighborhood." This is when God's presence is noticed in a particular place in a special way. Simply put, in the Bible, sometimes it looks like God decides to "go local" for people.

Christians sometimes call this God's "manifest presence"—when God is so powerfully present in a place that people can sense it, experience it, in a powerful and close-up way. This is often spoken of as happening in a place where the church community is. Churches speak of this kind of experience in terms of awe and reverence.

It is biblical. Scriptures call it God "dwelling" in a place. Whether that place is in Solomon's temple or the church community, or as an inner experience, it is a special sense of the presence of God.

"Going local" may seem different to how people tend to think about God. But, in the light of the Bible, you may realize that you have known about it, in a way, for a long time. An obvious example of God going local was in the garden of Eden where he is heard moving about (Gen 3:8). A quick re-retrace of our Bible journey is in order to see other examples of this.

God's manifest presence in the Old Testament was not restricted solely to the temple, as if that were the first place where God went local.

In the story of Moses going to the mountain to meet with God, his people had to stay back while he went closer to the mountain, and closer to the presence of God. Moses had to be wary of getting so close as to risk seeing God—he was warned the experience could kill a man—and that had to mean that God was there to be found, actually in that location, and if Moses looked in the right direction he would see where God was. That's the point. Otherwise, the story is practically meaningless.

God's presence in the cloud there was very different from the way God's presence would have been available elsewhere in the world. God had come to that locality—God was in the neighborhood—in a special way. You could almost go right up to him.

When the Name and the Glory came into the temple built by Solomon, God went local again. That's why, inside the tabernacle and temple, the Israelites had built the holy of holies for God's manifest presence to dwell in. And the priest Aaron was told not to come into the holy of holies too casually, for fear that he would see God there, with fatal consequences. This must mean the sight of the Glory. This instruction to Aaron would have made no sense unless God was actually there in the holy of holies in a distinct way.

From the beginning to the end of the Bible, the story unfolds of a God who wants to dwell with his people, who wants to go local with his people, right through to the ministry of Jesus in Galilee and the vision of God among his people in the New Jerusalem (Rev 21). And the people learned wisdom in how to approach God along the way.

Jesus as "the Name"

We have learned about the Name, the title given to God's presence in Jerusalem's temple. And we have seen in earlier chapters how, in the New Testament, it is revealed that the identity behind the Name is Jesus himself. Jesus is the ultimate example of God being in the neighborhood. So we can pose the question: where is Jesus?

During his ministry, Jesus of Nazareth could be found at an address in Galilee or on a mountain, in the temple or a synagogue, in a boat or on the road. Always in a particular location. Now, Jesus is present wherever "two or three are gathered" in his name (Matt 18:20).

Jesus is God's local presence. But why Jesus? Why isn't God the Father the local presence?[3]

Another question sometimes asked by young people lights the way. One such question is on similar lines: why was Jesus the one who came to live and die as a man, and not God the Father instead? We already have the background information to answer this. Of the three kinds of presence—heavenly, worldwide, and local—which was suited to come as a man on

---

3. In the chapter on the creeds, a second reason is given too, a reason from Solomon's temple. It is that it is the Name who receives his role from God, so it is the Name who comes in human form.

the ground? Only God's local presence. And in Solomon's temple, that's the Name. In Galilee, that's Jesus. It's a job for him. Only God's local presence could become Jesus of Nazareth. In the words of the Psalm, the Name is near (Ps 75:1).

What about now, in the church community? How can God have a localized presence? Just as a rainstorm can produce localized flooding, a church community can be flooded with God's presence raining down from heaven. According to Scripture, this is the power and presence of Jesus, brought spiritually by the Holy Spirit.

He was not promising to be omnipresent, though he always has that possibility through the Holy Spirit. He was promising to be present where Christians gather, two or three in his name even. So today, in the church community, Jesus still goes local. From his base in heaven, Jesus can be present in an infinite number of places at once through the Holy Spirit, as and when he wishes.

Drawing These Threads Together

Christians today speak of their own experience of God's presence in ways that are in tune with everything we have thought about. First, they are conscious that they pray to "our Father *in heaven*" as Jesus taught them to, so they know about God the Father being there. Second, they experience the inner presence of the Holy Spirit *in their hearts* and likewise the spiritual presence of Jesus *in the Christian community*. Third, they know God's Spirit is present working *in the whole world*—they may even sense his presence in a garden or another place—and they know that this is something else apart from their inner experience.

They know that God is not limited. There is nowhere in creation that the Father and Son could not be present through the Holy Spirit. Present in heaven, and locally and worldwide at the same time, this is the three persons of God. And they remain one God. It is a picture most vividly clear at Solomon's temple, with the Name and the Glory present, while God is in heaven. But there is another part to the explanation of where God is.

4. HEAVEN AND EARTH ARE JOINED TOGETHER

The early Christians' understanding was that the divine presence in the Jerusalem temple explained a lot. And for anyone wanting to know more about the mechanics of how God would be present in different places at the same time, the temple is the key. Especially, it was the place where heaven and earth were joined together.

So how does this work? First thing to always understand: God's heavenly presence and his earthly presence are inseparable. They cannot be split off from each other. But where is heaven? Judging by what is in the Bible, heaven is not some place far away us. In the Bible's perspective, heaven and earth are interlocking and overlapping levels of reality, not completely separate places.[4]

This isn't just some modern idea from novels like the Narnia books, where different worlds exist on either side of a wardrobe, or from science fiction with its tales of people passing from one universe into another. But that sort of imaginative picture may help some readers to picture what the Bible is saying.

This becomes easier to grasp for anyone who has known God speaking to them in a personal inner experience. Christians sometimes speak of the "still small voice" of God. This is the thing: God's words reach people as soon as he speaks them—his words do not have to travel billions of miles across space, taking a very long time, before people hear anything. He is heard on earth the instant he speaks in heaven. Heaven is right here, overlapping with our world.

Likewise, when someone on earth prays to God, it does not take millions of years for their words to reach heaven, as if it were billions of miles away. God hears right away. There are many conversations in the Bible between people on earth and God in heaven, and there is no time delay in those conversations as if they were waiting for a signal to catch up from the other side of the universe to reach them. Heaven and earth are interlocked and overlapping levels of reality.

But where are they joined together at their closest? A particular place? In Solomon's days, Jerusalem's temple was the place, in the holy of holies. God the Father would hear prayers in heaven, while God's Name and his Glory would dwell in the holy of holies. Heaven and earth were joined.

So, in what places are heaven and earth joined closely now? The Bible's answer: in the church community. Jesus and the Holy Spirit dwell spiritually in the church community, while God the Father hears prayers in heaven. This brings Christians into closer contact with heaven's realities. This makes the interlocking nature of heaven and earth a daily part of church life.

Heaven and earth will ultimately be joined completely in Christ (Col 1:20 and Eph 1:9). But heaven and earth are already joined to a degree, and God's presence passes from one to the other seamlessly.

---

4. Wright, "On Earth as in Heaven."

So, when the Holy Spirit is poured out from heaven to earth, the Spirit is received instantly on earth. It does not take the Holy Spirit millions of years to cross vast distances to reach people. He is right there instantly when believers ask him into their hearts. The Spirit is endlessly flowing from heaven to earth, present in both, joining heaven and earth together.

There would be no need to worry that God would be split in half—or into thirds!—by being in more than one place at the same time. Heaven and earth don't have the power to split God apart. God has the power to join heaven and earth together.

It is worth reminding ourselves of a few Bible verses in order to see how it portrays heaven and earth as joined together, and what this has to do with the temple. These were Jesus' words about God's presence being both in the temple and in heaven:

> he who swears by *the temple* swears by it and by *the one who dwells in it*.
> And he who swears by *heaven* swears by God's throne and by *the one who sits on it*. (Matt 23:21–22 NIV)

Two places are as one—heaven and the temple—joined by God's presence in both. Jesus follows the classic Old Testament pattern:

> The LORD is in his holy temple;
> The LORD is on his heavenly throne. (Ps 11:4 NIV)

God is present in both at the same time.[5] Ps 20 pictures this in a dramatic way. Here you can tell Yahweh and the Name apart, even as you can tell heaven and earth apart. The answer to prayer comes from heaven, where Yahweh is (v. 1, 6). The protection and help come from the earthly sanctuary, where the Name is (v. 1–2). (This sanctuary was in the temple, that is, in Zion, in Israel.)

> *May the LORD answer you* in the day of trouble!
> *May the name* of the God of Jacob *protect* you.
> May he send you *help from the sanctuary* and give you support from Zion! . . .
> Now I know that the LORD saves his anointed; he will answer him *from his holy heaven* . . .
> we trust in *the name* . . . (Ps 20:1–7 NIV)

There is no disconnect between heaven and earth when the Name is in the temple.

---

5. Wilson, *Out of the Midst of the Fire*, 68–70.

Thin Places

On the subject of heaven and earth being joined together, it would be a failing on my part not to mention what some call "thin places." This is a phrase popular with Christians who explore Celtic Christian spirituality, the traditions that have been passed down from Christians in ancient Ireland and Wales especially.

Many report that when a building—not just churches—has had Christian prayer in it for a long time, God's presence can stay there powerfully. It becomes a special place for Christians to go and spend time, for a deeper sense of God's presence around them. In Celtic Christian spirituality, these are called "thin places"—places where the boundaries between heaven and earth seem to have become especially thin, because heaven and earth are so closely joined together.

God wants to redeem the whole world, as well as the people in it, so it is not surprising that his presence can be found in places where his presence is sought.

In Solomon's day, God provided a way for people to be closer to him by having the temple built, which they could visit to experience a powerful manifestation of his presence. You could think of the holy of holies, the temple's innermost room, as a thin place. This way of God's presence remaining in the world, in physical places, lives on. God is present in both people and places.

The God Who Is Close

The Bible stands in opposition to an idea that was popular in the era of Queen Victoria, which was that God designed the world so that he could remain distant from it and leave it to run itself like clockwork. The story of the Old Testament teaches us the opposite: for God, being Israel's God meant that he dwelled among them.[6] Understanding this ought to give Christians confidence in God's wish to develop a closer relationship with them.

The story of God dwelling amongst the Israelites strikes a chord in church communities today. God frequently says it: "I will walk among you and will be your God, and you shall be my people" (Lev 26:12). It is by being amongst his people that he gets to be their God in the way that he intends. Any thought of God wanting the world to work without him, as clever as it might sound, does not come from the Bible.

---

6. Wilson, *Out of the Midst of the Fire*, 135.

We have covered the question "Where does God live?" in a way that does justice to the three-in-one God of the temple, so let's turn to some ways that churches have turned their knowledge of these things into action.

5. 3D SPIRITUALITY

This part is about church life, about praise and worship, prayer and Christian meditation, starting with sharing bread and wine. Experience of these things can be deeper when we know more about the three-in-one God of the temple.

Bread and Wine

In church services, typically on the first day of the week in honor of Jesus' resurrection, Christians take bread and wine together.

If Jesus is present where two or three are gathered in his name, then one of the times we would expect his presence is in the bread and wine meetings. For the church community, being the temple where his presence is welcome, times together like this are of special value.[7]

Remembering Jesus' sacrifice in these meetings, Christians sometimes call him the Passover Lamb. They compare him with the sacrificial lamb in the Old Testament Passover meal (1 Cor 5:7). It's a deliberate link between the Christian communion service and the Jewish Passover meal.

This brings us to a fascinating clue that puts us right on the triune trail. The ancient Israelites took part in the Passover meal in a place God chose for his Name to dwell:

> Sacrifice as the Passover to the LORD your God an animal from your flock or herd at the place the LORD will choose as a *dwelling for his Name*. (Deut 16:2 NIV)

It's no coincidence that early Christians taking part in the bread and wine meeting thanked God for making the Name dwell in the church community:

---

7. Hurtado, *At the Origins*, 79, 84–85. The power of Christ can be present when people meet in his name, present enough to be reckoned with as a force (1 Cor 5:4). An indication of Jesus being involved in the bread and wine meeting is in Paul saying the church risks being judged by the Lord, by behaving as if it were no better than a pagan meal (1 Cor 10:22, 11:32–33). Jesus was present, and wanted their hearts for himself, to the exclusion of pagan so-called gods.

> And when you have had enough to eat, you should give thanks
> as follows: "We give you thanks, Holy Father, for *your holy name*
> which you have made *reside in our hearts*." (Did. 10:2)[8]

It's a telling match: a meal, with sacrifice at its center, where the Name dwells. As it was for the Passover meal, so too for the bread and wine of the Christian gathering. Where the Didache was used, they believed that the Christian community was the place where God put his Name to dwell.[9] The early Christians were continuing to have this deep connection with the language of the Old Testament, the language of God's presence in the form of his Name.

Church services nowadays mention the Father in heaven and the Son present in the church community, with much the same meaning. There is an opportunity here for churches today to remember the triune meaning: the Name is dwelling in the hearts of Christians as they meet together to remember his sacrifice. Not a bad message to teach in a church service, to connect with authentic first-century Christian spirituality!

Worship

Acts of worship have an important part to play in trinitarian spirituality. The Father, the Son, and the Holy Spirit all feature in worship.

In the Bible, there are few verses that specifically name the Father as the one to direct our devotions towards, or the Son for that matter. A rare verse naming the Father as a focus of worship is John 4:21.

To find trinitarian worship in the Bible, we want to get back on the trail of the Name and the Glory. While we wouldn't say that those worshiping in Old Testament times would have been consciously thinking about worshiping God as trinitarians as such, their temple devotions were leading in that direction.[10] After all, the Name was treasured by Israelites for being "near" to them, as God's presence: "we give thanks, for Your Name is near" (Ps 75:1). God, his Name, and his Glory all feature in biblical worship.

---

8. Ehrman, *Apostolic Fathers Vol. 2*, 431–33.
9. Gieschen, "Divine Name," 146.
10. Forster, *Trinity*, 108–9.

Making Music to the Name

The Psalms are a rich and ready resource for acts of worship that include the Name. They show that in Solomon's temple, people offered praise to both Yahweh and to his Name.[11]

> Praise, servants of Yahweh, *praise the name* of Yahweh. *Blessed be the name* of Yahweh, henceforth and for ever. From the rising of the sun to its setting *praised be the name* of Yahweh! Supreme over all nations is Yahweh, supreme over the heavens his glory. (Ps 113:1–4 NJB)

It was completely in order to express devotion to the Name along with God. Similar positive attitudes turn up in both devotion to the Name and devotion to Jesus, as well as recurring details such as the throne of God. This is the scene in the heavenly sanctuary from the book of Revelation:

> "*To him who sits on the throne and to the Lamb* be blessing and honor and glory and might, forever and ever!" And the four living creatures said, "Amen!" and the elders fell down and worshiped. (Rev 5:13–14)

Jesus the Lamb alongside his Father: many modern songs used in churches express this devotion to them. The throne and the temple have an important connection. In this next verse, the Mercy Seat, with its fine models of the cherubim, make up the throne of God in the temple:

> The LORD reigns, let the nations tremble; he sits *enthroned between the cherubim* . . .
> Let them praise your great and awesome name. (Ps 99:1–3 NIV)

It was not the Father in heaven who was enthroned on the Mercy Seat in the earthly temple, it was the earthly presence of God—the Name. Here was the Name, in the Glory, in the holy of holies.

We read of the Israelites praising Yahweh who would be in heaven, and bowing towards the temple, which would be the dwelling place of his Name:

> *I give you thanks, O LORD,* with my whole heart . . .
> *I bow down towards your holy temple* and *give thanks to your name* for your steadfast love and your faithfulness,
> for *you have exalted above all things your name* and your word.
> (Ps 138:1–2)

---

11. Gieschen, "Divine Name," 122.

We can breathe fresh life into Christian worship by thinking about the temple and the throne, and thinking about the Name enthroned in the Glory there.

As seen, the Israelites could worship the one true God by praising God and his Name. As an update of this, Christians are called to worship the one true God by praising God and his Lamb Jesus. St. Paul captured the idea of singing to the Lord Jesus, like this:

> Sing and *make music* in your heart *to the Lord*
> always giving thanks to God the Father for everything,
> in the name of *our Lord* Jesus Christ. (Eph 5:19–20 NIV)

And for a comparison from the Psalms, praise was sung both to God and his Name:

> Sing to God, play music to his name. (Ps 68:4 NJB)
> I will praise God's name in song. (Ps 69:30)

This is what Christian worship is about, honoring God and his Name, identified as the Father and his Son: "that all may honor the Son just as they honor the Father" (John 5:23).

There may be many styles of Christian worship, from the silent to the very noisy. One thing different styles have in common is devotion to the Father and the Son. That's the heart of Christian worship. And we can be inspired, as we read Scriptures that express devotion to God and his Name at Solomon's temple, to worship God the Father and his Son.

There are many Scriptures of praise to the Name.[12] Why not read and speak some in worship, which truly follows the triune pattern of the Bible.

Revering the Glory

The Israelites also revered God by way of revering his Glory. And reverence towards the Glory amounts to reverence towards the Holy Spirit, because the Glory is a sign of the presence of the Holy Spirit. This is not like worshiping two gods as separate beings: God and his Glory cannot be split off into two completely separate things, just like God and his Name cannot be divided from each other. They are as one. Revering the Glory was part of the Israelites' worship of God.

So, here is a Scripture revering God's Glory:

---

12. E.g., on the Name: Pss 68:4; 76:1; 96:2; 99:3; 102:15. Also Pss 13:5; 66:1; 72:17–19; 115:1, which may be noted for where a temple context is not explicit.

> But You, O LORD, are enthroned forever . . . Nations will *fear the name* of the LORD,
> and all the kings of the earth will *fear your glory*.
> For the LORD builds up Zion; he appears *in his glory* . . .
> he looked down from His holy height;
> from heaven the LORD looked at the earth . . . (Ps 102:12–19)

This is all about the worship at the Jerusalem temple. With words such as "enthroned . . . rebuild Zion," it is looking forward to the Glory returning to the temple. The three-in-one God is at the center of it. God looking to earth from heaven, while the Name and the Glory are revered at the temple. Isa 59:19 repeats that people will fear the name *and the glory*. And Ezekiel says: "May *the glory* of Yahweh *be praised* in his dwelling place" (Ezek 3:12 NIV).

But here's a thing: worship of the Holy Spirit features in Christian meetings much less than worship of the Father and the Son. Perhaps it was more straightforward to revere the Glory when it was "out there" in the temple premises (as in the Old Testament), rather than "in here," an inner experience in people's hearts (as in the New Testament). We recall that Christians generally experience the Holy Spirit as an inner experience.

There may be another reason why the Holy Spirit is less a focus in worship. Christians speak of the Holy Spirit directing their focus to the Father and the Son. It is the Holy Spirit who leads Christians in worship, and the Spirit is not given to taking for himself the adoration. The Christian who ventures to address the Spirit in worship may have the uncomfortable sense of not following the Holy Spirit's leading, because the Spirit is pointing to the Father and the Son rather than to himself. This can be true in experience and Scripture.[13] But the Spirit truly deserves reverence.

There are a great many worship songs and hymns that are a rich resource for putting into practice the worship of Father, Son, and Spirit. A good choice reflects their relationship to each other. Let's think about the Father in heaven and the Son and the Spirit in their temple—the church community. Many hymns recognize the Father being in heaven. Simply saying the Lord's prayer recognizes the Father being in heaven.

Songs that welcome Jesus in gatherings hit the right note too. An older example, which I mention because it will be well-known to a wide range of readers, is titled "Jesus, we enthrone you," and it pictures Jesus standing among Christians worshiping him. This puts front and center the idea that Jesus' presence is being welcomed in the church community.

---

13. Swain, "Mystery of the Trinity." See page 196.

The presence of the Holy Spirit with the individual believer is well captured in the words of the song, "Spirit of the living God." Here, everyone singing addresses him/herself to the Holy Spirit, welcoming an inner experience of the Spirit. Some songs sung to the Holy Spirit get inspiration from a Scripture where the prophet Ezekiel says to the Spirit, "Breathe on these dead, so that they may come to life!" (Ezek 37:9 NJB)

There are songs too that express wonder at the works of the Holy Spirit worldwide, through all of creation.

Some songs bring to mind the Name and the Glory: "Jesus, Name above all names"; or the old Pentecost hymn "Thou Christ of burning cleansing flame, send the fire."

There is plenty to choose from, from Psalms to songs, to be spoken or sung. A well-chosen selection gives Christian worship an appreciation of the triune God's presence. Songs benefit from knowing whom we are singing to, or singing about.

We benefit so much if we keep in mind that God is the three-in-one God of the temple. God is on his heavenly throne and God dwells in his temple, just as the psalm says, just as Jesus says. God is also so much closer to us than we could imagine, and higher than us than we could imagine. Even as we sing songs of drawing close to Father, Son, and Spirit, there is room to be so inspired with awe that we can feel nothing less than deep respect for all that God is.

Talking to the Trinity

For saying prayers and listening to God, Christians can hardly do better than follow the good example of Jesus' disciples as seen in the book of Acts. In its pages, what we unearth is that the church hears not only from the Father in heaven, but continues to hear from Jesus and the Holy Spirit too.

Jesus in heaven speaks to the disciples (to Ananias and Paul), and they speak to him (Stephen, Ananias, and Paul do), and this happens spiritually, such as in visions. Paul said, "I consider everything a loss compared to the surpassing greatness of knowing Christ Jesus my Lord" (Phil 3:8 NIV).

At the end of his life, Stephen spoke to Jesus. He said: "Lord Jesus, receive my spirit ... Lord, do not hold this sin against them" (Acts 7:59–60). The thought of Jesus hearing him was not strange to him. He was not a stranger to Jesus. Stephen had probably spoken to Jesus this way before, in prayer. It would make no sense to suppose that he only began to talk to Jesus for the first time then.

Also in Acts, the Holy Spirit speaks, showing himself to have a firm relationship with the disciples:

> the Holy Spirit said, "Set apart for me Barnabas and Saul for the work to which I have called them." (Acts 13:2)

Speaking and listening to the Father, Son, and Spirit is the Christian way. It is open to Christians to follow the disciples' example, and not wait for a command to do so. For the most part, it is still right to address prayers to God the Father in heaven as Jesus taught, but Jesus allows people to make requests of him too (John 14:13–14).

So, St. Paul expects the Lord Jesus in heaven to hear him when he asks him in prayer to remove a "thorn in his flesh" (2 Cor 12:7–9 NIV). And the matter-of-fact way he writes about asking Jesus for help is really telling: it goes to show that Paul's churches wouldn't think it was an unusual thing to do.[14] And Paul reports that he heard Christ's reply, which was about his power being enough to help Paul, in Paul's weakness. Paul doesn't assume that Christians would need him to explain how he could be having this conversation with Christ. He just mentions having the conversation. It was obviously not such an unusual thing to happen. Many Christians today are aware of engaging Jesus in conversation (in prayer) too.

So, trinitarian spirituality has this richness, always having room for the Father, the Son, and the Holy Spirit. Nothing less is fully Christian.

Christian Meditation: Thinking God's Thoughts in God's Presence

What can a Christian do in their private prayer time as a temple of the Holy Spirit? Alongside prayer and worship, the Bible suggests this: "Within your temple, O God, we meditate on your unfailing love." And: "I may meditate on your promises" (Ps 48:9, and Ps 119:148 NIV). Let's think about Christian meditation. Christian meditation is thinking godly thoughts in God's presence, especially God's own thoughts as found in the Bible. That's what it is about—it is part of a relationship with the triune God. His presence is more at home with us when we enjoy his thoughts. So, Scriptures that give us God's thoughts are perfect subjects to meditate about.

This is at the heart of being temples of the three-in-one God. God dwells in his temple, has made a home in his people. God is sharing our inner space with everything else we might bring into it, including what we are thinking about. Thinking God's thoughts can help to spruce up his home inside us spiritually.

---

14. Hurtado, *At the Origins*, 75.

Christians sometimes practice this without calling it meditation: simply reading the Bible, which is full of God's thoughts. So they prove by their experience that they know how to practice Christian meditation. It may take a short or a long time. Sometimes, reading the Bible out loud helps.

Before you start, have a Bible to hand. Pen and paper can be handy. Ask God to fill you with his Holy Spirit, and thank him for the gift of his presence. Read something from the Bible that you find positive, to begin with. For example, this verse about God, his Name, and his Glory:

> Blessed be his glorious name forever;
> May the whole earth be filled with his glory! (Ps 72:19)

Verses about the Name and the Glory, that you find all through this book, make good subjects for Christian meditation.

The Bible calls us to be still and relate to God. For Christian meditation, we clear our minds of distractions, but we don't willfully empty our minds altogether. This differs from the requirements of some non-Christian philosophies, which advocate turning off our minds. In the Bible, God does not ask us to share empty minds with him, but rather our attention and love. We are better company that way. The brain can't stay empty for long in any case; when you have a vacuum, things just end up creeping in, and we are left open to things that could be to our detriment. But instead, God invites us take his thoughts to occupy our minds. So we need to be a bit active, not passive, and take his words in. Read words spoken by Jesus, think about them, speak them out. This is Christian meditation. For example:

> Whoever believes in me, as the Scripture has said, "Out of his heart will flow rivers of living water." (John 7:38)

Some find that being creative can help too, using a Scripture as inspiration for painting or drawing a picture. This too is Christian meditation. Thinking God's thoughts in God's presence helps to change us for the better, to love ourselves and others as Jesus would do; and to love and care for his creation, as a place God intended to be as holy and pure as his very temple, the place of his Glory.

God's presence isn't a mere "state of mind" that Christians aspire to—it's more than that. God's presence can't be manufactured by sitting a certain way, or by saying special words. God has already made his choice to be with people.

The first Christians did not *only* experience the Holy Spirit. Individual Christians and the church community also very much sensed that Jesus was spiritually present with them. They spoke of the Spirit of God's Son, Jesus Christ (Phil 1:19; Rom 8:9; Gal 4:6; Acts 16:7).

A moment needs to be spent thinking about what being a temple of the Holy Spirit means for Christian community and holy discipleship.

Community Life

The triune God created this world to share love in. It fits that the church is meant to be a community, ideally not isolated individuals, because a community can mirror the love between the Father, the Son, and the Holy Spirit. Worshiping the three-in-one God leads people to want to be a community in God's presence.

It is as a spiritual community that the church can really thrive. This is not a new idea. It goes all the way back to the Old Testament. Solomon's temple was a place of gathering, a place for the Israelites to travel to and meet together with God and bring sacrifices. This is echoed in how Christians today make their gatherings a place for meeting God in each other, recognizing each other as temples of the Spirit. Indeed, when the Bible says that Christian gatherings make "spiritual sacrifices" of praise and worship, it is an obvious link with the temple worship of Solomon's day.

A community that seeks to live in keeping with being a temple of the triune God can be a truly wonderful environment to grow and thrive in. A community that looks like Jesus, one that has the quality of Jesus' presence about it, is a place many people are drawn to. A community that practices his teachings, where there is discipleship producing more people like Jesus, is a place people would seek out. A place where no one made in the image of God should be downtrodden, a community that has the power and strength to go and love others, is something the world needs. Christians can ask for the sense of the presence of Jesus to increase in the church community, for such a community to thrive.

This is at the heart of the church's work, which is about bringing heaven's realities to earth. That is why the church prays—as Jesus taught—"your will be done on earth as it is in heaven."

The church may do good deeds in society, but it can do so with a value that is unique. When Christian work brings with it God's manifest presence, it is different from anything else the world can offer—it has the quality of Jesus' life about it. This quality cannot be manufactured—it only comes when he is present. When people are touched by the spiritual presence of Jesus, they want to know what has just happened, and want to know how they can have more of it. When people don't just receive charity but sense

God's presence too, they realize that God is interested in them personally. The reality is that he wants to bring something new and good to their lives.

There are many great books that go into this, and I would particularly recommend *The Grace Outpouring* by Roy Godwin and Dave Roberts (David C. Cook, 2008) on the subject of the presence of God.

Discipleship

Jesus still wants disciples. There is no mystery to how to be one. To be a disciple, you have to have a teacher. In other words, if you don't have a teacher, you are not a disciple. Not just any teacher will do. If you do not have Jesus for a teacher, you are not a disciple of Jesus. If Jesus is your teacher, then you are Jesus' disciple. And so reading Jesus' teachings, and learning from them, is the bottom line of discipleship. This is ideally learned as a group of disciples, as a church, learning from Jesus together, but also in private.

With discipleship comes Christian morality. If we are temples of the triune God, what is the right sort of moral life to live as God's temple? That is, how should a Christian act? One way a disciple learns is by asking: what is Jesus' morality, and how did he act? Well, in the New Testament, Jesus talks as a first-century Israelite. When Jesus was asked about how he lived, his answers were drawn from what we call the Old Testament. He listened to God speak through Scripture, as a first-century Israelite would. Jesus is the same yesterday, today, and forever. When he returns in glory, he will come with the same understanding of the Bible that he had when he left and ascended to heaven. The understanding of the Bible that we really want to get hold of is his understanding of it.[15]

Jesus knew that Jerusalem's temple was especially holy and sacred, with no room for unholy things. Church communities are temples of the Holy Spirit, and so they should be places that never knowingly practice or preach unholy things. We can experience the way of Christian life, where lives are already being transformed by the Holy Spirit in a way that was barely known in Old Testament times. The new way that began when Jesus bore our sins on his cross. The new way that continues with his Holy Spirit dwelling within us. And we can enter his temple with our imperfections now, ready and willing to be taught and changed. We can start to live heavenly realities now, as we get transformed to be more like Jesus.

Jesus knows what he is discipling people towards, and the Holy Spirit is nudging people in the same direction, towards Jesus' purity of spirit, his

---

15. John Wenham devotes a useful chapter to uncovering Jesus' understanding of Scripture in *Christ and the Bible* (Eagle, 1993).

freedom from sin, his compassionate heart for a world lost in so many ways. That is, to be a church which is in the right condition for God's Spirit to alight on and to rest there, just as the Glory rested over the tabernacle. Lives that follow Christ's teachings are God's work. Of course, none of us is ever perfect—God's forgiving grace covers that. But so as to know what Jesus is discipling us towards, we need to listen to his teachings, written in the gospels. His morality is the final word on the church's morality. It builds us a path to become living temples for the Holy Spirit to be really at home in.

6. 3D THINKING—HELPING PEOPLE TO UNDERSTAND THE TRINITY

In a world where the Trinity is often treated with unbelief and skepticism—by groups such as the Jehovah's Witnesses and by Islam—Christians should be confident in sharing why it is a well-founded truth. You can help people to understand the Trinity.

Christians sometimes feel stumped if they are asked to explain the Trinity. But if you have an opportunity for sharing the answers, don't be afraid. Let's look at how we might go about telling people this.

Observe and Understand

A point we can make, if people are concerned at the start that the Trinity will be hard to understand, is to say how we can come to understand things. Science teaches us a great lesson about how we do this. In science, even if at first something is not understood, what we do is observe it. We watch carefully. When we do that, we may start to understand it. After making our observations, we understand what we are looking at better.

In books or on television or in colleges, we see many examples of this scientific way of observing and understanding things. For instance, deep under the sea, there are some very strange creatures. We may not understand them at first, but we can observe them. And when we have watched them carefully, we start to understand them. Or mention the example of the bumblebee, how no one understood how its little wings could lift its bulky body off the ground, until we had modern cameras. Now they have been observed better. Now we understand how they fly.

Scripture helps us to observe the Trinity. It gives us the temple of Solomon as a place to do our observations. It teaches us that a temple is where God lives. In that temple, we observe God, his Name, and his Glory. We have the evidence right here: God in heaven sent his Name and his Glory to dwell in the temple. We notice that God, his Name, and his Glory can only ever be one God. It's his own Name and his own Glory, no one else's.

From our observations, our finding is that this is a three-in-one God. They can only be one God. By observing, understanding grows.

And in the New Testament, we carry out more observations, and we find the results matching our earlier findings. We observe that the church community is a true temple. We observe that the Father in heaven sends his Son and his Spirit to dwell in the church community. Understanding comes from that. Christians are a temple inhabited by this three-in-one God. So, we understand how the Father, Son, and Spirit are a Trinity, one God in three persons. Father, Son, and Spirit in one temple can only by one God. We can observe the Trinity, and we can go from there.

If you are talking to a Christian, this should be easier. You may know a Christian who says they are not sure they understand the Trinity. But they are probably closer to understanding it than they might think. Remind them that Christians may speak of themselves as a "temple of the Holy Spirit," and can pray to be "filled" with the Holy Spirit. And remind them that a church community may think of itself as a temple where Jesus is present.

With knowledge of the Bible, a Christian who knows the inner experience of the Holy Spirit in his or her heart and can appreciate the presence of Jesus in the church community is observing the right things. They can appreciate what the early church did: the double presence of God living among us. Explain that this is like what we see with the Name and the Glory in Solomon's temple.

This knowledge leaves Christians well placed to take the same step of understanding which the early Christians took. Using their knowledge of Solomon's temple, that step is to connect the *Holy Spirit* with the temple's indwelling Glory; and to connect *Jesus* with the temple's indwelling presence, the Name. That way, a Christian knows where to find the Trinity in the Bible: revealed in the presence in the temple.

Explain that the Old Testament picture was of the Glory ushering the Name into Solomon's temple, sent by God in heaven: the Trinity in action. The New Testament picture is of the Holy Spirit ushering the spiritual presence of Jesus into the church community, sent by God the Father in heaven.

Help people to picture the double presence in the temple, the Name and the Glory, and how they are both distinct from God in heaven. Picture the double presence of Christ and the Holy Spirit in the church community, and how both are distinct from our Father in heaven. That is the Trinity in two pictures.

This understanding of the Trinity has been there all the time. Thanks to our observations in Scripture, we realize that God has these *three spiritual presences*: God in heaven, the Name dwelling in the temple, the Glory filling the temple. Once we know this, we understand the Trinity better. The Trinity is God, his Name, and his Glory—understood to be the Father, the Son, and the Spirit.

Thanks to our observations, we can recognize that these are *three persons* who communicate with each other. Now we understand better still. God has three personal presences who communicate with each other. We have observed it, we can understand it.

Use the Bible

When helping people to understand the Trinity, bear in mind that people may not have thought much about the Name and the Glory before. So, show Scriptures that give this title to God's presence that would dwell in the temple—"the Name." You could use any of these verses:

> And rejoice before the LORD your God at *the place* he will choose as a *dwelling* for his *Name* . . . (Deut 16:11 NIV)

> I have chosen Jerusalem *for my Name to be there*. (2 Chr 6:6 NIV)

> we give thanks, for *your Name is near*. (Ps 75:1 NIV)

> May God, who has caused *his Name to dwell there*, overthrow any king or people who lifts a hand to change this decree or to destroy *this temple in Jerusalem*. (Ezra 6:12 NIV)

Show people that God sent his Name and his Glory to Solomon's temple. For Solomon prays this in 2 Chr 6–7 (NIV):

> "May your eyes be open towards *this temple* day and night, this place of which you said you would *put your Name there*. . . Hear from heaven, your dwelling place." (2 Chr 6:20–21)

> "Now arise, O LORD God, and come to your resting place." (2 Chr 6:41)

> When Solomon finished praying, fire came down from heaven . . . and the glory of the LORD filled the temple. (2 Chr 7:1)

Show that both the Name and the Glory were dwelling in the temple. It was: "the place where your glory dwells"; and "the dwelling place of your

Name" (Ps 26:8, and Ps 74:7). They dwell as a double presence: God's double presence, in God's temple.

When talking about the Name and the Glory in the temple, remind people that there is only one true God, according to the Bible. And, so, this is the simple equation:

God + his Name + his Glory = one God.

They can't be three gods, because it's God's own Name, and God's own Glory. Tell people that the early Christians pinned the identity of the Name and the Glory on Christ and the Spirit respectively. So that is the Trinity there in Solomon's temple.

Say that the temple helped the early church to understand this; a god dwells in a temple, and the church is a temple of all three who dwell in it: Father, Son, and Holy Spirit. You could mention that famous Christians in the early church said so, including St. Augustine. And so, these three are one God:

God + his Son + his Spirit = one God.

The church is their temple, and they are its God. So, a way that many Christians will understand it is this:

At Solomon's stone temple	*In the church community—a temple of living stones*
1) God in heaven hears prayers	Our Father in heaven hears prayers
2) *The Name dwells* in the temple	*Christ dwells* in the church community
3) *The Glory fills* the temple	*The Holy Spirit fills* the church community

You can use Scriptures that show that Christians are temples of both Christ and the Spirit—a double presence from God—just like the Jerusalem temple was the home of both the Name and the Glory. You could use Rom 8:9–10 to show Christ and the Holy Spirit dwelling in the church:

Who Paul is talking about	*What Paul says*	*Verse*
The church community is the temple	"in you"	Rom 8:9–10
1) It is God's temple	"the *Spirit* of *God* dwells in you"	Rom 8:9
2) The Son dwells in it	"*Christ* is in you"	Rom 8:10
3) The Spirit dwells in it	"the *Spirit* of God dwells in you"	Rom 8:9

This shows that Christ and the Spirit are the double presence in their temple. If you want to show more from Paul's letters, you could use 2 Corinthians:

Who Paul is talking about	What Paul says	Verse
The church community is the temple	"*we are the temple* of the living God"	2 Cor 6:16
1) It is God's temple	"the living *God*"	2 Cor 6:16
2) The Son dwells in it	"Jesus *Christ* is in you"	2 Cor 13:5
3) The Spirit dwells in it	"his *Spirit* in our hearts"	2 Cor 1:22

Again, this shows that Christ and the Spirit are the double presence "in you," in the church, their temple.

So that is the Trinity, and it can be observed. In the Old Testament: God, his Name, and his Glory. In the New Testament: the Father, the Son, and the Spirit. It is the same Trinity. It is easy to show them side-by-side like this:

God	Father
Name	Jesus
Glory	Holy Spirit

Tell people it is good news to know the Trinity. Good news because of what it means to our relationship with God. God does not stay away, remote from us, because while the Father is in heaven, Jesus and the Holy Spirit are here with believers.

Using the logic above, here are places where you can put your finger on a page of the Bible and say, "I can see the Trinity there": 2 Chr 6–7 (Solomon's temple); and Rom 8:9–10.

Use the Bible or the Creeds First?

I have heard people sounding a bit defensive trying to explain the Trinity by justifying the creeds. Using temple words instead is less of a problem. No one should sound defensive telling people about the Trinity as the God of the temple. With this message, the church can be well equipped for talking about the Trinity.

There should be no need to reach first for the Nicene Creed instead of the Bible. The creeds are good, but even if anyone asks you about the creeds, it will probably help first to open the Bible, and tell people about the temple and the Name and the Glory. Then you may find that people are satisfied anyway and are not, after all, asking you to talk about the complicated technical explanations that the Nicene Creed leads to. Deep discussions about the creeds sometimes need explanations about words in foreign languages that not many people understand—ancient Greek and Latin. The church's long-standing habit of starting explanations with the creeds instead of the Bible may not be helpful for many people today. When people hear of a three-in-one God, they want to put a finger on a page in the Bible and say, "I can see a three-in-one God here." Show people just that, telling them about the temple, and about God, his Name, and his Glory.

Why Some People Have a Problem With the Trinity

We have seen plenty of evidence, from the Bible through to the church fathers. However, despite the very clear and helpful quotes from the likes of St. Augustine and other famous Christian thinkers, those quotes do not appear at all in encyclopedia entries about the Trinity. What is worse is that this lack of good information is the sort of thing that makes Jehovah's Witnesses (for example) think that the Trinity is a problem. Christian people are needed to explain the Trinity helpfully.

There are some confusing statements out there. Articles in encyclopedias tend to leave the mistaken impression that belief in the Trinity only started long after Jesus' ministry. Because they imagine a long gap in time, they create for themselves a problem of how to fill in the gap of years between the apostles and the creeds. They fill the gap with guesswork, especially an old theory about how the church came to believe in the Nicene doctrine of the Trinity. It is hard to say where this theory first appeared, but it hasn't got better with time. It goes like this: the first Christians supposedly didn't really have any thoughts about a triune God, but after the resurrection, they had experienced the spiritual power and presence of the Holy Spirit and Jesus, and this supposedly left them with the job of creating a doctrine to explain their experiences.[16] And this need gradually deepened as they did baptisms in the name of the Father, Son, and Holy Spirit. So, supposedly, church thinkers wrestled with a problem of how to combine their experience of Jesus and the Holy Spirit with their belief in one God.[17] And supposedly, this problem prompted them to start thinking along the

---

16. Wainwright, *Trinity in the New Testament*, 10.
17. Wainwright, *Trinity in the New Testament*, 3–7.

lines of the Father, Son, and Spirit being a Trinity.[18] The theory goes that there are just hints of a "development" in this direction in some of the verses in the New Testament. The Trinity got defined in fourth-century creeds, and the church had come a long way, and had really progressed a long way from experiences to doctrines. This is "fake news" and now we can see why.

For one thing, it is just a theory to fill in gaps when there aren't really any gaps to fill, except the big holes in the theory. Like many theories, it does have a few facts to show for it, such as that the church's thinkers over the centuries did the hard work that got a nailed-on definition for the Trinity in the terms of the Nicene Creed. But the theory gives the wrong explanation for what got the thinkers started, as if it was only because of out-of-the-blue spiritual experiences that Christians were forced to think about the Father, Son, and Spirit being one God, as if it was all a bit of a shock to them, as if it left them casting around in the dark for a solution.

If it really had happened like that, you would expect some of the earliest Christians to have said that they needed a doctrine to explain their experiences. But in all their writings, no one said that. And we have plenty of their writings to go by. No one said their spiritual experiences were leading them to look for a new doctrine. None of them thought they were going through that kind of process at all. That is a gaping hole in the old theory.

The early Christians were Trinitarians, and they didn't lack confidence about it. But we miss that if we are looking for the wrong language in their writings. We shouldn't be looking for the ideas of the Nicene Creed in the Bible. We should be looking at Hebrew thinking about a temple-dwelling God. We know why later debates about the Trinity really started, and what led to the Nicene Creed: it was because they began answering problems raised by philosophers, and this led to new arguments that only written creeds could settle.

Perhaps the reason why some theologians have not recognized that the first Christians were Trinitarians is simply that they have been looking for the wrong language. They were looking for evidence of the language of the Nicene Creed, when the actual trinitarian language of the first century was the language of the temple. Jesus and his followers used the language of their own day, the language of the temple, the language of God, his Name, and his Glory. There was no gap of years between Jesus and the Trinitarians. They were Trinitarians. All that changed later was the language, the words that people used to talk about it.

We can wave goodbye to the old theory about a bunch of baffled Christians having odd experiences and thinking up a new doctrine to justify it.

---

18. Wainwright, *Trinity in the New Testament*, 9.

Records don't show anything like that ever happened. We can welcome the evidence of the New Testament and the early church writings, which is that the first Christians were primed by the temple stories of the Old Testament, and prepared by Jesus, to know what was happening, when their Father in heaven made them a spiritual temple which Jesus and the Holy Spirit dwelled in.

The first Christians wouldn't have needed to write anything like the Nicene Creed, because the triune teaching they had was already making sense to them. The things they knew about the temple taught them what they needed to know. And so they had no problem with the spiritual presence of Jesus and the Holy Spirit in them. They were not confused by the experience. They had been prepared for it. They knew about God in heaven and his double presence—the Name and the Glory—in the temple. They knew familiar words about Jerusalem's temple, which called it "the place where your glory dwells" and "the dwelling place of your Name" (Ps 26:8 and 74:7).

This was the world from which Christians such as St. Paul came. Christ and God's Holy Spirit are in you, Paul says to Christians. It is how the first Christians understood the triune God of the temple. Like them, we can celebrate the Trinity: God's presence with us.

Reflection and Application

- What Bible passages might help you to meditate on the Trinity of God, his Name, and his Glory?
- Typically, we think of the Father's presence in heaven, and Jesus' presence in the church, and the Holy Spirit's presence in Christian hearts. How does the Trinity of God, his Name, and his Glory help us to understand what this means?
- How does thinking of the whole Trinity, the Father and his Son and Spirit, help us to worship God with reverence?
- How might the church think about itself differently, if it thinks of itself as a sacred space where God chose to put his Name and Glory?

Chapter 8

Church Creeds and Beyond

1. THE ROAD TO THE NICENE CREED

We have thought about the triune God of Solomon's temple. Now we will look at the triune God of the church's creeds. It's the same God, but it is a very different way of talking about God. From temple to creeds—it is like going into a completely different world. The old world had the stories of the Israelites; it celebrated the holy house where the Name dwells and the Glory dwells. In the Old Testament, God said that he wanted to be the Israelites' God dwelling among them, and these were the stories ordinary people talked about. But in the church after the apostles, intellectuals took center stage, with new ways of talking about God.

So let's get a taste of the difference. The older world was not a world so much of intellectual ideas about God. It was a world of knowing God's presence amongst the people, and God's faithfulness to them.

It really can seem like passing through a door into a different kind of world when we read some of the words in church creeds. The strong impression comes over that the church had invited a world of professors to organize a creed party.[1] To be fair, there was more to them than intellect alone.

---

[1] Obviously, there was no shortage of intellect among the Israelites. The wisdom of King Solomon, like the beautiful writing of the Psalms, tells us plenty about that. Israelites such as Joseph and Daniel put their wise minds to use in the work of foreign governments—Egypt and Babylon. But intellect was never the main thing. If Israel had a unique selling point, it was this: their relationship with God was meant to be a light to the world, so that the whole world would want to be in the presence of the one true God. Even though the church's philosophers would say the same for themselves, they

We are talking about the likes of Athanasius, a Christian from Egypt, who was not just a brilliant mind but a devoted man who suffered persecution for his faith. He was at the forefront of the work on the Nicene Creed when he was only in his twenties. He had to live in exile—exiled five times by four Roman emperors who persecuted him for his beliefs! He held to what he believed to be right, even when that put him at odds with powerful people in high places in the Roman Empire. You could compare him to Daniel in the Old Testament—staying true to his beliefs even in exile and in danger.

Athanasius lived in an era of sweeping changes. The Roman Empire for the first time invited churches to the table of power, thinking the empire could do the churches some good and the churches could do the empire some good. That was a decision with many consequences that we won't go into here. That would be for another book. It's enough to say for now that changes at the top of the Roman Empire kept throwing churches into disarray. That was what came with being at the top table.

One moment there would be a Roman emperor who supported Athanasius and his pro-Trinity followers. Then there would be an emperor who turned against them. Then there would be another emperor on their side . . . and so on. The boot of power swung back and forth. In earlier times, church communities had been persecuted and never returned evil for evil. But now sometimes, Christians saw persecution going in their favor, and other times swinging against them again. Un-Christian attitudes set in, real meanness towards people who disagreed with their ideas about God. While there were still Christian voices who spoke out against violent words and deeds, the effects were felt far and wide on all sides.

It was in a world of turmoil that the Christian creeds mattered so much. They were attempts to restore unity, to give Christians something that they could unite around and speak about together, and to sideline ideas that would not have been acceptable to earlier Christians. It was a vote to stick with the historic beliefs of the churches, in new words, new phrases.

This was the world of the fourth century. They produced some of the wording of the church's most famous creed, the Nicene Creed, still used to this day (with a few additional words now).

In their drafting of the Creed, there is no sign of the old temple vocabulary, that is, the Name and the Glory. When the Nicene Creed was written, the church was largely populated with gentiles, not Jews, and they needed words that reflected how people were talking in their own day.

---

sometimes give the impression of putting their intellect before their relationship with God (albeit in God's service).

Questions and Answers

Before we look at the words of the Nicene Creed, let's remind ourselves about God and his Name and his Glory again, because now they can help us in an unexpected way. They give us great answers to new kinds of questions that the Creed was trying to answer.

The new sorts of questions were these. In what way are the Father and Son actually "one"? Had God always had his Son, or did he make his Son after a while? Is the Son some kind of inferior creature?

It might seem surprising to us that these questions needed to be addressed. After all, we have spent time considering God's triune presence in the temple where God and his Name and his Glory are definitely three in one. And we have seen that what goes for God and his Name and his Glory goes the same for Father, Son, and Spirit—the same three in one. So why were there problems later, in the fourth century? The thing was, the church was deep in arguments with Greek thinkers, and Greek thinkers raised new objections. Philosophers did not believe that an ideal God would ever come in human form or ever live in a less than ideal world like ours. They answered those questions in the words of the creeds, which we will come to. But first, let's use our knowledge, and do what they didn't do, and try to answer the questions by making use of our knowledge of the temple and the Name and the Glory.

Question: In what way are the Father and Son actually "one"?

Answer: It has to be right to say that God and his Name (and his Glory) exist as one God. They cannot be pulled apart. It is God's own Name, not someone else's. It's God's own Glory, not someone else's. Of course they are one together. They always exist as one.

If we focus on the Name, God's presence in the temple, we can say these things. God and the Name are not like two different species. The Name is the temple-dwelling presence that flows endlessly out of the Father's heavenly presence. The Name is as much God's presence as anything you could wish God's presence to be. This has always been the case and always will.

Question: Had God always had his Name, or was there a time before he had his Name?

Answer: God always had his presence in the form of the Name.

Question: Is the Name some kind of inferior creature?

Answer: No, the Name is God's own presence. Yahweh God is fully himself as God in heaven. Equally, Yahweh God is fully himself as the Name in Solomon's temple. The Name is not inferior. It is God's own Name. God does not have a Name that is below him.

The Nicene Creed

Let's see how the Nicene Creed answers these questions in a different way. These words will be more familiar to people who attend traditional churches where the Creed is read aloud in services. The words to particularly watch out for are these: "eternally begotten of the Father," and "God from God, Light from Light," and "true God from true God, begotten, not made," and "of one being with the Father." This then is the Nicene Creed:[2]

> We believe in one God, the Father, the Almighty,
> maker of heaven and earth, of all that is, seen and unseen.
> We believe in one Lord, Jesus Christ, the only son of God,
> eternally begotten of the Father,
> God from God, Light from Light,
> true God from true God,
> begotten, not made,
> of one being with the Father.
> Through him all things were made.
> For us and for our salvation he came down from heaven:
> by the power of the Holy Spirit he became incarnate from the Virgin Mary, and was made man.
> For our sake he was crucified under Pontius Pilate; he suffered death and was buried.
> On the third day he rose again in accordance with the Scriptures;
> he ascended into heaven and is seated at the right hand of the Father.
> He will come again in glory to judge the living and the dead,
> and his kingdom will have no end.
> We believe in the Holy Spirit, the Lord, the giver of life,
> who proceeds from the Father [and the Son][3].
> With the Father and the Son he is worshiped and glorified.
> He has spoken through the Prophets.
> We believe in one holy catholic[4] and apostolic Church.
> We acknowledge one baptism for the forgiveness of sins.
> We look for the resurrection of the dead, and the life of the world to come.
> Amen.

2. Nicene Creed: http://www.creeds.net/ancient/nicene.htm.

3. The words "and the Son" were included later by Western churches, but not included by Eastern churches.

4. "Catholic" here means the opposite of a denomination. It does not mean "Roman Catholics" alone, it means universal and worldwide.

Most of those words are also found in the Bible—but not all of them. When the Creed was written, a lot of care was taken so that it did not contradict the words of the Bible. Now, specific words that we were watching out for are obviously in the Creed for a reason. It is to answer those difficult sorts of questions about God and Jesus.

What do we make today of words like "eternally begotten of the Father," and "God from God, Light from Light," and "true God from true God, begotten, not made," and "of one being with the Father"?

These words and phrases are of such a different kind from words like Name and Glory. It is a sign that the church's scholars had a different focus: not the language of Solomon's temple, but the language of Greek thinkers.

Where Were Problems Coming From?

Greek pagan thinkers had reasoned that the material world we live in is less than ideal, and so (they thought) an ideal god would never touch it: for that reason, they rejected the long-held Christian belief that God had come to earth as Jesus. Their new claim was that the one who came to earth must have been created by God at some moment in the distant past as some inferior being that could cope with an imperfect world. They supposed that Jesus must have been some kind of creature better than men, but not really human, and not really like God either. They thought this was the only way to hang onto the belief that there was one true God—by excluding Jesus from it. This was more or less the philosophy of a thinker called Arius. The church had to respond to his strange philosophy because he had a growing influence, which was devaluing Jesus and rejecting the Trinity.

Arius may have had good intentions, thinking so deeply about God being one. But he didn't understand the three-in-one. He believed his way of thinking honored God. But much of the Christian message of salvation was lost in his philosophy. Especially he risked losing sight of the fact God had come into the world as Jesus to redeem creation, to make the physical world fit to be in his divine presence.

Arius was not trying to be completely unorthodox, but the way he used words was looking like it was mixing Christianity with pagan or gnostic influences. The Nicene Creed was written to save the church's historic beliefs from these thinkers.

The Creed's Solution

The Creed used words that could be understood by both sides. Christian scholars answered their challenges by using their opponents' own kind of words—words that could be used in Greek philosophy. Hence, they used words like "eternally begotten," and "God from God, Light from Light," and "true God from true God, begotten, not made," and "of one being with the Father."

To get breakthrough in the church's deliberations, even the Roman emperor Constantine threw in a word, the word translated as "one being"! This bothered some of the Christians who were part of the debate, because it was novel, and they did not like to go further than words that they had used before. There are barely words good enough to describe God, but at least there are biblical words for the job, together with words that Christians had long used in their debates.

Some Christians down the ages have shared their discomfort. So it is not out of place—even to this day—to say so. That is not throwing away this creed, this historic agreement between all the churches who met, churches that had pedigrees going back to the first century of the church. They saved the message of salvation from being muddied by philosophies.

So, some parts of the Creed sound quite foreign in places to the biblical language this book has been about. But it really had never been completely unacceptable for Christians to use words that are shared between both the Bible and Greek philosophy. Christians, to assist in spreading the gospel, had long done so. For example, the word *logos*, which we find in the Greek words of John 1:1. Another example is in Hebrews, where the word "shadows" has something in common with Greek philosophy. As a classic example, St. Paul quoted a Greek poet and a philosopher (in Acts 17:28) to try to win converts to Christianity. The issue in every case is not really the words used, but the intended meanings when the words are used.

Temple Language and the Creed Compared

Again, knowing what kind of questions the Creed was trying to answer, how might the Name and the Glory shed more light on the questions?

The Creed's newer words tie in nicely with the Old Testament revelation of God and his Name. It is not difficult to say that God and his Name must be of "one being." The Name is the presence of God that flows from the Father's heavenly presence into the temple. They exist as one. Let's see some things about the Name that tie in nicely with the Creed and what it says about Jesus:

What we can say of the Name:	What the Creed says of Jesus. He is:
God has always eternally existed, and so his Name has always existed. God's Name is his presence, which flows endlessly out of the Father's heavenly presence.	"eternally begotten of the Father"
The Name is God's own presence flowing out from God in heaven. God's Name was not something manufactured by someone.	"begotten, not made"
The Name is God's own temple presence, which flows out of God's heavenly presence. Like light flowing out from light.	"God from God" (meaning "Godness from Godness") "Light from Light"
The Name is the *true* presence of God in the temple flowing from the true presence of God in heaven.	"true God from true God" (meaning "true Godness from true Godness")
God and his Name exist as a unity. One does not exist without the other. God and his Name cannot be pulled apart, split off and divided from each other to have two totally separate existences.	"of one being with the Father"

A closer look at the Creed's unusual words is in order.

God From God, True God From True God

For Christians there is only one true God. Some complain about the wording "God from God," because it gives the mistaken impression of Christians having more than one God, the impression that Jesus is a second additional God. We need not let ourselves be confused over this, just because it uses the word "God" twice. The good news is that it does *not* mean there are two gods. In fact it is written this way so that Arius's followers would be shown to be in the wrong if they said that Jesus was a lower god next to a higher god. And Arius's beliefs could easily look like a belief in two gods.

We can get into the inner meaning of the Creed if we take the phrase as meaning "true Godness from true Godness." That is what it means. It does it justice to say that it stands for "true divinity from true divinity."

It is intended to mean this about the one true God: Yahweh God is fully himself as the Father, and likewise Yahweh God is fully himself as the Son. This is one God, and this God is known to us in more than one presence.

What the Creed means is that Jesus is not a separate, different, lower kind of heavenly being next to God. The Creed puts things this way so that we don't reduce Jesus into a second god. If it did, we would have to deal with two gods! If we made that mistake, we would need two gods for our salvation. That is the dangerous position which Arius's ideas get into. Here is an example. If Arius had had his way, this Scripture would unfortunately be mistaken to mean bowing to worship two separate gods:

> "To him who sits on the throne and *to the Lamb* be blessing and honor and glory and might, forever and ever!" And the four living creatures said, "Amen!" and the elders fell down and worshiped. (Rev 5:13–14)

The Creed helps us to steer clear of any thought of this being two gods. God and the Lamb are as one, and not two gods. They are worshiped as one God.

Begotten, Not Made

So, God and his Name are not like two different species, as if the Name were something totally separate from God, as if it could be a second kind of god. You can see why Arius was wrong. Perhaps if Arius had thought about the Name and the Glory, as well as thinking about philosophy, he would have been in agreement with the Trinitarians. The Name is God's own presence, not something artificial that God had to make one day. God did not wake up one day and invent his presence, his "Name." Instead, we say it is "born" of God.

So, meaning "born," John's Gospel provided the word "begotten." It comes where it says (in the ancient church's reading) that Jesus is "the only begotten Son" (John 1:14).

So, the Name was born of God, not manufactured by God like a little piece of creation.

Eternally Begotten

What do these words in the Creed mean, "*eternally* begotten"? Well, God keeps existing, and so his Name keeps existing because of that, always and forever. That is how the Name is eternal. So, the Son is eternal.

God's Name is his temple presence that flows endlessly out of the Father's heavenly presence. This can be compared with offspring coming from the womb, not as a one-off birth event, but a *continuous* process of God's presence *always* flowing, *always* being born, *endlessly* out of his heavenly presence. The Creed means this when it says the Son is "*eternally* begotten of the Father."

Of One Being With His Father

God and his Name exist as a unity. One does not exist without the other. God and his Name cannot be separated from each other to have two separate existences. So the Creed can say that the Son is of "one being" with the Father. (It may be worth knowing that this strange word "being" means "existence." They are of one "existence." That sounds a bit strange, so it's better-sounding English to say that they are of one "being.")

A Name and Glory Creed

So we have seen what the Creed says about the relationship of God and his Son. We can test this by putting the biblical term "the Name" alongside the words of the Creed. For fresh light on the Creed, we can look at it this way:

The Name is eternally begotten of the Father
The Name is God from God ("Godness" from "Godness"), Light from Light
The Name is true God from true God (true "Godness" from true "Godness")
The Name is begotten, not made
The Name is of one being with the Father

To use other words appropriate to the triune God of the temple:

The temple presence is eternally begotten of the Father
The temple presence is God from God, Light from Light
The temple presence is true God from true God
The temple presence is begotten, not made
The temple presence is of one being with the Father

This illustrates that there is really no contradiction between the God of the Creed and the God of Solomon's temple.

The Creed is helpful for staying free of mistakes about the Trinity. It maintains the personal distinctions between the Father, and the Son, and the Holy Spirit. The Nicene Creed makes clear that the Son is not the Father by saying the Son is "begotten" of the Father. This is based on John 1:14. The Father and the Son never get each other's titles the wrong way round![5]

And the Nicene Creed makes clear that the Holy Spirit is not the Father, because it says the Holy Spirit "proceeds" from the Father. This is based on John 15:26.[6]

As the Athanasian Creed says: "For there is one person of the Father, another of the Son, and another of the Holy Spirit." We will come to this creed next.

2. THE ROAD TO THE ATHANASIAN CREED

As we have advanced along the triune trail, we have seen how Christian ways of using words were changing. Greek philosophy can seem a world away from where we started with the God of Solomon's temple. All the same, like detectives following a trail, we follow the clues wherever they lead. And our journey into the world of great Christian thinkers has further to go.

In ancient times, confusion sprang up around the word "being," because when the word was translated from Greek into Latin it came out as *substantia*. And the problem was that it unintentionally sounded like "stuff" that you could handle or touch—it's where we get our word "substance" from. But that was just a case of things getting lost in translation. All that was meant at first was to speak of the fact of God's "existence."

Their use of the word "being" was meant to clarify that they were talking about the existence of a "real" God and not an imaginary one. We could say something similar when answering this question: "Is your God imaginary or does he exist?" Their answer, to say that God exists, was to say God has "being."

These sorts of conversations were going on. Christian scholars were striving to avoid misunderstandings with each other. To foster mutual understanding instead of confusion, the best words needed to be found. People

---

5. Scholars have a technical word for this: filiation, meaning that Jesus is the Son to the Father. It is an aspect of how each of them has "personal properties" that make them distinct from each other. See: Swain, "Mystery of the Trinity."

6. Scholars have a technical word for this too: spiration, meaning that the Spirit is the Spirit of the Father and the Son. It is another example of different personal properties. Again, see Swain, "The Mystery of the Trinity." God has "personal properties" that make the three distinct from each other as persons, and "common properties" which make them identically divine as one God. Sometimes, scholars sum this up as persons and essence. But they struggle to define what they mean by essence. The relation between Father, Son, and Spirit is the essence of what God is in the view of Thomas Aquinas. See Gignilliat, "Trinity and the Old Testament."

needed to agree what the words meant, so it is clear that one thing is being discussed and not another. But it is not surprising that, even in those days, there were misunderstandings in the discussions![7] Perhaps it might have been easier working with words such as Name and Glory!

These discussions were pushing words further than before. They did this so that Arius and his followers would not devalue Jesus, even accidentally.

Discussions like this led to another creed being written which was linked with Athanasius' name—the Athanasian Creed—though he didn't write it himself.

This creed is long and we don't need to go through all of it here. It is mainly about the Trinity being three persons united in one God, and about Jesus being both man and God at the same time. The following excerpts from the Creed give us enough to consider here:[8]

On the Trinity

> we worship one God in Trinity, and Trinity in Unity . . .
>
> For there is one person of the Father, another of the Son, and another of the Holy Spirit . . .
>
> The Father uncreated, the Son uncreated, and the Holy Spirit uncreated . . .
>
> The Father eternal, the Son eternal, and the Holy Spirit eternal.
>
> And yet they are not three eternals but one eternal . . .
>
> So the Father is God, the Son is God, and the Holy Spirit is God;
>
> And yet they are not three Gods, but one God . . .

7. Athanasius sought to clear up much of the confusion. To do this, he used two different Greek words that could both mean "being." They were *ousia* (which had been used in the Nicene Creed) and *hypostasis*. He wrote that one God "exists" (*ousia*) and, in the one God, each of the Father and Son and Spirit "exists" (*hypostasis*)—one God in three persons. By using two different words, he wanted people to understand when he was talking about one God and when he was talking about three persons. So that he would not be misunderstood when talking about "being," Athanasius said, "*hypostasis* is *ousia* and means nothing else but simple being." He just wanted to use one word when talking about one God, and another word when talking about three persons. Such words can be found in the Bible, with the meanings of a different century (for example *hypostasis* is in Heb 1:3, which says Jesus is "the stamp of what God is"—author's translation). After Athanasius and to this day, theologians have dug for deeper meanings in these words, and words such as the "essence" of God, with meanings developing, changing over time. But this book is interested only in what the ancient church was thinking about the Trinity.

8. Athanasian Creed: http://www.ccel.org/creeds/athanasian.creed.html.

And in this Trinity none is afore or after another; none is greater or less than another.

But the whole three persons are co-eternal, and co-equal...

On Jesus

For the right faith is that we believe and confess that our Lord Jesus Christ, the Son of God, is God and man.

God of the substance of the Father, begotten before the worlds; and man of substance of His mother, born in the world...

Equal to the Father as touching His Godhead, and inferior to the Father as touching His manhood.

Who, although He is God and man, yet He is not two, but one Christ.

Once again, knowing what kind of questions the creeds were trying to answer, how might the Name and the Glory help with the answers?

We can take the first part of the Creed above, and substitute the words Name and Glory for Son and Spirit. It then goes like this:

we worship one God in Trinity, and Trinity in Unity...

For there is one person of the Father, another of the Name, and another of the Glory...

The Father uncreated, the Name uncreated, and the Glory uncreated...

The Father eternal, the Name eternal, and the Glory eternal.

And yet they are not three eternals but one eternal...

So the Father is God, the Name is God, and the Glory is God;

And yet they are not three Gods, but one God...

And in this Trinity none is afore or after another; none is greater or less than another.

But the whole three persons are co-eternal, and co-equal...

It is difficult to deny its logic when the Name and the Glory are in place. It has to be right that the Name and the Glory are "uncreated" in much the same sense as God is "uncreated." God did not figure out one day that he needed to manufacture his Name and his Glory for the first time. His Name and his Glory always exist because he exists. His Glory is a permanent aspect of his existence, and much the same can be said about his Name, his presence.

And, essentially, it has to be right that God and his Name and his Glory can only be one God. They cannot be pulled apart, split off, and separated to make three gods. God does not give his Name and his Glory away.

This is the three-in-one God.

God, his Name and Glory are co-equal and co-eternal as one God. We need to confirm this against some checks. The following pages will do those checks.

3. THE INCARNATION OF JESUS

Using the language of the Name and the Glory can help people understand the church's traditional teaching and its traditional words.

This would help make sense of some more of the language used by the church when talking about the Trinity. Some Christian teachers sound like they have swallowed a dictionary. This is what sometimes happens when the church talks about the Trinity in its traditional way—as in the creeds. You need a Christian dictionary!

Let's start with the word "incarnation." It just means "in the flesh." Sometimes people say Jesus came "incarnate." Sometimes they say he came "in the flesh." It means the same thing. The word "incarnation" is biblical. It is a way of translating 1 John 4:2 which says that Jesus has come "in the flesh."

Let's remind ourselves that Christians believe that Jesus is both God and man, human and divine. We don't split off God from Jesus. As we saw earlier, speaking about "God and Jesus" is equivalent to speaking about "God and his Name." Jesus is the Name. In John's Gospel, we saw Jesus as God's Name, with his Glory.

Following on from that, we need to come to the doctrine of the three persons of the Trinity being "co-eternal" and "co-equal." These strange words are found in the Athanasian Creed. Questions we can ask about them:

- What do the words mean?
- Do they have any backup in Scripture?
- Can knowing about God and his Name and his Glory help us to understand these things better?

The answer is a resounding yes to that!

Co-eternal

The Athanasian Creed says that the Father and the Son and the Holy Spirit are co-eternal. This makes sense because God and his Name and his Glory are eternal. In Old Testament language, God says, "this is my Name *forever*" (Exod 3:15). In the New Testament, we find that God's Glory is the "*eternal* glory" (1 Pet 5:10).

All three are eternal together, God and his own Name and his own Glory. They are not eternal in a separate way from each other. They are eternal in a joined-up way, all together. That is why we can say "co-eternal," and not just "eternal."

In the New Testament, when we read about God the Father, his Son Jesus, and his Holy Spirit, they are eternal. They are each described there with a Greek word for eternal, which is *aionion*. That goes for the Father in Rom 16:26. It goes for the Son in 1 John 1:2. It goes for the Holy Spirit in Heb 9:14. They are each eternal. Together, they are one God and as such they are co-eternal.

Co-equal

The next word to explain is "co-equal." The Athanasian Creed says that the Father and the Son and the Holy Spirit are equal. But it does not actually say much at all about the ways in which they are equal. What ways are these? How are they like each other?

It does not say if they are the same, or equal *in everything*. Actually, they are not the same in everything.

There are differences, such as the Son being "begotten" of the Father. The Father is not begotten of the Son; the Son is begotten of the Father. It is only ever that way round.

But in other ways they are equal. Think of the Name and the Glory, as that always helps. God's Name is not unequal to God; it couldn't be. It is *his own Name*. God does not have a Name that is below him. God's Name is not inferior to him—it is his own Name, and his own presence! It is inescapable: there is an equality to speak of between God and his Name. Insofar as Jesus is the Name, this equality has to be true for him.

Likewise, God does not have a Glory that is below him, or inferior to God. It cannot be, otherwise it would fall short of what it should be.

So, it has to be right to say of God and his own Name and his own Glory that there is an equality between them. But it would not be right to say they are exactly the same as each other. Better to say that they have a sameness about them.

What About Jesus Being Human?

Could Jesus be equal to God in any way *if Jesus was human*? The Athanasian Creed was intended to answer exactly that question, so we will want to understand it better. How might the Name and the Glory help with understanding it? The fact is that the Name is equal to God, but at the same time there is a way that the Name is unequal. That may seem confusing at first. Don't let that unsettle you—this will make sense. We have to think about the Name's role.

You may know that the question of equality in the Trinity troubles some people, when they think about Jesus and his Father. Jesus said, "the Father is greater." How does that fit with equality?

It is to do with Jesus being human. Recognizing that the Name of God came in the flesh, as Jesus, we have to think about whether this means something new for the status of the Name. What happens to the Name's equality with God now? After all, flesh-and-blood human nature is not equal to God. This is where the Athanasian Creed comes in with an answer. It talks about Jesus being both human and divine. In plain language he is both God and man:

> For the right faith is that we believe and confess that our Lord Jesus Christ, the Son of God, is God and man.
>
> God of the substance of the Father, begotten before the worlds; and man of substance of His mother, born in the world . . .
>
> Equal to the Father as touching His Godhead [Godhood], and inferior to the Father as touching His manhood.
>
> Who, although He is God and man, yet He is not two, but one Christ.

The Creed's explanation of equality and inequality is in this line—"equal to the Father as touching His Godhood, and inferior to the Father as touching His manhood." That in itself may satisfy many people, but let's go further to answer the questions that some people might have. Especially, how can Jesus be equal and unequal at the same time? What does this really mean?

Being "inferior to the Father" is in tune with his human nature (what the creed calls his "manhood"). No one need have any argument with that being true of human nature, that Jesus can say, "the Father is greater than I" (John 14:28). But how then is that in tune with Jesus being God's presence, God's Name, as he was when present in Solomon's temple with the Glory?

We already have part of the answer. God was still in heaven while the Name was given a home chosen for him by God, in Solomon's temple. A distinction between them comes into view there. God the Father is the heavenly presence; the Name is the earthly presence. It was when God in heaven answered Solomon's prayer that the Name (and the Glory) entered the temple. God in heaven listens and answers, and the Name and the Glory act in response.

So God the Father has a clear leading role in this. He gives direction and more besides. God sends his presence, his Name. Scripture says that the Name was given a home chosen for him by God; God puts his Name in his dwelling place. God in heaven leads, the Name responds.

God's leading role tells us something about the Name: on the one hand equal to God in the sense of being God's own Name and presence; but at the same time being sent and receiving his role from God.

God in heaven has this precedence in terms of a leading role, being the giver, providing his Name with a home, as his presence in his temple.

The Name and God are equal	The name has the lower role—the unequal role
The Name is God's own Name, God's own presence	The Name was given a home chosen for him by God

This is the vital evidence we need to understand the matter. It carries over to Jesus. It puts our thoughts about Jesus in a bigger picture. *This is Jesus: equal to God in being his Name, his presence; yet having the lower role, in being given a place chosen for him by God in heaven.* It is clear that this is the lower role, receiving a role from God in heaven, being given an earthly home chosen by God in heaven. Here's the thing: anything that can be true for the Name can be true for Jesus. If the Name can be equal to God the Father in one way and unequal in another, then so can Jesus.

To be the Name is to be the one who takes a lower role. To be human is also to be the one who takes a lower role. Like a glove that fits, being the Name and being human were true for Jesus at the same time.

So, in the life of Jesus, the Name took on human nature. That way, the stage is set for Jesus speaking of God the Father in heaven as greater. It's all in the biblical words.

The Name and God are equal	The name has the lower role—the unequal role
The Name is God's own Name, God's own presence	The Name took on human nature—being Jesus

Why Did Jesus Make Himself Equal With God and Yet Say the Father Is Greater?

Words can bring truth out of the shadows. First, John's Gospel picked up their equality, with this observation:

> [Jesus] was even calling God his own Father, making himself equal with God. (John 5:18 ESV)

That fits. God is equal to his own Name. Jesus could make himself to be equal with God, as the Name.

On the other side of the coin, Jesus illustrates *how* the Father is *greater* than him. *It is all about the Father being the ultimate giver.* God the Father *gave to Jesus* his role, his earthly place. He also *gave to Jesus* his followers. Jesus said so:

> My Father, who has *given* them to me, is *greater* than all; and no-one is able to snatch them out of my Father's hand. I and the Father are one. (John 10:29–30 ESV)

The Father is greater, and how he is greater than Jesus is in being the ultimate giver. The ultimate giver of all good gifts (Jas 1:17). The temple was a good gift given by God in heaven, a gift to the Name.

Unequal and equal at the same time in different ways: compared to God the Father, the Name is unequal in being given his role and his place on earth, but equal in being God's Name. With that truth brought out of the shadows, Jesus' equality and inequality make perfect sense. We observe it in the temple. We observe it in Jesus. And because we can observe it, we can understand it.

It is the perfect match in the status of Jesus and the status of the Name. The Father is the giver and the Son is the one who receives. If it wasn't for our being able to observe the Name, we might not understand the different things that Jesus is saying, about being equal with the Father and yet the Father being greater. It's true of the Name. It's true of Jesus.

The Giver is Greater

We saw earlier why Jesus was the one who came to live and die as a man, and not God the Father: of the three kinds of God's presence—heavenly, worldwide, and local presences—only the local presence is particularly suited to coming to earth in human form. Of God, his Name, and his Glory, it has to be the Name for this job, being God's local presence.

And there is a second reason why it was not the Father who came in human form. It is as we have already seen. If someone is to take the lower role, we would expect it to be the Name, not God in heaven.

It is so in the lower role of being the Name, given a dwelling place chosen for him. And it is so in the lower role of being human. In other words, it is not the Father but the Son who takes this lower role.

That is why it was—it had to be—Jesus who came in human form, rather than the Father doing so. It is a role for the Name, the one who receives his role from God, the one whose temple home is chosen for him as a gift from his Father.

The Giver is the greater. But they are still one. They have higher and lower roles, but that never means that they are split off into two completely separate beings: they are one. God and his Name are always one.

Where he says "The Father is greater than I," the real point of what Jesus said is apparent—all we have to do is read John 14:28–29 as a whole. Jesus is actually in the middle of explaining that after he goes to join his Father in heaven, his presence will return to the disciples (at Pentecost):

> You heard me say, 'I am going away and *I am coming back to you*.' If you loved me, you would be glad that I am going to the Father, for the Father is greater than I. I have told you now before it happens, so that when it does happen you will believe. (John 14:28–29 NIV)

And we know what that means. It means that Jesus would return by his spiritual presence, to dwell in the church, his temple, just as the Name dwelled in Solomon's temple.

It is nothing less than Jesus anticipating the time after his resurrection when he would ascend to heaven and afterwards return to them spiritually through the Holy Spirit:[9] "that I may be in them." That's what he said that same night, at the Last Supper.

The Father gives and Jesus receives. Jesus receives the Holy Spirit from the Father, and gives it to the church.

---

9. Jesus' promised return in this verse cannot mean his appearances between his resurrection and his ascension, as some have argued, since he describes it taking place after going to the Father (after which he will send the Spirit, note: 15:26). His journey to the Father still lay in the future even after the resurrection (John 20:17). Nor can it mean his future "second coming," as some have argued, since he advises those assembled in the upper room that he is telling this to them so that they will believe when it happens, i.e., in their lifetime (14:28–29). That leaves one meaning: his return, through the Spirit, from Pentecost onwards (14:15–17). He anticipates his own spiritual presence coming to them (15:23). His references to resurrection appearances may come at 16:16 onwards.

When we say that Jesus receives his role from the Father, this is true for him on the level of his humanity, and true for him on the level of his divinity as the Name. To understand Jesus, we hold these two things together: equal in nature, yet always ready for the role that is lower. And suitably, as the one who takes the lower role, it was Jesus who came in human form.

So Jesus' being equal to the Father but taking a lower role—just as the Name is equal to God but takes a lower role—is eternally part of who Jesus is, and an essential part of what Jesus does.

The disciples would be his temple; and he would return to be in them—that is the context in which Jesus speaks of himself as the divine presence and of his Father as greater.

As a human being, he has always acted and spoken in a way that is in harmony with him being the Name, never doing or saying anything that would be at odds with him being the Name.

It is a harmony that has been hidden in plain sight: the Son "*tabernacles*" in the church community, as the Father *sends* him to do; it is just as the Name is *put* in the temple as the place where *God chooses* for him to dwell.

It is a snapshot of the Trinity, a truly dynamic picture. The Father is seen to have the leading role. The Son's loving service is exemplified in his becoming human, and also in how he receives his role from the Father.

But that still isn't the end of the story. God doesn't leave it there. The way that the Name—as God's presence—takes his role *never* means the Name is putting himself down and staying down. The Father honors the Name as equivalent to himself:

> you have exalted above all things your name . . . (Ps 138:2)

> far above all rule and authority and power and dominion, and above every name that is named . . . (Eph 1:20–21)

God does not have a Name that is below him. The Name lowers himself and the Father lifts him up again.

"God is not a man"

There's an important truth to remember, so that we don't speak wrongly about God. It's in Num 23:19: "God is not a man, that he should lie." It is helpful to come to this, to remind ourselves what happened when Jesus came in human form. God and human nature were fastened together in him—in perfect unity—you can't see the join, so to speak. That's the right kind of thing to say. Here are some of the things we don't say if we are being really careful to get our words right about Jesus: we don't say that humanity became God; or God became human. That is not quite the right thing to say about Jesus. Why? Because God's nature is still God's nature. And humanity is not God, it's still human. And Jesus had both natures—that's the point. Jesus gives us both his own humanity and his own divinity as his two natures, and all in one package.

God and human nature fastened together in a unique way. There's no muddle between them. You can't mix together humanity and divinity like paint in a pot, and make a different color. What is special about Jesus is that his humanity stays human and his divinity stays divine. So it is still true where Numbers 23 says that "God is not a man"—as there are two natures in Jesus, and one nature is divine, and it stays divine. His God nature has not become human. His other nature is human and it stays human.[10] God and man are joined together—in Jesus, they are joined as one, in one person. It is two natures perfectly fastened together, perfect union.[11] He's not half-man half-God. That would be selling out on his humanity and on everything about him. The point is that he is never less than fully human. His human nature is simply fastened to his God-nature, which he had always had, and they are a perfect fit for Jesus, for the Name.

And the really wonderful thing is this: God has taken humanity into his very heart through Jesus. Christians are joined to Jesus and so with him we are taken into the very heart of God.

So, let's talk about it in terms of God and his Name. The Name is not humanity. The Name is divine. But the Name took on human nature. In Jesus, humanity and the Name are joined together. But the Name is still divine. The divine Name is one nature of Jesus, and humanity is the other. Never mixed like paint in a pot. Always seamlessly joined together as one person. It is right to say that Jesus is the Name come in the flesh.

Some parts of the ancient creeds are not so easy to follow. But knowing the Trinity as God, his Name, and his Glory unlocks answers to puzzles that have sometimes confused people.

That is to take nothing away from the creeds' importance and value. Churches use them as a yardstick for recognizing when a message about salvation deviates from what the early church could have accepted. The creeds

---

10. Christians who experience the Holy Spirit within them have a little bit of insight into how this is possible, since they can tell that the Holy Spirit has a mind of its own, sometimes at odds with us, and yet when we are born of the Spirit, it is impossible to completely dissect what we do into what we did ourselves and what the Spirit did when we walk "in step with the Spirit." It is a seamless relationship when we do. This is not the same as Jesus' experience, but it is a little insight into what is possible for two natures being in harmony.

11. I'm not here intending to enter into a critique of the theology of theosis, but rather simply stating fundamental Christology.

guard against ill-thought-out new doctrines that, in one way or another, undermine the message of salvation. To avoid them, the words of the creeds mark a path with boundaries that help to tell when a wayward doctrine is being preached.

With our knowledge of God, his Name, and his Glory from Solomon's temple, we have a biblical vocabulary that shines a clear light on the subject of the creeds. The ancient creeds themselves shine beautifully in this light.

This is the Trinity. Over the years, only the vocabulary has really changed, from God and Name and Glory, then to Father, Son, and Holy Spirit, and then to the philosophical words of the creeds.

4. ONE TRUE GOD

The ancient creeds remind us to choose words thoughtfully when we try to describe God, so that we don't give a wrong impression. Words matter. They put ideas across. Choosing a word carelessly can convey an idea we don't intend, just as finding the right word puts across an idea the way it is meant. That is why so much work went into writing the church's creeds. It is worth spending a moment looking at some words that crop up when people are on the right or wrong path when talking about the Trinity.

Monotheism

The Athanasian Creed rightly emphasizes that there is only one true God. Belief in only one God is called monotheism by scholars. This is a good trinitarian word. We can talk rightly of both monotheism and Trinitarianism fitting together, which means there are three persons included in the identity of the one true God.

But some past discussions about the Father, Son, and Holy Spirit have gone off-track and become mistaken doctrines or heresies. Even today, new versions of these old heresies pop up, so it as well to know how to spot them and where they go off-track. Each has an old name.

Modalism—this old heresy wipes out the difference between the Father and the Son and the Holy Spirit. You would think the trinitarian truth is obvious, that the Father is not the Son: for one thing, they talk to each other! But instead, modalism actually thinks the Father and the Son are the same person. And modalists count in the Holy Spirit too, making all three into just one person. Trinitarians take it this way instead: the Father knows who is his Son. And the Son knows who is his Father. They never get each other the wrong way round! And the Holy Spirit itself knows that it is not the

Father or the Son. They never get each other the wrong way round either. All three of them know who they are and how they differ from each other.[12] So rightly, we count the Father, and the Son, and the Spirit, and there are three. Three persons in one God. They are always and forever interacting with each other. We can use the words God and Name and Glory, and we can use the words Father, Son, and Spirit, and be sure that we are talking about three persons in one God, each doing different things for each other at the same time, and so we can tell them apart from each other. So, the old heresy stumbled by saying that one God equals only one person. Next we come to a heresy that stumbles by saying that three persons equals three gods.

Tri-theism—this old heresy makes the mistake of thinking that Father, Son and Spirit add up to three gods. This is wrong and different from the Trinity, which affirms there is one God, *and the three are one God together.*[13] The Father and Son and Spirit are not three *gods*. They are a three, but this is three *persons*, not three gods. Using the words of the Athanasian Creed, people sometimes speak of the one true God who exists in three persons like this:

> God the Father
> God the Son and
> God the Holy Spirit

That is often spoken in the blessing at the end of a church service. The wording can trouble people, because by using the word God three times, the mistaken impression could be taken that it is about three Gods. It is in fact about only one God. If the wording seems clumsy, could speaking of the Name and the Glory help? To put it another way:

> God the Father
> God the Name and
> God the Glory

With the God of Solomon's temple unlocking the answer like that, it obviously is not three gods, but one God: God, his Name, and his Glory. We can count the word God being used three times, but that is just counting a word. That is no more an issue here than when Yahweh uses the word "God"

---

12. Modalism, also known as Sabellianism, makes the mistake of being blind to their "personal properties" that make the three distinct from each other. See: Swain, "Mystery of the Trinity."

13. Tri-theism makes the mistake of being blind to their "common properties," blind to their being "identically divine." See: Swain, "Mystery of the Trinity."

three times calling himself "the God of Abraham, the God of Isaac and the God of Jacob" (Exod 3:6).

The fact is that when you think of God, his Name, and his Glory, they can only be one God, not three gods. We can give tri-theism a miss.

Subordinationism—this old heresy is a real mess. It gets one main thing right and one main thing wrong. It gets right that the Father is not Son and they are not the Spirit. It goes wrong by being blind to the truth that the three of them are identically divine, as one God together. From that mistake, it ends up with a second-class Jesus in every way and a second-class Holy Spirit, and it starts to sound like they are two or three gods, with a pecking order of one at the top and one or two at the bottom, depending how they carve them up. The Jehovah's Witnesses see things this way a bit (one at the top, one at the bottom, and wiping out the Holy Spirit from being a person altogether as if he's never spoken to them!). This study has already covered how the Name is co-equal, yet takes a lower role: therein lies an answer.

Pantheism—this heresy stumbles by saying wrongly that its "god" is really everything we see around us and everything we see is part of god, even the trees and the grass, the tables and the chairs, the rats and the people. This is bad. It sounds like admiring creation but don't be fooled. This is dragging everything about God down to the level of a germ or an insect or anything in creation. This is wiping out the special difference between the Creator and creation. We need to recognize the shining truth of this difference. The truth is that there is a line and we respect what is on either side of the line. On one side of the line is God, his Name, and his Glory. On the other side of the line is creation, including us and where we live. A wonderful thing about the Trinity here is when God graciously crosses over that line, coming into his creation to support humanity, as Jesus. This is what Christians celebrate at Christmas, Jesus coming from heaven to earth to save us all from Satan's power when we had gone astray; that in this world of sin, the dear Christ enters in; mercy mild, God and sinners reconciled (as the Christmas carols go). That reason to celebrate is lost when pantheism rubs out that line. You more or less lose the essence of what the Bible tells us about the Father, the Son, and the Holy Spirit.

Pantheism is as bad as saying that the Creator doesn't exist at all, because it wipes out the difference between creation and Creator. It erases our picture of the Creator, whom we know as wonderfully set apart from creation, but intimately working in creation to bless it and save it.

There are plenty of heresies, but this short list just goes to show that there are ways of missing the right path, and the right path is speak of one Creator God, which is three persons, the Trinity. There are also other words that can help us, and words to avoid when speaking of the Trinity. Let's see some.

Distinct

This is a helpful word. To keep things on the straight and narrow, when speaking of the three persons—Father, Son and Spirit—we do not speak of them being "separate" from each other. They are always one. A better word is to say that they are "distinct" from each other. If we say they are distinct, that is fine, because then we are not saying that they can be pulled apart, split off, and divided from each other to have three totally separate existences.

When saying they are distinct from each other, we can rightly see differences between God and his Name and his Glory. So, it is good to say that the Father, Son, and Spirit are "distinct" from each other, not "separate" from each other. In a better choice of words, we find the right meanings.

Presence

This is another helpful word. To add in a little more biblical language, we can use the word "presence" when talking about the three persons. So, then we can say this:

> God the Father, the presence in heaven
>
> God the Name, the presence in the temple
>
> God the Glory, the presence that fills the temple and all the world

So, "one God in three persons" can also be put this way: "one God in three presences." We will look into that again later to try to clear up any confusion.

The trail that started with the Name and the Glory, and Solomon's temple, has led us further. The trail of clues continued in the New Testament: it led us to Pentecost, to Jesus, and to the Holy Spirit. But it didn't stop there.

We have discovered the creeds, but there is always much more that Christians say about God, and the next part looks at another puzzle that is well-known to many Christians. And the key that unlocks the answer is once again the Trinity of Solomon's temple: God, his Name, and his Glory.

5. BEYOND THE CREEDS

One of the things that sometimes comes up in discussions about the Trinity is a group of words: omniscient, omnipotent, omnipresent.

These mean all-knowing, all-powerful, present everywhere. So:

- Omniscient = all-knowing
- Omnipotent = all-powerful
- Omnipresent = present everywhere

These words are not from the creeds. Some say that God is defined by these things. Others say the more important thing to understand about God is the relationships between Father, Son, and Spirit.

Some people ask how is Jesus omniscient, omnipotent, and omnipresent? And answers are unlocked by our familiar key: God, his Name, and his Glory.

Omnipotent (All-powerful)

It is through the power of his Holy Spirit that God can do all things. As the Bible says: "Where is he who set his Holy Spirit among them, who sent his glorious arm of power . . . ?" (Isa 63:11–12 NIV).

Usually, if anyone is called God's power, it is the Holy Spirit. But this would not mean that the Father is any less "God." God the Father can *send* his Holy Spirit!

And whatever the Father can do through the Holy Spirit, the Son can do through the Holy Spirit. This is the essence of omnipotence. So, of Jesus, St. John wrote that he has the Spirit "without limit" (John 3:34 NIV). The power of the Spirit is unlimited for the Son as for the Father. Another way to look at the omnipotence of Jesus is this:

> the Spirit = the power of God = the Breath of God = the Breath of Jesus.

So Christ breathes out the Breath of God. Only God, or God's Name, breathes out the Breath of God. So Jesus is no less "God" as such, and no less omnipotent (John 20:22, Isa 30:27).

It is through each other that the Father, the Son, and the Spirit are all that they are. So it should be no surprise that God's Name is omnipotent. One way that the Bible speaks of the Name's power is this: *"your name is great in might"* (Jer 10:6), or to put it another way, "your name is mighty in power" (Jer 10:6 NIV).

Omnipresent (Present Everywhere)

The Name and the Glory can be present everywhere and anywhere. A little glimpse of this may be had in Ps 8:1 which speaks of the Name: "O LORD, our Lord, how majestic is *your name in all the earth*!" And Num 14:21 which speaks of the Glory: "the *earth shall be filled with the glory* of the LORD." (We have explored how important it was for the Name sometimes to be present in a particular place, not just everywhere.)

Wherever the Father chooses to be present through the Holy Spirit, the Son can choose to be present through the Holy Spirit. As the writer of the Psalm said to God, "Where can I go from your Spirit? Where can I flee from your presence?" (Ps 139:7 NIV). This is unlimited for each of them. The Father and the Son can be present with us. This is possible through the Spirit.

And it would not mean that the Father is any less God whenever he is described as being in heaven rather than strictly omnipresent. God the Father is the one who sends the omnipresent Holy Spirit. Something similar can be said for Jesus. People might ask why Jesus was in Nazareth instead of being omnipresent, but this is really no different from supposing it's a problem for the Father to be in heaven rather than omnipresent. Through the Holy Spirit, Jesus' spiritual presence can now be everywhere as and when he wishes, just as the Father can. This is the essence of omnipresence.

For example, the Son chooses to be present "where two or three come together in my name" (Matt 18:20). So the Son has unlimited ability to be present through the Holy Spirit in all Christian communities at the same time, or anywhere else in creation. God will be where he wills to be.

Omniscient (All-knowing)

"Omniscient" means being all-knowing. God can know everything that is happening in all creation. This is true for the Father, the Son, and the Holy Spirit. All that the Father wishes to know through the Holy Spirit, the Son can know through the Holy Spirit. This is the essence of omniscience. St. John's book of Revelation puts it like this in regard to the Son and the Spirit. It uses the number seven, a symbol of completeness, to refer to the Holy Spirit as seven Spirits. In this passage, the Son is mentioned as "the Lamb." The Lamb's eyes are the Holy Spirit's:

> I saw a Lamb standing, as though it had been slain, with seven horns and with seven eyes, which are the seven spirits of God sent out into all the earth. (Rev 5:6)

To put it another way, the Holy Spirit is like Jesus' eyes, seeing everyone in the world. These are not literally "eyes" in someone's head! The word "eyes" here simply means seeing, that the Lamb sees. So the Lamb's "eyes" can see everything, everywhere, and know all things. And those "eyes" are seeing what the Holy Spirit sees. So the Holy Spirit sees everything everywhere. The Son and the Spirit in heaven are omniscient.

St. John was drawing on the words of the book of Zechariah, in Zech 4:1–14:[14]

> These *seven are the eyes* of Yahweh, which range over the whole world. (Zech 4:10 NJB)

In so many words, Jesus is Yahweh God, and in heaven he sees the whole world. The eyes through which God looks over the whole earth, the eyes that make God omniscient, are the Holy Spirit's.[15]

Sometimes a child will ask the most profound questions. One of them is this: how does God in heaven see everything that happens on the earth? And that was the answer: through the Holy Spirit. They do all things together.

The Trinity: Omniscient, Omnipotent, Omnipresent

The Holy Spirit is key, then, in understanding how God is omniscient, omnipotent, and omnipresent. The Holy Spirit is spoken of in the Bible as God's eyes, God's power, and God's presence. Through the Holy Spirit, God interacts throughout the world we live in. And these qualities apply equally to Father, Son, and Spirit. Through each other, the Father, Son, and Spirit are what they are. So we can say this:

> God is all-knowing, all-powerful and present everywhere.
> God's Name is all-knowing, all-powerful and present everywhere.
> God's Spirit is all-knowing, all-powerful and present everywhere.

God can be understood. God wants to be understood. Jesus came to reveal God to us.

Next we need a last look at the idea of three "persons," which we saw in the Athanasian Creed.

---

14. Bauckham, *Revelation*, 109–11.
15. Bauckham, *Revelation*, 112.

6. WHAT IS A PERSON?

Sometimes, a treasure map takes us into a forest, and the trail winds this way and that. Going through the thoughts of ancient scholars can seem like going through a forest of words. But we have the map to the treasure and the keys to unlock the puzzles. Our trail brings us to one tree in this forest in particular. This tree has one word written on it: "persons." It is a clue, an important clue, for understanding the Trinity better.

The Athanasian Creed speaks of one God who exists in three "persons." But what does "person" mean here? The word needs investigating.

Nowadays when someone talks about a "person," it is with modern meanings in mind that are not found in the Bible. Meanings that are hardly in tune with the way people thought at all in the days of Jesus. Just speaking of "persons" can start to give us the wrong impression about the Trinity, and there are better words. So let's see the difficulty with the word person.

The problem with the modern meaning of "person" is this: it is common to think of a person as a private individual, with private thoughts and emotions that divide each of us from everyone else.

That just isn't the way the Bible thinks of persons at all. It is much more integrated; people are much more united together in the Bible. Of course, each member of the human race is precious and unique, called by name by God. But that is not the same thing as the modern idea of private individuals. In the ancient world, people were considered best understood in relation to each other and to God. They would not think of you as a private individual. It mattered what tribe you were in, what town you came from, whose family you were from, who your friends were, what God you followed. Those things mattered to understand a person.

When we speak of one God in three "persons," we mean in the sense understood in the early church. The Trinity is not three private individuals. The Father, Son, and Spirit are not completely separate entities. It's not as if you could pull them apart and divide them from each other. The triune God is three distinctive presences that share in one identity. They relate to each other in that shared identity. That identity that they share together is being Yahweh. And they are a bit like a community who can only be properly understood in relation to each other.

If anyone objects to speaking of Father, Son, and Spirit as three persons, it may be that they are really rejecting the idea of God as three separate private individuals. People would be right to reject that picture of three completely separate individuals.

What we need instead is to think of the Father, Son, and Spirit in a more biblical sense of "persons." We're coming to just that.

Why the Church Started Using the Word "Person" for God

We can explain how Christians ended up using the word "person" for God. It's to do with the good old Latin language. It came into the story long ago when a biblical Greek word—*prosopon*—was translated into Latin. *Prosopon* in Greek became *persona* in Latin. *Persona* is what you find in Latin translations of the Bible. We get the English word "person" from *persona*. But what if we go back, before the Latin, back to the Greek? Here we will find a better understanding of a biblical word that helps us to think of the three "presences" of God: as the Father, Son, and Holy Spirit.

The Greek Word: Prosopon

What is good here about the Greek word *prosopon* is that we can rightly translate it into English as the word "presence." And the word presence doesn't bring the confusion caused by the word person. We would never take the word "presence" to just mean an isolated private individual.

Prosopon was formed from two smaller Greek words—*pros ops*—meaning "with eyes." To make sense in English translations, they often translate it as "face" (as in 1 Cor 13:12), or "presence," or "person" as in Mark 12:14 (KJV): "thou regardest not the person [*prosopon*] of men."

The good thing, since our focus is the Father, Son, and Spirit, is that *prosopon* is used of all three in the New Testament and the Greek version of the Old Testament.

Prosopon is used of the Son's presence in 2 Thess 1:9–10, and the Father's presence in Heb 9:24. The Greek Old Testament gives us these interesting uses of *prosopon* in relation to the Spirit:

> Do not cast me from your presence [*prosopon*]; or take your Holy Spirit from me. (Ps 51:11 NIV)

> Where can I go from your Spirit? Where can I flee from your presence [*prosopon*]? (Ps 139:7 NIV).

By the way, each of those verses shows, in classic Hebrew style, how to say the same thing twice! Spirit and presence (*prosopon*) are both referring to the Holy Spirit. We now have the keys to understand the biblical way of talking about God as personal presences, and things fall into place. So, when we say "person" of God, we don't mean like a private individual.

Presence and Place

This idea of "presence" has given us a memorable way that we can tell the Father, Son, and Spirit apart from each other. Think again about where God lives. Typically, we think of the Father's presence in heaven, the Holy Spirit's presence everywhere worldwide, and Jesus' presence in a particular place. Keeping together this idea of person and presence has a lot of benefits.

Presence and Relationships

There are advantages in remembering that the Father, Son, and Spirit are distinct persons from each other. For example, we see that the biblical conversations between them are genuine. Two thousand years ago in Galilee, the Father in heaven and the Son on earth spoke and listened to each other. They are two distinct persons, and yet shared one identity—Yahweh.

Knowing about these things can help us to understand ourselves better too. As human beings, we tend to see ourselves, rightly, as people who want relationships with others. Christians believe that the human race was made to be this way. Especially, this desire for company is a reflection of God's nature—because God, within, inside, is three-way relationships—between Father, Son, and Spirit. Because they are distinct from each other, it means there can be real relationships between them. And so we as human beings— made in God's image—seek each other's company.

The Holy Spirit Is a Person Too

Next, a few brief words on the importance of remembering that the Holy Spirit is a "person" too.

One heretical idea that readers may have come across, because it is held by some modern cults, is that the Holy Spirit has no personal characteristics, to the point of not being a person at all. They might make a claim that the Holy Spirit is just an impersonal force, which isn't right at all. Nothing about God is impersonal. Christians who speak of their personal experience of the Holy Spirit within them may express surprise that anyone could have a doctrine like that. The Christian experience can sometimes be likened to Acts 13:2–4 (NIV) where the Holy Spirit personally speaks a detailed instruction to the disciples:

> the Holy Spirit said, "Set apart for *me* Barnabas and Saul for the work to which *I* have called them."

The Holy Spirit calls himself personally "me" and "I" there. The Holy Spirit even personally specifies the things to be understood by those listening, in a way that a person does. The Spirit also has a voice in Acts 8:29 and 10:19, as well as in Mark 13:11 and Rom 8:26. (Many Christians get more of an inner impression of what the Spirit is saying than hearing actual words, but sometimes this includes hearing words—not out loud, but in an inner communication that others can't usually hear.)

The Holy Spirit, like Jesus, is God's own personal presence. And God does not have an impersonal side to him. You can't imagine anyone in Jesus' day who would ever have thought that the God of Israel had an impersonal presence. The dwelling of God in his church, in his temple, is personal. The Holy Spirit is a person, just like God the Father and his Son Jesus are too.

It can come as a surprise to discover that some people deny that there is evidence of personal characteristics in the way the Holy Spirit communicates. This is a common denial in religious cults, who tend to claim—and this is where it really starts to impact on people—that the Holy Spirit has no personal relationship with them. Cults also, at the same time, tend to deny that Jesus is God's presence amongst them.

This is how cults are. If they did not deny these things, it would make it more difficult for the cult leaders to control their members. This is because the truth would set cult members free: it would give opportunity for ordinary cult members to think that they can listen to the Holy Spirit for themselves, and call on Jesus as their own Lord. The truth would knock cult leaders off their pedestal and show that they are wrong to claim to have a better access to God than their members have. Knowing the Holy Spirit as a person for themselves helps to set people free from cults.

In the same way, a personal relationship with Jesus means people can call on Jesus as their Lord and their God personally. Cults don't like that. It makes Jesus the king, not the cult leader. This sets people free from the control of cults. So cults don't like people to believe that they too can have a personal relationship with Jesus or the Holy Spirit.

The unhealthy desire that some people have for control over other people can lead to some quite bizarre ideas. That is why some cults claim, wrongly, that the Holy Spirit is only a force, something that is just impersonal. Or they say that when the Holy Spirit speaks in the Bible, it is not a person speaking, it is only poetry, only "personifying" an impersonal thing like poems do. This is nonsense. An impersonal force does not address people with specific details, saying things like, "Set apart for *me* Barnabas and Saul for the work to which *I* have called them." That's how a person speaks. That's the Spirit speaking with words from Jesus, just as Jesus said the Spirit would (Mark 13:11 and Luke 21:15). And God does not have an impersonal side to him. God's Holy Spirit is personal.

The trinitarian spiritual life is person to person, the life of God in 3D.

Reflection and Application

- How do creeds help with church unity?
- How might your knowledge of God, his Name, and his Glory help you to understand the creeds better?
- How do the Name and the Glory help you to think about the Trinity being co-equal and co-eternal?
- God gives to his Son, his Name, a temple to dwell in. How does the status of the Name of God help with understanding the status of the Son of God?
- How might recapturing the language of the Name and the Glory help the church to understand the Trinity better?

Epilogue: Academic Case for the Thesis

Out of consideration to the general reader, I am placing here that which scholars would expect to read first. I hope I may be forgiven for this.

This epilogue, with academics in mind, opens up some preliminary questions that they may have about the primary and secondary sources for the historical data and theological background to this book. It draws on academic material that a theological or ministry training college might regard as too niche for a general syllabus. But there is no good reason why such material and its benefits should not be readily accessible to the mainstream. First I need to explain why some terminology in this book is couched in the way it is.

TERMS

This book explores a trajectory through Hebrew and Christian Scripture exposing the development of a very early trinitarian understanding of God. There are many reasons why readers may be interested in the origins of Christian belief in the Trinity, and as such this contribution to biblical and early Christian studies explores avenues for both study and practical Christianity. It is intended to be as accessible as possible to the non-specialist. For this reason, the use of Hebrew and Greek vocabulary is kept to a minimum, always in transliteration, and always with an explanation. I am also giving place to terms such as Bible, Old Testament, and New Testament. Of course, in the nuances of modern scholarship, there is a strong case for preferring words such as Scripture, Hebrew Scripture, early Christian writings, and so on. I hope it will be appreciated why the terms more familiar to the non-specialist are used. Unlike the chapters that follow, this epilogue goes with terms such as Hebrew Scripture. I have had similar regard to use of the calendar terms BC and AD (whereas in the epilogue you will find BCE and CE). In a book written to be straightforwardly accessible to the non-specialist, I have given place to the terms Christian and Christianity, even in relation to the earliest generations of the Jesus movements, while minimizing such usage because of the risk of anachronistically implying an early separation between "Christianity" and "Judaism." One could also, to avoid anachronism, prefer a term such as "assembly" to "church," but again, for much the same reason, I use "church," at some risk of the false impression of major religious institutions existing before their time. I am not claiming it is especially good to choose vocabulary in this direction, but I hope it will be understandable why I have done so in this book. The term "church fathers" is also used. I am aware that Western academia now tends to avoid unnecessary patriarchal connotations. However, a non-specialist who is aware of such writings will tend to know that as the umbrella term for them from the titles of volumes containing them.

PURPOSE

To better communicate their understanding of God should always be an aim of the Christian theologian and minister. This book serves that aim. In preparation for ministry, a Christian may be taught to think theologically, and, especially in relation to the Trinity, to be orthodox, but scarcely to communicate this information in accessible language to the inquisitive "layperson." The minister put on the spot to explain the Trinity should not be blushing with embarrassment. This book argues that we should avoid leaving the impression that the Trinity is entirely a mystery that cannot be understood, or that it defies logic, or that its comprehension requires very technical and abstract philosophical language. Anecdotal evidence suggests that it is not reassuring to leave someone hanging with a phrase such as "it might seem irrational to you," if a rational explanation of the Trinity is what they are reaching out for. It is less than ideal if an impression is left that the doctrine of the Trinity is nothing but a problem. People are also increasingly less likely simply to accept a doctrine on the basis of authority, but can find a doctrine appealing if it is attractive to the mind as well as the heart, acceptable to the intelligence of the devout or the curious, and this study is offered in that spirit.

Therefore the latter part of this study includes attention to common problems that an earnest seeker may have comprehending the Trinity. Some have got stuck, for example, on the very idea of God being both three and one; or on Jesus' saying "The Father is greater than I"; or on saying that Jesus is at one and the same time both man and God; or on making the leap from observing that the Holy Spirit is described with personal characteristics to calling the Spirit a "person." A non-specialist who asks clergy about it is apt to get a theological answer that "goes over their head" or no answer at all. This is unsettling for some conscientious Christians and their confusion becomes a tool used by proselytizing cults, and even other faiths (such as in some contemporary Islamic outreach). Christian confusion about the Trinity is played by Jehovah's Witnesses as a winning card in recruiting people away from churches and into their sect, for example, and with some success. This is a wholly unnecessary confusion that anyone should be spared. This study offers some reflections on these questions, reflections rooted in canonical writings that lend themselves to being simply and easily communicated. And if the ones asking the questions want their answers met from Scripture, we ought to try to meet them on those terms first.

Therefore, giving the layperson a confident rational answer explaining the Trinity is not merely an intellectual exercise but a pastoral necessity. I hope that many teachers and communicators would take advantage of a simple scriptural model of the Trinity such as that described in this study. I have found that being able to open a Bible and show how this model can be observed—as the three-in-one God of the temple—dispels confusion, and supports understanding. On one occasion, this satisfied the demands of a very anxious young man who had been led to believe that Trinitarians can't find the Trinity in the Bible. His church leader had directed him towards me for some quick on-the-spot Bible study and it was enough for his needs on that day.

This book provides the reader with tools to journey through scriptural narratives, finding the Trinity in "salvation history," rather than resorting directly to abstract concepts. Along this journey, I carefully lay out how the early church could find demonstrations of the Trinity in canonical texts as the three-in-one God of the temple. It is the intention that no one come away feeling that the doctrine of the Trinity is irrational, illogical, or unscriptural. This is not a book of apologetics, but I hope it will stir interest in studying a much-neglected early church apologetic for the Trinity. For the ease of the non-specialist, I aim at a conversational tone throughout. This is after all a subject which ministers may want Christians in general to feel able to have a constructive conversation about.

The book is structured to serve the non-specialist. Its first chapter—which I have rather boldly titled "People like you can understand the Trinity"—sets out the core scriptural data for appreciating the thesis, first in a very abbreviated form and then at length. The following four chapters spread the net to capture data in the book of Acts, Hebrew Scripture, and the canonical Epistles and Gospels in that order. Chapter 6 surveys a broader range of writings of the early Christian era, evidencing how much the church knew the approach to the Trinity that this book builds upon. It is the intention that this book be practical for Christian discipleship, and chapter 7 sets out how the themes of this book can inform personal and corporate discipleship, with an emphasis on worship and practical suggestions for purposes of churches that wish to explore themes liturgically, and on personal devotions that the general reader may find accessible. The chapters do not have to be read in that order, and scholars may find it helpful after reading this epilogue to proceed directly to chapter 6 to take stock of primary sources. This necessarily comprises mainly short quotes from a wide variety of sources from antiquity. Space does not permit me to set each in a wider context of each author's intentions and writings, but I think their inclusion is both informative and helpful.

Temple theology, a key element of this study, provides for an appreciation of both God's transcendence and immanence, that God is both above all things and at the same time desires to dwell with humanity. This facilitates a trinitarian hermeneutic and well-rounded worship. And those more familiar with Scripture may find here fresh readings that will revitalize their appreciation of well-known texts. God is *agape*, and we have an opportunity to explore the fellowship between the Father, Son, and Spirit in a fresh way. The final chapter tests to what degree the Name and Glory theology of this study shares significant patterns with the Nicene and Athanasian creeds. A study guide at the end of each chapter provides suggestions for reflection and application in Christian life.

Allow me to state what this study is not intended to be. It does not visit common proof texts for the Trinity.[1] Nor is it about external proofs of the Trinity through philosophy or analogy. This study does not enter into discussion about whether any external proof is possible.[2] There is no trying to persuade anyone problematically from any external analogy, least of all from such as ice, water, and steam! Where this study seeks to demonstrate anything, it is from how early Christian writings used Scripture. This study reflects on Hebraic roots of Christian faith in a triune God, as might be seen through an early church lens.

This study is not intended to be a thorough survey of a very wide variety of scriptural trinitarian themes.[3] Nor is it intended as a study of Nicene language, nor of modern theological controversies such as complementarianism or gendered pronouns. I am adhering to generally familiar use of pronouns in speaking of the persons of God. This of course is not meant to imply that divinity is particularly male in nature. In God's image they are

---

1. For an assessment of texts commonly used as proof texts, see Warfield, "Trinity."
2. For a rather negative assessment of external proofs, see Warfield, "Trinity."
3. For extensive treatment of such, I would recommend *The Essential Trinity* by Brandon D. Crowe and Carl R. Trueman (London: IVP, 2016).

created, male and female, and in creation God's image is evident in a unity of male and female. Coincidentally, two Hebrew nouns that loom large over this study, *shem* and *kabod*, are masculine nouns. From this detail I deduce absolutely nothing at all about God's nature.

This book is also not intended as an exposition of technical terms such as paternity, filiation, spiration, transcendence, immanence, procession, personal properties, common properties, substance, essence, *ousia*, *hypostasis*, or *homoousios*. Indeed, for ease of the non-specialist, any such terms appear only in this epilogue, and in footnotes (where relevant themes are being discussed in the main text). Those footnotes are mainly found in the later part of the book, for any who may want to follow through. Terms such as monotheism, modalism, and subordinationism are of necessity used in the main text. All the foregoing terms are of course integral to a scholarly appreciation of doctrines of the Trinity but the key themes they represent can be explored in plainer language to an adequate degree for the purposes of this study. Space is given to the use of the term person, since this is familiar in common usage, and its implications need to be covered more directly. This study is not about modern developments in the theological meanings of the foregoing terms, and insofar as they are mentioned at all, it is for the sake of excavating meanings that were obtained in the ancient church up to the time of the Cappadocian Fathers, and only explored at an introductory level. It suffices for the thesis of this book, which I will come to shortly.

This study attempts theology not in the abstract but as rooted in the Hebraic story of Yahweh's interaction with creation, especially with humanity, especially in Israel's ancient stories. It seeks for Hebraic salvation history to inform theology. Later in the book, this develops into a dialogue between Hebraic roots and Nicene theology. This study broadly falls into historical theology, with an eye on contemporary relevance.

As for method in handling scriptural texts, I have endeavored to avoid skipping from canonical book to book, text to text, as if proof-texting. I have sought as far as seems reasonable to stay with any book for some length before moving on to another, and where Scriptures are cross-referenced across books, it is because links are apparent in the texts or the themes bear comparison.

Finally on the purpose of this study, it may also make some small contribution that might speak into contemporary debates on Name theology.

MAIN TOPICS OF DISCUSSION

There are three main areas of discussion addressed in this epilogue. First, I will highlight a neglected early church apologetic for the Trinity, drawing on the concept of God dwelling in his temple. Second, I will outline some relevant scholarship in the fields of temple theology, Name theology, and Glory theology. These areas are core to this study. Third, this epilogue will state in brief my thesis presenting a much-overlooked type of the Trinity in Hebrew Scripture. The paradigm for this is in motifs of divine presence in Solomon's temple, in which the categories of Name and Glory are found together as presence. This type is the Trinity of God, his Name, and his Glory.

AN EARLY CHURCH APOLOGETIC FOR THE TRINITY

Although much scholarship has attended to the trajectories leading to Nicaea, there has been recent interest in the potential for an early Trinitarianism in the New Testament, exemplified by the essays in *The Essential Trinity: New Testament Foundations and Practical Relevance*. In this study, I wish to draw attention to a neglected demonstration of the Trinity from the early church. This accesses an ante-Nicene perspective on the Trinity that consciously takes its trajectory from Hebrew Scripture via Paul's letters and John's Gospel and other Christian Scripture, largely with little or no reference to categories that are most associated with the Nicene and Athanasian creeds and their associated debates. It goes like this. It observes that God dwells in a temple. Its premise: if we are talking about the temple of the God of Israel, then this temple ought of necessity to be indwelled by the one true God only and no one else. Observation: where this is a living temple, the Christian community, it is found in Scripture to be indwelt by, surprisingly, the Father, Son, and Holy Spirit: three. This compels us to think: the scriptural church is indwelled by those three, where we would expect it to be indwelled by a single God only. Conclusion: if it is shown that Father, Son, and Spirit dwell in a temple that exists for God alone to dwell in (in the church), then the three together must accordingly be that one God. It is their temple to dwell in, and they are its God. It is difficult to see how they would not qualify as one God, if a paradigm of Israel's temple for its one true God is operative. Their act of co-indwelling the temple is thus a demonstration of the Trinity, the three-in-one God of the temple. Father, Son, and Spirit in one temple can only be one God.

This apologetic is set out with additional argumentation and Scriptures in Ambrose, *On the Holy Spirit*, Book III.12.91–93. The apologetic is also rehearsed in brief in Augustine, *The Enchiridion: on Faith, Hope and Love*, 56; and Jerome, *Dialogue Against the Luciferians*, 6; and Cyril of Alexandria, "That Christ is One." The apologetic is already assumed in Cyprian, "Epistle 72.12, to Jubaianus"; and more than hinted at in Tertullian, "On Modesty," 21. The texts are reproduced in translation in the course of this study.

A narrower assumption of the apologetic had already appeared in Ignatius (Ign. *Eph* 15:3), illustrating the divinity of Christ, whereas it is those later authors who include the whole Trinity in this demonstration. Their apologetic draws on Paul's letters and John's Gospel to make the point, more so than other Scripture. Notably, they draw not only on Christian-authored Scripture but on Christian use of Hebrew Scripture.

Ambrose wraps the apologetic in an extra (perhaps superfluous) premise too: one temple for one God. Although Ambrose does not say so, this echoes Philo's commentary that God "foresaw that there could not be any great number of temples built either in many different places, or in the same place, thinking it fitting that as God is one, his temple also should be one." On this basis, Philo argues that Jews across the world had to come to the Jerusalem temple to sacrifice, rather than performing sacrifices in their own houses.[4]

It does not seem too much of a stretch to acknowledge the logic of the early church authors' argument from Scripture. This study hopefully goes a little way to raising awareness that the early church practiced the use of this simple apologetic, and that it provides a useful paradigm for detecting very early Christian appreciation of the Trinity. It also raises important questions for historical theology. For example, if the likes of Paul conceived of God as "one" (Rom 3:30), how could he be comfortable with complicating that deep belief with another idea, namely the understanding that the church was a

---

4. Philo, *On the Special Laws*, XII.66–68. Curiously, Philo—who lived in Alexandria—does not mention the presence of another Jewish temple standing in his lifetime, in Onias, Egypt. Philo is perhaps in principle harking back to the centralization of the cult in the time of Solomon's temple in Jerusalem. This was meant to be the single central location for God's Name to dwell. In the first century, notwithstanding Philo's rhetorical point, Jews had a broader flexible view. A temple is a sacred space where God dwells, and the Jerusalem temple was not unique in that. Paul could talk about individual Christians being temples of the Holy Spirit, decentralized, being in many places. And this was at the same time that some Jewish Christians were still worshiping in the Jerusalem temple. Also at the time, a synagogue could be a sacred space, a sort of temple. This could also go for the Jewish home at mealtimes. As Professor Tom O'Loughlin has pointed out to me, this was also the view held by the Qumran community about their refectory. But in terms of the idea of one temple for one God, Solomon's temple was still a paradigm of centralization that could legitimize the argumentation of Philo (and Ambrose's extra premise). Philo applies it only to an earthly temple, holding in the same passage that heaven is the truest temple.

temple in which *Christ and the Spirit* dwelled as divine (Rom 8:9–10; 1 Cor 3:16)? What made these ideas about God conceptually compatible to him? What was there in Paul's understanding of the Israelite God that could make it conceptually acceptable to him to speak of a "temple of the Holy Spirit" that Christ dwells in? Any answer has to come from Paul's own day, not from the fourth century when the Nicene Creed was written. Could there be a clue in earlier Jewish concepts of God dwelling in his temple that would be known in Paul's day? It is worth saying that in contemporary academic discourse, without the above trinitarian apologetic being drawn upon, we find the understanding that the activity of temple-dwelling is evidence of divinity of the temple-dweller.[5] If it is tempting to see here a unifying theory, one that unites some Hebraic and Christian concepts of God, we need to hold ourselves back a bit, at least until we have surveyed more of the evidence, and made sure that we know what we are attempting to say. It is more humble to approach this in terms of looking at how some early Christians could read Hebrew Scripture rather than to leap to conclusions about how everyone read it.

TEMPLE THEOLOGY

Temple theology is a wide-ranging subject, one that is fundamental for Hebraic understanding of divine presence from Eden, to the Jerusalem temple, to eschatological fulfillment of the hopes of Israel.[6] The Jerusalem temple, akin to Eden, was the locus where heaven and earth were joined together. Heaven and earth are designed to overlap and interlock.[7] It is not unintentional that, in Scripture, Israel's sanctuaries on earth mirror a heavenly sanctuary (Rev 11:19). God's presence in heaven and earth is integrated, and the temple mediates this. This sense of integration is necessary, because what is often being depicted in Scripture is a bifurcation between the transcendent God in heaven and the immanent presence of God in the temple on earth. God is depicted as being manifestly in two distinct locations simultaneously, with distinct presences, which we will see are distinctly named. This temple theology, with transcendence and immanence closely knit together, is found in the psalmist's words (Ps 11:4) which are echoed in Jesus' words (Matt 23:21–22).

---

5. See for example, in an exegesis of 1 Cor 16:9: "it should be noted that the 'god' of the somatic Temple is actually the Holy Spirit—it is his 'image' that is to be honored in the temple of the human body." Bonnington, "New Temples in Corinth." See page 157.

6. Richter, *Deuteronomistic History*, 11.

7. Wright, "On Earth as in Heaven."

In the church era, there is similarly a bifurcation between the transcendent "our Father in heaven" and the immanent Holy Spirit in the church community. This comes with the ascension of Christ from earth to heaven and the outpouring of the Spirit from heaven to earth, by which Christ's presence straddles earth and heaven.[8] N. T. Wright remarks on how the early church developed its theology of the Ascension and Pentecost as a temple-orientated phenomenon:

> . . . at the heart of Pentecost, in Acts . . . the coming of the Spirit is all about the launching of the new Temple. In Judaism, heaven and earth overlapped in the Temple; but now, says Luke, Jesus is the one who has taken earth, in his own person, his own human body, right into heaven; and the Spirit is the corollary of this, the life of heaven becoming manifest and powerful here on earth. Heaven and earth are thus locked together in a firm and unbreakable Trinitarian embrace . . .[9]

Such a narrative argues a radical first-century shift, away from the Jerusalem temple and towards the church, for the locus where heaven and earth meet in Israel. The idea of temple shifts from the Jerusalem temple to the church community. The outpouring of the Spirit upon Christ's followers makes them *a temple of living stones, inhabited by the Son and the Spirit of God*.[10] In what seems to be a remarkable parallel, Solomon made *a temple of actual stones, inhabited by the Name and the Glory of God*. It is a coincidence that is not asking to be left unexplained. To the elements of this we now turn. It is interesting to see how scholarship tackles the scriptural motifs of God's Name and Glory, God's *shem* and *kabod* respectively in Hebrew terms.

NAME THEOLOGY

The Name theology that this book is exploring is not that of Exodus 3 and 6, wherein God's Name is revealed to Moses. It is not about a personal name. This study's Name theology is framed—together with Glory theology—around the narratives of Solomon's temple in 2 Chr 5–7, wherein "the Name" is a dwelling presence in the temple. That is, this presence—the presence of God—is simply called "the Name."

Name theology finds that God's presences (plural intentional) in heaven and the temple are distinct from each other. It is a distinction between

---

8. O'Collins, *Tripersonal God*, 73.
9. Wright, "Spirit of Truth."
10. Wright, *New Testament and the People of God*, 368.

Yahweh in heaven and his *shem*—his "Name"—in the temple. Instances of this abound in Hebrew Scripture. Scholarly discussion of it usually centers upon Deuteronomy and Kings (and Chronicles), with reference also to certain psalms, and a couple of passages in Exodus and Isaiah, not to mention other points of reference. There has been much debate as to the unique relationship between God and his Name. The Name in the temple seems to be an invisible presence of God, and as invisible is not categorized as a *theophany*. By way of a description of the invisible Name, one sees the term *hypostasis* permitted in the scholarly literature, but at significant risk of imposing abstract western thought forms on ancient Semitic understandings of God. The consensus towards the Name being a form of God's spiritual presence on earth has been tested by a de-spiritualizing counter case that, in the relevant passages, the Name is simply an appellation for God, or a useful metaphor, and not to be identified as divine presence.

I will summarize in broad outlines some scholarly literature on those perspectives, with attention first to discussion of pre-Christian Hebraic context. For this purpose, I will review Eastern Orthodox and Western scholarship, beginning with the latter.

NAME THEOLOGY IN WESTERN SCHOLARSHIP

Name theology builds on the scriptural picture of transcendence in heaven and immanence on earth, by identifying these divine presences as Yahweh in heaven and Yahweh's "Name" in the temple, looked upon as a Semitic concept more or less equivalent to the idea of a *hypostasis*. In twentieth-century Western scholarship, this observation often went hand in hand with a source critical view, which needs to be briefly reviewed. It argues that a theological shift took place after the destruction of the Jerusalem temple in the sixth century BCE, away from an earlier belief in Yahweh visibly dwelling among the Israelites, towards a replacement belief that Yahweh had remained in heaven while Yahweh's Name had dwelled invisibly in the temple.

Some source critics, such as Gerhard von Rad, have argued that in said earlier era (which they associate with the so-called Priestly material), God's Glory was considered to dwell in the temple as the visible theophany of God; whereas the later era preferred to posit God's invisible Name being there in a tension with Yahweh being in heaven. In this view, the supposed shift is attributed to a Deuteronomist, shell-shocked by the exile, writing history on the understanding that Zion's abandoned temple must never have been somewhere where God was present in a sense previously understood. This argument is vulnerable to criticism on a number of levels, and not all source critics have agreed with this hypothetical history. Tryggyve N. D. Mettinger regards the Name and Glory theologies as more or less contemporaneous, but both as examples of grappling with the destruction of the sanctuary, written in exile.[11] Before coming to challenges to the source-critics, a closer look at the scholarly literature is in order.

Putting forward the source critical view, von Rad in 1953 made influential distinctions in a chapter tellingly entitled "Deuteronomy's 'Name' theology and the Priestly document's 'Kabod' theology."[12] Famously, he made these remarks on the "Name" and its relationship to Yahweh:

> How and where will Israel . . . have communion with Jahweh? It is well known that Deuteronomy gives this question . . . a definite answer—Jahweh will choose a place to 'cause' his name to dwell there . . . The idea of the name as the characteristic form in which Jahweh reveals himself is not in itself anything new . . . But what is decidedly new is the assumption of a constant and almost material presence of the name at the shrine. Earlier references speak more loosely of the name, in such a way that its relationship with the human world is much less easy to define . . . As we see it in Deuteronomy, it may be established in a particular place . . . it verges close on a hypostasis . . . It is not Jahweh who is present at the shrine, but only his name as the guarantee of his will to save . . . Deuteronomy is replacing the old crude idea of Jahweh's presence and dwelling at the shrine by a theologically sublimated idea.[13]

Ian Wilson notes that these "oft-quoted remarks are the classic formulation of Name theology, and well illustrate the typical deduction which is made from the data."[14] Nine times in Deuteronomy, God speaks of finding a home for his Name to dwell in.[15] In von Rad's view, the divine presence is spiritually maintained on earth by the Name, while ostensibly removing God to heaven. This is the bifurcation of God's presence. Transcendence and immanence are at arm's length from each other, so to speak, to emphasize transcendence. Von Rad's phrase "close on a hypostasis" is non-committal, but perhaps appropriately so, if we are to seek ancient Semitic understandings that pre-date Greek philosophy. That is, we are dealing with a Semitic

11. Mettinger, Review of The Deuteronomistic History.

12. von Rad, *Studies in Deuteronomy*, 37–44. Since this study is about perspectives available to early Christians, no discussion of source-criticism or other such approaches will be entered into beyond this epilogue, since these were not tools of their time.

13. von Rad, *Studies in Deuteronomy*, 38–39.

14. Wilson, *Out of the Midst of the Fire*, 3.

15. Deut 12:5, 11, 21; 14:23–24; 16:2, 6, 11; 26:2.

concept with some possible equivalence to the idea of a *hypostasis*. One sometimes encounters the term *quasi-hypostasis*, to express this sensitivity about the risk of reading the conceptual baggage of one culture into another.[16] This is not to say that "the Name" is less than would qualify as a *hypostasis* in Christian theological terms. Thus, Larry Hurtado, noting that various texts in Scripture "make the presence of God's name an interchangeable way of referring to the presence of God, especially the presence of God that is associated with the sanctuary," is able to develop this point by wrapping it around a quote from von Rad:

> since *Yahweh* was regarded as God's unique name, it was seen as participating directly in God's holiness, and "indeed it was, so to speak, a double of his being," with special associations with the temple and the approach to God that was particularized and especially efficacious there.[17]

Whereas the Name is an invisible double of Yahweh's "being" in von Rad's reading, that serves as a contrast to, for example, the visible theophanic appearance of the Angel of the Lord, which according to von Rad is "a manifestation of Yahweh himself."[18] We will return to theophany, in terms of God's Glory, shortly.

Mettinger usefully emphasizes how separate locations of God and his Name contribute to the sense of a tension between two things that are inseparable:

> the Deuteronomistic Name theology emphasized the idea that God himself dwells in heaven, while his Name is present in the Temple. The Name repeatedly appears as a quantity distinct from God yet intimately attached to him.[19]

G. H. Parke-Taylor typifies how the source-critics imagine a greater emphasis was brought to transcendence:

> The Deuteronomist, in introducing a "name-theology," is able to overcome any restrictive view of a localized presence of God and to retain the notion of transcendence by asserting that although his "name" is present in the central sanctuary (Deut.12:5) even the heaven and the highest heaven cannot contain him (1 Kgs 8:27–29).[20]

16. Leithart, "Placing the Name."
17. Hurtado, *Lord Jesus Christ*, 383–84.
18. von Rad, *Old Testament Theology*, 287.
19. Mettinger, *Dethronement of Sabaoth*, 129.
20. Parke-Taylor, *Yahweh: The Divine Name*, 63.

That there is a theological distinction between the transcendent God in heaven and the immanent Name in the temple is soundly based. However, it does not take source-criticism's historical reconstruction to get us to that conclusion. Non-rationalistic Russian Orthodox tradition had already identified this earlier, as we shall see. Moreover, the source-critical approach has been challenged, not least for a distortion that overstates a separation of transcendence and immanence in the texts. Ian Wilson, while not opining on Name theology itself, undermines the source critics' position by showing that Deuteronomy does *not* lift Yahweh's presence completely out of the earthly realm.[21] Yahweh's presence and the Name's presence feature in an integrated way in Israel's centers of worship in Deuteronomy. What is notable in Deuteronomy is that the Name is associated with the geographical centralization of God's place of meeting with his people, signposting ultimately towards the Jerusalem temple.[22]

Perhaps von Rad's paradigm overstates the removal of Yahweh to heaven, and Wilson rightly observes that such cannot be deduced from Deuteronomy. In the opposite direction, Charles Gieschen argues that Name theology serves to keep God's presence close, not far away. He writes of texts in which visible figures are in possession of the Name, with the assumption that the possessor of Yahweh's Name *is* Yahweh in some sense. He cites Exod 23:20–21, a passage foundational for Name theology (and cites its possible influence on Isa 30:27): "the texts themselves depict the Name as a theophanic form who manifested the presence of YHWH in a manner similar to the Angel of YHWH, the Glory of YHWH, and the Word of YHWH."[23] However, this may not be conclusive. It would not follow, say, that the Jerusalem temple is a theophanic form of the Name as and when the Name is in it; and it does not follow that the angel is a theophanic form of the Name either, nor that the angel is synonymous with the Name (in Exod 23:20-21). In general in Hebrew Scripture, the Name is invisibly present, and even if Gieschen could be right about the angel, visible theophany would be the exception rather than the norm for the Name. However, Gieschen is surely right to argue that Jesus is a theophanic form of the Name, with which Hurtado concurs, and we will come to Christology later.

The general point can be made that Name theology does not necessarily isolate God away from the earth, but has God in touch with the earth in a distinctive way. Transcendence and immanence are much more closely knit

---

21. Wilson, *Out of the Midst of the Fire*, 217.

22. Richter, *Deuteronomistic History*, 53.

23. Gieschen, "Divine Name." See page 123. Gieschen's essay is a valuable resource for examples of Name theology in Scripture and ante-Nicene literature.

together in this view. Therefore, simultaneously, there are distinct presences of God in heaven and earth, but without Yahweh being removed from the earth. A potential for christological development in this bifurcation will be attended to shortly, as, in this study, what will be of prime interest is how such texts might be interpreted in the early church era.

A challenge to the source-critics' Name theology has been posed by Sandra Richter. Her extensive research has established that literary use of an important "name" idiom in Deuteronomy can be traced further back to a borrowing, as a piece, from an Akkadian idiom meaning "placing the name" on a monument as an inscription, where it signified that a royal name inscribed on a text or on a monument was a sign of royal ownership over it and associated territory.[24] This more ancient trace of the idiom is evidenced in linguistic cuneiform parallels with various formulas.[25] Richter imports this information into her understanding of Hebraic categories. She treats texts referring to Yahweh placing his name in the temple as synonymous with a king visibly placing his name wherever he claims ownership over territory, effectively effacing the authoritative names previously found in the territory by inscribing his own.[26] We see this kind of thing in the El Amarna letters 1 and 9 (letters between the Egyptian government and its agents in Canaan and elsewhere, dating from the fourteenth century BCE): "the king has set his name in the land of Jerusalem for ever." Such an ancient text is informative but it is hazardous to deploy it wholesale as an interpretative control for texts written many centuries later, just as much as the Nicene Creed cannot comfortably be used as paradigmatic for reading into Hebrew Scripture.

Nonetheless, in a fundamental challenge to scholarship on Deuteronomic Name theology, Richter argues for carrying this meaning from Akkadian texts over into the very Hebrew Scriptures that are foundational for the Name theology of von Rad et al. In this view, "placing the name" *on* an object would be the actual Deuteronomic meaning, with scope for metaphorical meanings such as "name" meaning "reputation," but not for a motif of divine presence. Richter thus separates the Name from the motif of divine presence in the temple, divesting the Name of divine quality. It is not only the source-critics in her sights, but the broader appeal of the idea of a distinction between *YHWH* and his Name as divine presence. And it

---

24. This was a longstanding practice. Alexander the Great's name was said to have been inscribed on the temple of Athena in Priene at his request. See Stevenson, *Power and Place*, 79. Richter's point is not with the longevity of the practice but that the Akkadian formula controls the meaning in the biblical texts.

25. Richter, *Deuteronomistic History*, 55.

26. Richter, *Deuteronomistic History*, 55–57.

is not only the Deuteronomic histories she has in mind, although these are the focus of her study (Deuteronomy through to 2 Kings), but all of Hebrew Scripture that pertains to the Name. It is in Deuteronomy that she finds the essence of the Akkadian formula, but she believes it can "bind the rest of the tapestry together" in respect of Name theology, which is itself "composed of many threads" across Hebrew Scripture. This is ambitious. To do so, she has to dispense of the accepted notion of the Name being a Semitic equivalent of the idea of a *hypostasis* in any and all instances. But her attempt to do so has encountered criticism. There are too many mismatches. Whereas an Akkadian usage would be for example a king inscribing his name on many monuments in many places at home and abroad, Deuteronomy points towards Yahweh's Name having only a centralized locus which was ultimately at the Jerusalem temple,[27] allowing a lot of territories to pass by en route. This mismatch is not necessarily resolved by the temple standing for the whole land, upon which Richter relies.[28] In particular, there is no mention in Kings or Chronicles of any such visible inscription in the lengthy and detailed account of the temple's construction,[29] let alone the fact that this would have to be the inscription of Israel's God rather than that of a king.[30] Apart from these mismatches, John van Seters observes in his response to Richter's thesis that "the idea of building a house for the name of Yahweh . . . is not directly dependent upon any foreign usage and cannot be explained by Richter's metaphorical use" (metaphorical meanings such as "reputation").[31] In addition, in the crisis of King Manasseh bringing a carved idol into the Jerusalem temple, it is notable that this is juxtaposed not with Yahweh being in the temple, but rather Yahweh's Name (2 Chr 33:4–7). This juxtaposition has any force only if the idol is present in a temple in which another god should be present, and the only accounting for this in the text is the Name being there as the rival of the idol. The function of the text is not satisfied if Name is merely a metaphor for reputation or something similar. In other words, the thread of the Akkadian idiom does not succeed in binding the many threads of the Deuteronomic Name and temple material.

Mettinger illustrates his disagreement with Richter in examining 2 Sam 7. Richter pairs 2 Sam 7:13 ("a house for my Name") with the *reputational* meaning of the preceding 7:9, where Yahweh promises to make David's name the greatest of the names of men. Whereas Mettinger pairs it

27. Seters, Review of Deuteronomistic History.
28. Richter, *Deuteronomistic History*, 55.
29. Hurowitz, Review of Deuteronomistic History.
30. Hurowitz, Review of Deuteronomistic History.
31. Seters, Review of Deuteronomistic History.

with the preceding 7:5 ("Are you the one to build me a house to dwell in?"). There is perhaps something in both, but Mettinger at least has to be right that "a house for my Name" parallels "build me a house to dwell in" which is thematically foundational for the narrative.[32] Similarly, Mettinger urges that 1 Kgs 8 observes a contrast between the immanence of vv. 12-13, where the temple is built to fulfill Yahweh's promise to come and dwell, and the transcendence of God in heaven in vv. 39, 43, 49 of the same, which leaves a space in the temple to be filled by God abiding in another way, which is surely represented by the Name.[33] Ps 11:4 amply illustrates this bifurcation of God's presence between heaven and the temple. This bifurcation in temple theology corresponds with that in Name theology, one that cannot be readily dismissed.

In assessing Richter's thesis, we can follow her lead in taking into account material outside of the Deuteronomic histories, and the Psalms are a key port of call. The Akkadian idiomatic framework cannot comfortably bear the weight of Richter's argument against the Name as divine presence where it is contextualized among the Psalm's idioms referring to God dwelling in Zion.[34] In 2 Kgs 19:14-15, a letter is spread out in the temple before Yahweh who is enthroned between the cherubim, and we find this taken up in Ps 99:1-3, which couples this very image of divine presence with a summons to "praise your name." In Ps 138:2, bowing towards God's temple is an occasion for "praising your name." The name is sung to in Ps 68 in a context of divine presence in the temple (Ps 68:4-5, 16-17). Richter is not able to avoid this body of evidence, and asserts, *contra* Name theology and surely against the function of these texts, that the "Name" in such cases is merely an appellation of God uttered by the Israelites or a synonym for "reputation."

The evidence base that Richter has to somehow accommodate expands further. In Ps 20:1-2, being protected by the name is paralleled with aid to Israel coming from the sanctuary (cf. Pss 33:21 and 44:5). To this, Richter asserts that, *contra* Name Theology, the "Name" in such cases is merely an appellation of God or is perhaps "used in a near-substitutionary fashion for YHWH himself."[35] By now, the cumulative impact of these texts outweighs Richter's rationalization, and "near-substitutionary" seems not far from the

---

32. Mettinger, Review of Deuteronomistic History. Both meanings obtain if Leithart is right about this being a play on words. See Leithart, *House for My Name*, 31.
33. Mettinger, Review of Deuteronomistic History.
34. Mettinger, Review of Deuteronomistic History.
35. Richter, *Deuteronomistic History*, 11.

arguments that lead us back to the distinction between God and his Name as two forms of the divine presence.

The evidence-base goes wider still. The Name is something to which the Psalmist relates on a personal level as "near" (Ps 75:1). After the exile, the Israelites would "dwell close to the holy name of the Lord God" (Tob 13:10–11, NJB). God's Name can be in an angel (Exod 23:20–21). The Name of *YHWH* can come as judge in an anthropomorphized depiction (Isa 30:27), which Parke-Taylor describes as "the equivalent of YHWH, displaying his power in a theophanic disclosure."[36] Function, not merely content, determines meaning in a text, and if Richter's importing of Akkadian meaning was already strained in the previous examples, it lacks explanatory force in these instances in particular. It is difficult to see how it can provide a satisfactory explanation for such a range of "threads." Her insights on the Akkadian background to phrasing in Deuteronomy are surely complementary to Name theology, rather than its downfall.

Other criticisms of Richter's work have been ventured but perhaps with less impact unless we buy into source-criticism. Mettinger, who treats the Deuteronomic texts in question as reflections in exile, criticizes Richter for making the Israelites strangely devoid of any reflection on divine presence in an era where they were promoting the temple as central to Israelite worship.[37] Richter's interpretation of evidence delays such reflection until the rabbinic era, in the third century CE or later.[38] Of course, such reflection could have happened in-between times, in the earliest decades of the church era, and this study will argue a case for that. In the view of Hurowitz, Deuteronomy does remove Yahweh from the earth, and on this basis Richter's thesis is defective in that it voids the house of God as a place of divine dwelling. It makes the temple other than what it existed for, and too distant from the purpose of other temples in the ancient Near East.[39] However, Richter seems to follow Wilson in not seeing Deuteronomy as removing God from the earth, so such criticism would not seem to be valid within her framework.

In summary, Richter's thesis is vulnerable in that Israel goes through the land without inscribing the Name on any monument, and even when God has led them to the one place where he will place his Name—Jerusalem—the name is not inscribed on anything; and a house is built for the Name, which is a novel development. This is so remarkably different from

---

36. Parke-Taylor, *Yahweh*, 15.
37. Mettinger, Review of Deuteronomistic History.
38. Richter, *Deuteronomistic History*, 14.
39. Hurowitz, Review of Deuteronomistic History.

the Akkadian model that the differences cannot be set aside, and appear more relevant when we notice that something different is happening in Yahweh's relationship with his Name, where "a house for my Name" parallels "build me a house *to dwell in*," where "The Name of *YHWH*" can come as judge, and the Name can be personally "near," or "in" an angel. This is incongruous with the Akkadian formula. Compared to her own proposal, the very thesis that Richter is resisting has more explanatory power for the data. The bifurcation of God's presence between heaven and the temple, in 2 Sam 7 and Ps 11, provides a paradigm in which the Name as divine presence logically fits.

THE GLORY

To shift discussion from the Name to the Glory, we may return to von Rad. His influential source-critical contrast is displayed in his emphasis on the theophanic *kabod*, where the Glory is enthroned in human form in the temple, on God's throne. Ezek 1:26–28:

> High above on the form of a throne was a form with the appearance of a human being (NJB) . . . This was the appearance of the likeness of the glory of the LORD (NIV).

The Glory is visible, theophanic, in contrast to the invisible Name, in this view. In von Rad's argument for a shift from immanence to transcendence in Israelite history, he makes this assertion about what he sees as the earlier immanence of God conveyed by Glory theology: "The Priestly Document represents a totally different theology here. The Tabernacle is neither the dwelling place of Jahweh himself nor of his name, but the place on earth where, for the time being, the appearance of Jahweh's glory meets with his people."[40]

Mettinger expresses the source-critics' dichotomy succinctly: "The Kabod theology follows the theology of immanence . . . while the Name theology emphasizes instead God's transcendence."[41] In this paradigm, immanence goes with visibility. Thus, Von Rad remarks on the Glory as a visible dwelling presence in Ezekiel: "It is remarkable how this 'appearance' theology issues at the very end into a conception of 'dwelling'; the 'glory' comes to the new eschatological Jerusalem 'to dwell there for ever.'" Von Rad writes that in Israelite belief this was actually a divine dwelling, not only

---

40. von Rad, *Studies in Deuteronomy*, 39.
41. Mettinger, *Dethronement of Sabaoth*, 133.

a symbol of dwelling: "Solomon's temple was built as a so-called 'dwelling temple' and was also understood as such by Israel."[42]

Mettinger argues that "in the Priestly tradition as represented by Ezekiel, the place of honor on the throne has been given to the Glory of the Lord." God's throne belongs to God alone, and in this view, *kabod* has more or less become a nomenclature of God:

> ... *kabod* now designates God himself. Thus Ezekiel attests the development [of *kabod*] from divine attribute to divine name. He conceives of the Glory of the Lord as both speaking and acting: for example, the Kabod speaks in Ezek 9:3–7; 43:6–11; 44:4–5 ...[43]

By way of illustration, Mettinger observes, "The Glory is able to act decisively in judgment on the temple: . . . it simply abandons the chariot throne (Ezek 9:3; 19:4)."[44] Mettinger notes how the theme of the Glory in Ezekiel is moving towards personalization, depicted as seated on God's throne,[45] humanoid in form.[46] Jarl Fossum goes further: "The Kabod, then, according to Ezekiel, is the human form of God. As such it can be compared to the Angel of the Lord, God's human form of manifestation . . ."[47]

However, that is not quite such a sharp contrast to the entirety of Name theology. Isa 30:27 anthropomorphizes and personifies the Name as expressing wrath and acting in judgment. Comparable immanence is attributed to the Name and the Glory, even if not so much in terms of visibility. The source-critical approach overstates its contrast. In fact, the whole framework of source criticism thinking is vulnerable here. It is predicated on Name theology being a rejection of Glory theology, of transcendence trumping immanence. But this picture of theological evolution entirely depends on assuming this dichotomy, whereas McConville sees the Name and the Glory rather as complementary in Hebrew Scripture, each with its own functions.[48] Evidence of this is not lacking. In 1 Kgs 8, the Name and the Glory dwell in Solomon's temple in complementary fashion, the former coming to dwell in it and the latter marking the moment by filling it. Richter

---

42. von Rad, *Studies in Deuteronomy*, 42.
43. Mettinger, *Dethronement of Sabaoth*, 106–7.
44. Mettinger, *Dethronement of Sabaoth*, 107.
45. Mettinger, *Dethronement of Sabaoth*, 106.
46. Mettinger, *Dethronement of Sabaoth*, 113.
47. Fossum, *Name of God*, 177. This extensively researched work traces developments of Name theology into Samaritan and gnostic texts from earlier roots including christological thought.
48. McConville, "God's 'Name' and God's 'Glory,'" 153–57.

endorses McConville's use of Exod 33:19–23 to dispense with the dichotomy. Here, the Glory lends itself to dramatic portrayal of God's presence rather more than the Name does. Thus, Richter sees this as lending support to her reasons for why there was no evolution towards transcendence evident in the Name tradition: "the shift to name in the deuteronomic narrative is the result of context and emphasis."[49]

However, unlike Richter, McConville sees the Name as a form of God's presence. This is clear in his explanation of how the Name and the Glory appear in a complementary fashion in Exod 33:19–23.[50] In it, Moses makes this request of God: "Now show me your Glory." But God replies to him, "I will make all my goodness pass before you, and will summon the Name, Yahweh . . . but you cannot see my face" (Exod 33:19, translation adjusted by this author).[51] God and his Name are distinct from each other, the latter summoned by God. This is subsequent to Yahweh's words that are so foundational in Name theology: "I am sending an angel ahead of you to guard you along the way and to bring you to the place I have prepared. Pay attention to him . . . since *my Name is in him*" (Exod 23:20–21, NIV). Meanwhile, God's "face" is associated with the Glory (Exod 33:18–23). Moses was denied a direct view of the Glory, of God's "face." But the Name did not present the same danger when summoned by Yahweh, coming "in" the angel. The Glory is so dramatic that it can keep the Israelites at a distance. But the Name is a facet of Yahweh that allows their closer walk with God.[52] In light of evidence such as this, I concur with Wilson, McConville, and Richter that from Exodus to Deuteronomy there was no fundamental shift in Name theology, as if there were a post-exilic evolution from immanence to transcendence. The source critics' argument for such an evolution fails to recognize the complementary function of the Name and the Glory. Richter, however, throws out the baby with the bathwater by arguing that the Name does not represent a bifurcation of God's presence, a conclusion that does not sit well with the evidence base.

This study will draw on early Christian understandings, and as such I must leave discussion of source criticism to this epilogue alone. This book takes an integrated approach to the Name and the Glory, not setting them in opposition as the source critics have done. Paradigmatic for this is 2 Chr 5–7 (similarly, 1 Kgs 8). It lies in how the text deals with the tension between

---

49. Richter, *Deuteronomistic History*, 29 n.107.

50. McConville, "God's 'Name' and God's 'Glory,'" 153–57.

51. Many translations say "proclaim my Name" instead, but without doing justice to the sense of the verse. "I will summon the Name" is in keeping with how the same Hebrew word "summon," or "call upon," is used elsewhere in Hebrew Scripture.

52. McConville, "God's 'Name' and God's 'Glory,'" 153–57.

its clear expectation that God's presence *does* rest in the temple (6:1–2, 41) alongside its conception that a temple cannot contain God (6:18). This tension is overcome by the abiding of both the Name and the Glory within the temple (6:5–6; 7:1), whilst God hears prayer from his heavenly dwelling both before and after the arrival of the Name and the Glory (6:21, 7:14). Thus, in the paradigm of Solomon's temple, God is emphasized as transcendent in heaven, while both his Name and his Glory are together immanent, such that the Name dwells in the earthly temple and the Glory fills the temple. With the theology of Name and Glory integrated here, God's presence in heaven and earth is united, and the temple is the central point where heaven and earth are joined. On this basis, 2 Chr 5–7 will be used as a lens for this study.

This study generally refers to the scene as told in 2 Chronicles rather than 1 Kings. This is not because of particular differences between them. Rather, the preference is because the composition of Chronicles took place somewhat closer to the Christian era, and the focus of study here is upon perceptions found in and around the early Christian era, making Chronicles a more appropriate choice for the exercise. Chronicles is the work with which the *Tanakh* ends, a climactic position, unlike in the Christian Bible where it is found amidst the histories. It makes the final verse of the *Tanakh* an instruction for rebuilding the temple, something picked up thematically by Matthew's Gospel in the view of G. K. Beale.[53]

In early Christian writings, the picture of the joining of heaven and earth in God's temple expands. It does so in giving us an inside view, so to speak, of Christ and the Spirit in heaven, after the Ascension, with their presence flowing spiritually from heaven to earth, uniting both places. And the locus in which this finds expression is in the church, the temple of living stones.

NAME THEOLOGY IN EASTERN ORTHODOX SCHOLARSHIP

Name theology in the Russian Orthodox Church comes with an extraordinary background. It begins in 1907 with the publication of *On the Caucasus Mountains* by a monk called Ilarion who was part of an island monastery at Athos. In his book, based on his spiritual experience in speaking a name of God out loud, he asserted that "the Name of God is God himself and can produce miracles." This led to a practice called *Imiaslavie*—Russian for "praising the Name," where the sound of a name of God was believed

---

53. Beale, *Temple and the Church's Mission*, 177.

to become a *hypostasis* when uttered.[54] By 1913, this belief had been ruled heretical in the Russian Orthodox Church, and the group of monks behind it was suppressed, literally, as the Russian navy was sent onto the island with bayonets, and the book was banned.[55]

The Orthodox church did plan to take another look at the issue in 1917. But then the Russian Revolution happened, so the further look didn't happen. The Communist era in the Soviet Union virtually put theology on ice. Then after the Soviet Union collapsed, there was a resurgence of interest in Imiaslavie, and since the 1990s a century-old debate has been revived in parts of the Russian Orthodox Church.[56] In-between those years, a few theologians in the Russian Orthodox tradition published on the subject, including Sergius Bulgakov, whose essay, *The Name of God*, was written in the 1920s as part of a larger work, *The Philosophy of the Name*. In *The Name of God*, with remarkable depth of insight on different meanings of the Name in Scripture, Bulgakov interprets many of the same verses touched on above (and elsewhere in this study). I can only review a few relevant examples here. In working with the Bible as inspired by God, in the Orthodox tradition, his work resists Western rationalism. Source criticism could not be further from his mind. Yet it is interesting to see recognizable conclusions in his work.

In brief on Imiaslavie, Bulgakov did not hold with the version sponsored by the monks, but he did not dispense with the venture altogether. Modifying their controversial phrase "the Name of God is God himself," he dispensed with the word "himself," and changed the meaning to "the Name of God is divinity," undermining any suggestion of the sound of the Name

---

54. Bulgakov, "Name of God," 160. I cannot begin to do justice to the nuances of Russian Orthodox tradition, or its categories of "divine energies" and "synergy" and icons, but I will try to give a sense of the theological issue. Imiaslavie claims that if any of the names of God is spoken in veneration, then in that moment of it being spoken, "the Name of God is God himself," and it claims that God's spoken name that makes the sound has always existed from eternity. Critics say that if the Name of God is simply a word that can be spoken in a human language, as the word *Jesus* exists in a human language, it should be treated as part of creation, not as God. Being a sound in human language reinforces this impression of being part of creation, rather than it being "God himself" as if we were talking about a hypostasis.

55. Kenworthy, "Debating the Theology of the Name," 250–65. Critics said that the monks were reducing God's name to a magic word. Other critics said this spirituality was not ascetic enough, or not theological enough, or too much like folk religion or magic rather than prayer, or quite simply not thought through and not approved by church authorities or by a wider church consensus.

56. Kenworthy, "Debating the Theology of the Name." Even today, some in the Russian Orthodox Church see it as an unresolved issue and others see it as a closed case, while others have no official position.

itself amounting to a *hypostasis*. He allowed merely that God is present when the sound of his Name is spoken out loud in veneration and prayer, in much the same way as Bulgakov saw icons having a role in Orthodox devotions.[57] However, he is clear that the spoken Name is not a *hypostasis*.[58] Whereas there is no *hypostasis* in Imiaslavie, it is an altogether different matter where the Name dwelling in the temple is concerned, according to Bulgakov:

> The expression "Name of God" has a wholly special meaning in connection with the temple and with cult in general. Here there cannot be any question of *pars pro toto*, of directly using this expression instead of "God" . . . The temple is the dwelling place of the Name of God, and it was built for the Name of God.[59]

Bulgakov leaves no room for doubt that the Name literally was dwelling in the temple: "If . . . there are no obstacles to regarding the temple as God's house, there are also no obstacles to regarding it as the dwelling place of the Name of God."[60] Indeed, that is the very purpose of the temple: "This sanctuary, tabernacle, and, later, the temple are made in order that the Name of God may dwell in them."[61] Bulgakov's historical theology is starkly different to the source-critics':

> . . . for the Jews with their religious realism there was never any possibility of conceiving the temple as anything other than the dwelling place of the Name of God, as is attested by the sacred chronicles. As early as Deuteronomy we find Moses' testament: ". . . there shall be a place which the Lord your God shall choose to cause His Name to dwell there" . . . The first book of Kings tells about the building of the temple by Solomon . . .[62]

Bulgakov then expounds at length on the accounts in Kings and Chronicles of the founding of the temple, and concludes, "What we have here is the express dwelling of the Name of God in the temple, along with the Glory of God . . ."[63] I will return to how Bulgakov regards the temple as the dwelling place of both the Name and the Glory of God, which is coincidentally central to my thesis.

---

57. Bulgakov, "Name of God," 163–66.
58. Bulgakov, "Name of God," 165.
59. Bulgakov, "Name of God," 137.
60. Bulgakov, "Name of God," 142.
61. Bulgakov, "Name of God," 134.
62. Bulgakov, "Name of God," 138.
63. Bulgakov, "Name of God," 141.

Bulgakov, somewhat pre-empting the source critics, captures the vital relationship between the transcendence of God and the immanence of the Name in the temple, present for Israel's religious activities, putting it this way:

> The Biblical usage with this juxtaposition of the expressions "God" and "Name of God" expresses the correlation between the transcendent . . . of God in and for Himself, and the God of religion and cult, who, in practical terms, is represented precisely by the Name of God. Therefore, in essence, this expression signifies nothing other than God worshiped by man.[64]

In practical terms, such as in temple worship, the Name of God *is* God and is worshiped as such. Bulgakov's reflections on the Name seem to have flown under the radar of the source critics, understandably given the specific twentieth-century background, but they will stand us in good stead, and I will return to them shortly.

TOWARDS A CHRISTOLOGICAL AND TRINITARIAN UNDERSTANDING OF NAME THEOLOGY

With implications for Name theology, Aubrey R. Johnson has drawn from an ancient understanding of agency in which a person's representative standing in for them is in effect that person in a more personal and profound sense than the job description implies. Johnson sees the Name as illustrative of this relationship: "In the same way, the 'Name' is an important 'Extension' of Yahweh's Personality analogous to that which is observable in the case of man. On that basis, a knowledge of the 'Name' is a matter of ritual importance."[65] Johnson reviews a number of examples, and draws a crucial conclusion relevant to this study:

> we can see how it was possible for a Jewish Christian to relate his Messiah so closely with the divine Being as to afford a basis for the later (and Greek) metaphysical formulation of the doctrine of the Trinity.[66]

---

64. Bulgakov, "Name of God," 144.

65. Johnson, *One and the Many*, 17–18. Richter is opposed to this understanding of Semitic thinking. *Deuteronomistic History*, 21. Her criticism is answered in turn by Mettinger who cites extra-biblical parallels. See Mettinger, Review of Deuteronomistic History.

66. Johnson, *One and the Many*, 37.

G. A. F. Knight had already, in lectures delivered in 1950, similarly interpreted the Name in the temple christologically, and went so far as paralleling the concepts of the "Word of God" and the "Name of God." Here, Knight, arguing for a trinitarian trajectory in this theology, finds a place for the Name in the concept of diversity within unity:

> We recall that the name represented the essence of the personality. The "personality" of God was above even the heaven of heavens, yet His "essence" was present in the Temple. God had "extended" Himself, had placed His *alter ego* in the Temple. Or, to use modern terms for such pictorial thinking, the nature of God is to be conceived in terms of diversity in unity.[67]

Meanwhile, Knight implicitly inches toward pneumatology in regard to the Glory: "the glory of God cannot be dead matter either, but must be conceived in personality just as much as the Spirit of God."[68] Knight's Christian perception of the Glory as personal in a way parallel with the Spirit leads him to this interpretation: "the indwelling Presence of God in the OT was identified with the Glory of God."[69] Support for this position may be inferred from Mark Bonnington.[70] This is Knight's insight regarding the Name and the Glory: the Name is God's "*alter ego* in the Temple," and the Glory is "the indwelling Presence of God." Knight even observes parallels between the concepts of Name and Word and between the Glory and the Spirit. However, Knight does not find his way to asking whether the Trinity of Father, Word, and Spirit is parallel to the Trinity of God, Name, and Glory, but the potential for the question is there. And he is clear about the direction in which he is leading the reader, in regard to his take on what he calls "Hebraic metaphysical thinking." Thus: "But though their thought forms are strange to us, we must recognize by means of them the Hebrews are seeking to express what to them was essentially true of their God, viz., that He is not to be thought of as a Monad of being . . ."[71]

Indeed, in exploring what he refers to as examples of an *alter ego* of God in Hebrew Scripture, Knight asserts something in ancient Israel akin to a nascent Trinitarianism: "Let us be content with saying that since this OT pictorial representation of the Nature of God is true to our knowledge of

---

67. Knight, *Biblical Approach*, 14.
68. Knight, *Biblical Approach*, 38.
69. Knight, *Biblical Approach*, 44–45.
70. Bonnington, "New Temples in Corinth," 157: "the Spirit is never directly identified with the presence of God in the Temple, but is rather linked through a mediating idea, such as *doxa* or holiness."
71. Knight, *Biblical Approach*, 16–17.

God as we have it revealed to us in Christ, it means that the mystery of the Holy Trinity was not entirely hidden from the minds of God's people even before His coming to earth in Christ."[72]

In looking towards a christological and trinitarian understanding of Name theology, we cannot lose sight of the fact that the discovery of a distinction of persons is vital if Trinitarianism is not to find itself slipping towards the embrace of modalism. The distinction of persons is found only in glimpses in Hebrew Scripture at the best of times. Arthur W. Wainwright argues how such a vital development took place: "The idea of extension of divine personality is Hebraic. The idea of interaction within the extended personality is neither Hebraic nor Hellenistic but Christian."[73] Wainwright applies this to the figure of Jesus thus: "Although Jesus was an extension of the divine personality, he exhibited more than extension. In his dealings with his Father there was an interaction within the divine personality. There was a dialogue within the Godhead."[74]

In early Christian writings, such theological development is grounded, not least, in the paralleling of Christ and the Name. Hurtado, in support of Fossum, highlights John 1:14: "In light of the frequency of reference to God's name as "dwelling" upon the earth among Israel, Fossum is surely correct to contend that this tradition about the divine name should be seen as a likely background of the statement in John 1:14 that the Word "dwelt [eskenosen] among us.""

In other words, for "Word" we may substitute "Name."[75] Gieschen, Fossum, and Hurtado are in agreement on this point, and in Gieschen's phrase: "the Son as the Word/Name existed before creation and "became flesh.""[76] Thus, the incarnated Jesus is the Name made flesh, so to speak. It is striking, then, how "Word" can be aligned with "Name" theology.

This paralleling informs a Christian reading of a distinction of persons in Hebrew Scripture when reading of God and his Name. Hurtado argues that in John's Gospel Jesus identifies himself as the Name, referring to John 12:23–28: "The hour has come for the Son of Man to be glorified . . . for this purpose I have come to this hour. Father, glorify Your name!" Hurtado's view is that

---

72. Knight, *Biblical Approach*, 33.

73. Wainwright, *Trinity in the New Testament*, 40.

74. Wainwright, *Trinity in the New Testament*, 38.

75. Hurtado, *Lord Jesus Christ*, 384, relying on Fossum, "In the Beginning was the Name."

76. Gieschen, "Divine Name," 135.

EPILOGUE: ACADEMIC CASE FOR THE THESIS   243

> "God glorifying "the Son of Man" (12:23) and God's own name (12:28), are probably to be taken as synonymous. In GJohn this "son of man" bears, manifests, and in some profoundly unique sense is the divine name in earthly expression . . ."[77]

Gieschen makes the same argument from the same material, with effect that Jesus "can simply be identified as "the Name," as was the divine presence in Deuteronomy . . ."[78]

Clear about the trajectory here, Hurtado states that "the author [of John] is appropriating and creatively adapting biblical and Jewish divine-name tradition to express what he considers an important Christological conviction."[79] Following the trajectory beyond Scripture, Hurtado also picks out that Justin Martyr identifies Jesus as a Name figure depicted in Isaiah.[80] More examples of such associations in early Christian literature are provided in this study.

Bulgakov has another perspective. He contrasts the presence of Jesus in the church and that of the Name in the temple, as it were closeness against remoteness:

> "It is necessary to become aware of and to feel all the power and acuteness of this difference, even this oppositeness, between the Name of the transcendent God, which (according to the perfectly definite testimony of the Word of God) was remote and terrible and dwelled only in the temple, and the Name Jesus, the temple for which is every human heart, and every member of the faithful, as having this Name imprinted in his heart, is a priest of this temple."[81]

Bulgakov's assertion about the Name being remote seems to miss the theological purpose that the Name signified the dwelling of God among the Israelites. As a psalmist put it, God's "Name is near" (Ps 75:1, NIV). This study will focus on a reading in which the presence of Jesus in the church and the presence of the Name in the temple are closely associated and I will argue that they are one and the same in an early Christian reading.

---

77. Hurtado, *Lord Jesus Christ*, 386.
78. Gieschen, "Divine Name," 135–36.
79. Hurtado, *Lord Jesus Christ*, 382.
80. Hurtado, *Lord Jesus Christ*, 387.
81. Bulgakov, "Name of God," 157.

TOWARDS A PNEUMATIC UNDERSTANDING OF THE GLORY

On the close association of the Glory and the Holy Spirit, brief notes must suffice, further to what is noted above. I will argue that the visible Glory of God is a sign of the presence of the Holy Spirit. Why wouldn't it be? That might be what a theologian would say. But we can be more specific in a key narrative. A clear parallel with the temple-launching Glory (in 2 Chronicles) is found in Luke's account of the Spirit's coming at Pentecost. Both come visibly as fire, the former filling Solomon's temple, the latter filling the believers. N. T. Wright draws out the parallel: "at the heart of Pentecost, in Acts . . . the coming of the Spirit is all about the launching of the new Temple."[82] Wright amplifies the point:

> When Solomon built the Temple and dedicated it, it was filled with the cloud which veiled God's presence . . . And Luke, writing the story [Pentecost], wants us to think: this is the glory of the Lord coming back to fill the Temple![83]

The believers become a temple of the Holy Spirit, to employ the Pauline phrase, a temple where the Glory can dwell. This proves very important to the construction of Luke's narrative in Acts 2–6, and a brief anticipation of its evidence must be briefly stated here. Two sightings by the church of the visible Glory of God sit in that narrative like bookends, at Pentecost in Acts 2 and at the death of Stephen in Acts 7:55–56. Before Stephen dies, he sees into heaven and sees the visible Glory there.[84] There are a number of parallels of the Glory with the Spirit to be found, for further exploration later.

THE THESIS

Various scholars have written about Solomon's temple being the dwelling place of both the Name and the Glory without their writing about it as a type or a theophany of the Trinity. Sergius Bulgakov wrote about "the express dwelling of the Name of God in the temple, along with the Glory of God."[85] Bertil Gärtner says about the temple: "Yahweh himself dwelt there:

---

82. Wright, "Spirit of Truth."
83. Wright, "New Law, New Temple."
84. Smith, *Fate of the Jerusalem Temple*, 177.
85. Bulgakov, "Name of God," 141.

there were his kabod and shem."[86] Oskar Skarsaune refers to "the glory and name of God dwelling in the tabernacle/temple."[87] From a source-critical perspective, Mettinger wrote about "the concepts of the Presence implicit in the "Name" and "Glory" theologies [of the temple]."[88] Gregory Stevenson notes that the temple "is the residence of God's glory . . . the place where God's *name* resides . . . "[89] Without reference to the temple, Hurtado establishes a christological direction for the divine Name and Glory, speaking of the blessed people "who saw Jesus as given God's name and glory (John 17:11–12)."[90]

Bulgakov regards the Name and the Glory as God's presence in the temple, referring to "cases where the expression "Name of God" can in no wise be interpreted just as a synonym, as a descriptive expression replacing "God," but signifies a special mode of God's presence . . . The Name of God is united with and likened to the concept of God's Glory, which even lovers of simplified synonymology cannot refer just to descriptive expressions . . ."[91] Bulgakov is categorizing both the Name and the Glory as God's presence in the temple. He also saw them as paired in the Moses episode that was addressed by McConville: "Here the appearance of God's Glory and the uttering of the Name of God are juxtaposed as two sides of the theopany . . ."[92] Here, the term "summoning" would, I suggest, be an appropriate translation in place of "uttering," but the key thing to observe is that for Bulgakov the Name and the Glory are jointly part of a theophany.

In light of all of the foregoing, it ought not to be very surprising to see how my thesis develops, tidying up loose threads in a trinitarian reflection. This study builds upon the early church apologetic which established a demonstration of the Trinity in the fact that three divine persons are co-indwelling a temple built for only one God. That is, it is difficult to see how these three would not qualify as one God when they share the one God's temple as their rightful dwelling. It's their temple, and they are its God. And this temple is the church.

The Hebraic Trinity of God, his Name, and his Glory avails of the same demonstration, because it likewise qualifies as one God dwelling in the one

---

86. Gärtner, *Temple and the Community in Qumran*, 1.

87. Skarsaune, *In the Shadow of the Temple*, 328.

88. Mettinger, *Dethronement of Sabaoth*, 17.

89. Stevenson, *Power and Place*, 122. Stevenson shares the common view that the presence of the Name resolves the tension between God's immanence and transcendence.

90. Hurtado, *Lord Jesus Christ*, 389.

91. Bulgakov, "Name of God," 136.

92. Bulgakov, "Name of God," 136.

true God's temple, insofar as we can count God in the heavenly sanctuary and his Name and Glory in the earthly sanctuary, a unity of temples.

The Name and Glory theology of Solomon's temple (2 Chron 5–7) will be used as a reference point and control text for analyzing early Christian thinking. My thesis is that, in all but name, there is a very early Christian Trinitarianism rooted in temple motifs. This is not discerned if we are looking for something like the Nicene Creed in Scripture—that is not there, and there is no reason to expect to find it there. Rather, in this paradigm text, a three-in-one God is found in three operations in a temple context: whereas God himself listens from heaven to Solomon's prayer, his Name dwells in the temple, and his Glory fills the temple. Logically, these three amount to one God, not three gods, as it is God's own Name and his own Glory. The question is, can it be the same three-in-one God as Father, Son, and Spirit, in an early Christian reading?

The question has to be asked in order to better understand perception of the Trinity in the early Christian era. In light of Wainwright's caution, it is important to argue that we need not think about God and his Name and his Glory in a modalistic fashion, when it is the very thing onto which early Christian writings congruently map the names of three distinct persons: Father, Son, and Spirit. Thus, in the development of early Christian thought, a distinction of persons emerges in our picture of God and his Name and his Glory. In a sense, ancient Hebraic distinctions between God and his Name and his Glory become *personalized* distinctions. The threeness of God and Name and Glory can be found in Hebrew Scripture read through this early Christian filter, communicated through early Christian writings.

There also appear to be grounds for a transference of concepts in both directions. In the other direction—from ancient Hebraic thought—the oneness of God could be read across, and I would argue that this is the underpinning that makes it conceptually acceptable to the likes of Paul to have a "temple of the Holy Spirit" in which Christ dwells as divine, without suspicion of blasphemy. In the first place, God and his own Name and his own Glory can be only one God. Christian Scripture imprints Father, Son, and Spirit on top of God, his Name, and his Glory. In that light, Father, Son, and Spirit are seen to be one because God, Name, and Glory are one. The oneness and threeness of the Trinity sit comfortably together in this reading. This explanation of three-in-oneness may be appealing to Christian ministers as potential teaching material, a picture of the Trinity that should be easy for the non-specialist to observe. (The teacher may wish to note how easy it is to illustrate the match pictorially, with three being mapped on top of three.)

Comparison with the Solomonic picture of transcendence and immanence is warranted. Whilst Solomon's God is in heaven and transcendent, Solomon's temple is a place of immanence, indwelled by the Name, and filled by the Glory (2 Chr 5–7). This fits a Christian picture of the transcendent and immanent Trinity, which has firstly "our Father in heaven" as transcendent; and secondly the church as living temple, as a place of immanence indwelled by the risen Christ, and filled by the Holy Spirit.

To digress briefly, theologians today may be quick to point out the importance of theological nuances that ought to have place in this discourse; this picture of divine presence has to be hedged with qualifications about the Trinity cooperating in God's every action, with the Father's presence in no way required to be entirely absent from the earth, for heaven and earth are joined together; and there is a unifying effect that acts upon the heavens and the earth as Son and Spirit flow spiritually from the former to the latter. I don't want to risk over-systematizing. Early Christian thought is not rigidly organized. I merely observe above all else how the Solomonic temple narrative carries over into an early Christian conceptualization of how the presences of Father, Son, and Spirit are placed.

This divine theophany, then, is a Trinity of *God and his Name* (indwelling the temple), *and his Glory* (filling the temple). God's *Name* is read as a type of Christ, and God's *Glory* is read as a type of the Holy Spirit. Collectively, this three of God, Name, and Glory (in Solomon's temple) are a type of Father, Son, and Spirit (in the church as temple). Two models of a three-in-one God, both of which are located in scriptural concepts of temple and divine presence.[93] It is a coincidence that is not asking to be left unexplained, especially as the comparison will reveal multiple points of correspondence and close resemblance.

Seemingly presupposed in early Christian writings is this particular Hebraic model of the three-in-one God of the temple. Temple texts are the scriptural framework, at the church's inception, for its grasp of a God with a three-in-one basis. In continuity with centuries of Hebraic reflection, early Christian interpretation of Solomonic temple motifs provided a blueprint that made acceptable the church's earliest self-understanding as a true temple in which Christ and the Spirit dwell with divine status. I would assert that no other proposal to date has similar explanatory power for how such a thing could be conceptually acceptable to a Paul who advocates that God is one. Hebraic categories are definitive for early Christian reflection on

---

93. Wherever using the word divine, I mean in the particular sense that YHWH is uniquely divine, deity-ness if you like. In such a sense, divinity includes being worthy of exclusive worship as the sole Creator and sole sovereign Ruler of all things, the God who chose Israel as his people. See Bauckham, *God Crucified*, 9–13.

a God that is triune. More than a type, God and his Name and his Glory are a theophany of what the Father, the Son, and the Spirit are, and *vice versa*.

My thesis, then, is how early Christian reflection could interpret Hebrew Scripture. It is not necessary to claim that the Chronicler comprehended the scene at Solomon's temple in such trinitarian terms. My argument here is not that the authors of Hebrew Scripture consciously anticipated such thinking about God and his Name and Glory, but that this is how early Christian authors could interpret it. As such, the objective of this study is principally to explore this Christian adoption of temple motifs. In this reading, Solomon's temple provides a paradigm worked out in the Jesus movement, canonical, and non-canonical writings of the early church.

In any case, whether or not the authors of Hebrew Scripture understood God's temple presence as the Name to be a bifurcation of the divine presence, and whether or not they had the nascent Trinitarianism described by Knight, this thesis does not stand or fall on that. As it happens, I would answer in the affirmative to each of these points, but any reservations about that are not a stumbling block to what follows. What matters here is how the first Christians were able to interpret the data of Hebrew Scripture. If we interpret the data more or less the same way, then it so happens that we are aligning ourselves with them. We can recognize what they were doing whether we approve them doing so or not.

A case in point is what Luke does with themes of temple, Name, and Glory in Acts 2–7. One of the focal points here is in Acts 7:48 in which Stephen's speech emphatically endorses Solomon's perception that an earthly temple is insufficient to be the exclusive house of God (2 Chr 6:18).[94] Luke is going to diverge from 2 Chronicles. Whereas Chronicles resolves the problem of the insufficiency of a hand-built temple by presenting the immanence of the Name and the Glory (while God is in heaven), Luke in Acts takes a different direction. He deploys 2 Chronicles' motif of the temple's insufficiency to divest Herod's temple altogether of God and Name and Glory, and redeploys the Name and the Glory to the church community. He does so with a three-pronged attack. One: Acts 7:48 excludes the presence of God from the temple. Two: in respect of the Glory, the Pentecost narrative of Acts 2 springs the surprise that the return of the Glory to Jerusalem happens not in the stone temple but in the Christian community.[95]

Three: the relocation of God's Name from the Jerusalem temple to the Christian community, which is striking in its sophistication. Luke weaves

---

94. For a summary review of academic literature on the significance of Acts 7:48 to the fate of the Jerusalem temple, see Smith, *Fate of the Jerusalem Temple*, 167–70.

95. That the temple is divested of the Glory is also implied by Stephen seeing the Glory only in heaven in Acts 7:55. Smith, *Fate of the Jerusalem Temple*, 177.

this into the narrative of Peter and John's controversy at the Jerusalem temple, in Acts 3–5. In these three chapters, the word "temple" (*hieron*) is used precisely twelve times, and the word "name" (*onoma*) twelve times in respect of Jesus. As I shall argue in greater detail, Luke is indicating that the Name that holds the right to dwell in God's ideal temple is the Name of Jesus. Said temple is the church community, founded by twelve apostles. The ancient story of the presence of the Name and the Glory at the inauguration of Solomon's temple is taken up in Luke's story of the inauguration of the church as a temple, with the motif of the Glory locked onto the Spirit and the motif of the Name locked onto Jesus. Luke voids the Jerusalem temple as a locus of God's immanence, and invests that immanence in the church community.[96] It is implicitly consecrated as the home of God, his Name, and his Glory, explicitly as the home of God, his Christ, and his Spirit. It is a surprisingly early exposition of the oneness and the threeness of Luke's God, and evidence of how Christians could read the Hebraic temple narratives.

CHRIST AND THE GLORY

In light of this study's association of the Glory and the Spirit, I need in brief to anticipate questions about early Christian writings' close association of the Glory and Christ, as some scholars may have in mind to identify the Glory with Christ instead of, or as well as, the Spirit. As a preliminary response to that, and by way of a comparison, a close association between, say, the Name and the Glory does not in itself make them synonymous, and we see Scripture texts in which they are clearly differentiated[97]; and for another example, a close relationship between Christ and the Holy Spirit does not make *them* synonymous. Likewise, a close association between Christ and the Glory does not in itself make them synonymous. These close relationships are, not unexpectedly, there to be observed but not overstated. Certainly, Christ exhibits the Glory in the transfiguration, and he is the Lord of the Glory according to James (Jas 2:1), but that close association is not synonymous with his *being* the Glory itself. If anything, being the "Lord of the Glory" is open to interpretation as a distinction between the nominative noun and the genitive noun.

For the purposes of this study, Solomonic temple motifs supply the paradigm that informs any comparison or association with the Glory. Luke

---

96. This does not prevent the Jerusalem temple having usefulness to the disciples. Smith, *Fate of the Jerusalem Temple*, 177. Indeed it still has value as sacred space in Acts, on which see n.4 above.

97. See for example McConville, "God's 'Name' and God's 'Glory,'" 153-58.

clearly parallels the arrival of the fiery Spirit at Pentecost with the Glory fire of Solomon's temple. This theme of Acts 2 will be explored at length. Meanwhile, Luke clearly locks the motif of the Name onto Jesus.[98] So, although Scripture has diverse things to say to us, in contexts profoundly informed by Hebraic temple theology we find that the Name and the Glory are specifically paralleled in Jesus and the Spirit respectively. In this temple context, the distinction between Jesus and the Glory is intact.

ADDITIONAL NOTE ON THE NAME

Bringing us into the present day, it is intriguing that the words "the Name" are used in the daily devotions of practicing Jews. That is to say, use is made in prayer of the Hebrew words *ha Shem*. Indeed, this is to say *ha Shem* instead of uttering God's personal name YHWH. This circumlocution is an ancient rabbinic practice[99] but it does not really tell us anything about how the first Christians were thinking, nor does early church thinking tell us how to interpret what such a practice means in contemporary Judaism. It should not be assumed that the scriptural bifurcation between YHWH and his Name can be read into this practice. Observation of this modern ritual contributes little to the present study, but it is suggestive of a trace of a thread somehow linking the past and the present. It is outside the scope of this study to explore that.

THE ROAD TO NICAEA

The focus for this study is the Name and the Glory, evidence for a paradigm explored during the first Christian century. It is important not to treat this anachronistically, as if it were an outflow of Nicene categories that reflect later philosophical thinking. In fact, Name theology precedes the Nicene Creed in most interesting ways. Hurtado makes a salient point:

> In the next century or two after GJohn, Christians began appropriating and adapting terms and conceptual categories from the Greek philosophical traditions (e.g., "being" [*ousia*], "essence" [*hypostasis*; Lat. *substantia*]). But it is perhaps not excessive to suggest that the Johannine use of divine-name tradition is in its

---

98. As mentioned, Luke in narrating the temple controversy of Acts 3–5 deploys the word temple and the word name (in respect of Jesus) precisely twelve times each. This study undertakes to explore what this says about Jesus, Name, and temple in Luke's writing.

99. Richter, *Deuteronomistic History*, 11.

own terms an equivalently radical and direct claim about the linkage of Jesus to God.[100]

Fossum strikes a harmonious note in discussing Name theology in the gnostic Gospel of Truth:

> Since the Son is the Name, there is no distinction in nature or mode of being between the Father and the Son. We have here the doctrine of the consubstantiality of God and Christ expressed about two hundred years before the production of the Nicene Creed by means of the Semitic concept of the "Name," which, however, primarily is ontic, while the Greek concept of "nature" (*ousia, substantia*) used in the Creed is ontological.[101]

Therefore, it is not unwarranted for the study of nascent Trinitarianism to be reconsidered according to Israelite categories, as preceding gentile ones. Israelite categories can be as sophisticated and definitive as anything Nicaea would offer.[102] This is not to pitch one against the other. In fact they will be found to be complementary for appreciating the breadth of Christian thinking in the early church era.

In much modern scholarship, the story of Christian knowledge of the Trinity is often told in terms of cause and effect, the experience of early Christians, knowing and worshiping Jesus as the Son of God and experiencing the power of the Holy Spirit, which prompted the early church to try to reconcile this with their monotheism and to do so from the second century onwards by scouring Greco-Roman culture for instruments of philosophical thought until the doctrine of the Trinity was inevitable, cemented centuries later at Nicaea. That leads to an assumption that Greek philosophy was a necessary gateway to Trinitarianism. But that looks dubiously like writing history from the perspective of what has evolved rather than evaluating what was happening in earlier moments, taking each stage of the past on its own terms. It also looks latent with an unwarranted suspicion that without the journey through the possibilities of Greek philosophical categories, some "unorthodoxy" would have been the inevitable destination from earliest times, as if Hebraic categories cannot assure what has been historically known as mainstream orthodoxy. This is problematic if Christian theology is to avoid the impression of jettisoning confidence in Semitic expressions of God's self-revelation. It is also problematic in overlooking the

---

100. Hurtado, *Lord Jesus Christ*, 385.
101. Fossum, *Name of God*, 107–8.
102. Bauckham, *God Crucified*, 77–78.

vital appreciation of a three-in-one God that was there from the emergence of the Jesus movement in its Jewish context.

This study offers another perspective on events, attempting a historiography of Trinitarian belief founded in a first-century Israelite worldview. Nicaea cemented gentile categories into the definition of the Trinity, but that is only half the story. The first Christians had Hebraic temple categories by which Paul, John, Luke, and others appreciated God as tri-personal, categories that were (in all but name) as much full expressions of Trinitarianism as anything Nicaea offered. In contrast, using Nicene categories as a lens through which to peer to uncover the Trinity in the Hebrew Scriptures would be not only an imposition, but also can leave hidden in plain view categories that were an open book to authors of early Christian writings.

FURTHER READING

A bibliography is provided, but for further reading on temple theology, I would especially recommend two books: G. K. Beale's *The Temple and the Church's Mission*,[103] and the wide-ranging essays in *Heaven on Earth*.[104] I have already alluded to some of their themes, but, as an example directly relevant to this study, the differentiation of God's earthly presence between his worldwide and his localized presence in the temple is instructively covered by Beale's essay in the latter publication. He develops this as a key theme for understanding God's great mission for his temple presence to flow out into the world.[105]

On how temple theology has christological implications, Bill Salier's essay "The Temple in the Gospel According to John" has a number of relevant insights.[106]

FUTURE DEVELOPMENT

No study of the Trinity can be exhaustive. The remit of this book is essentially to open discussion for how the Trinity can be observed in Hebraic motifs of

---

103. Beale, *Temple and the Church's Mission*.

104. Alexander and Gathercole, *Heaven on Earth*.

105. Beale, "Final Vision of the Apocalypse," see page 206–7. In the same volume, Daniel Strange prefers to argue that this spatial distinction of divine presence is metaphorical. Daniel Strange, "Little Dwelling on the Divine Presence," see page 216. I am drawn to agree with Beale's view, more fully and compellingly set out in his *The Temple and the Church's Mission*, that the divine mission for God's real temple presence to flow out from the temple into the whole world is a key theme from Genesis to Revelation.

106. Salier, "Temple in the Gospel According to John."

temple, Name, and Glory in Scripture, and I hope readers will come to agree that it is a question that merits discussion. It is hoped that this study will help stimulate discussion about the Trinity in at least some of the following respects: for the study of Christian origins, to locate trinitarian temple theology at the heart of the Jesus movement; for theologians, to examine how Hebraic categories and Nicene categories surprisingly complement each other for trinitarian reflections; for interest in Scripture as foundational for trinitarian doctrine, and to meet a demand to locate the Trinity explicitly in Scripture, not least Hebrew Scripture; for teachers of Christianity, to challenge the assumption that a three-in-one God is something that the human mind cannot comprehend, when the Solomonic paradigm seems to offer something that can be comprehended without too much of a strain; also for those involved in dialogue with other faiths or those of unorthodox traditions, to provide a tool that may disarm hostility to the idea of God as Trinity. If this seems over-ambitious, I can only argue that the need for such discussions is real. The doctrine of the Trinity is contested ground on many fronts, and any tool that assists in progressing discussion positively is worth consideration. Above all, as stated earlier, I aim to dispel unnecessary confusion about the Trinity, and present it as something that the non-specialist can be confident in understanding and explaining, instead of defending it as a mystery incomprehensible to reason.

It is hoped that this study will be of interest to those in dialogue between Christianity, Judaism, and Islam, as a model of the Trinity that disengages the objection of tri-theism, and also disengages the objection that Christian belief in the Trinity is not rooted in Hebrew Scripture. Thus, it would be a matter of some joy if it be found that here we have a hermeneutic tool for better understanding in cross-cultural dialogue for, say, a Christian in dialogue with a Muslim for dispelling the mistaken preconception that the Trinity amounts to tri-theism: the concept of God, his Name, and his Glory could not be further from that. Not only for the Muslim, but for the Jewish observer who has only ever thought that the Trinity is most unlike Israel's God, this opens up a potential line of dialogue reconciling this God with ante-Nicene Trinitarianism. And for anyone of an unorthodox church tradition who has thought the Trinity compromises monotheism, there are grounds here to reappraise their position. The clear potential here is to establish common ground in re-reading sacred text, towards an understanding that the Trinity is recognizably congruent with Israel's God as portrayed at the temple of Solomon, even one God in three "persons." In God, his Name, and his Glory, there is a language for the church to revisit.

In preparing this study, I took account of feedback from academics, theologians, and church leaders. It began life as a dissertation and presentation for a course at Ichthus Christian Fellowship, and I am particularly grateful for their feedback, especially the input of Roger Forster. My master's dissertation in church history at the University of Nottingham explored themes of divine presence in Israel pre-70 CE that are further developed here. I touched upon the thesis of this study with my professor at university, who recommended I develop it further. It is too wide-ranging for a doctoral study, and is thus offered in this form.

I am more than happy to be contacted by email at researcher@trinity-research.co.uk to discuss this study.

COLIN GREEN
2019

Bibliography

BOOKS AND ONLINE RESOURCES

Alexander, T. Desmond, and Simon Gathercole, eds. *Heaven on Earth*. Carlisle: Paternoster, 2004.

Ambrose. *On the Holy Spirit*. Nicene and Post-Nicene Fathers: Second Series 10, 93–158. Buffalo, NY: Christian Literature, 1896.

The Apocrypha: The Apocryphal/Deuterocanonical Books of the Old Testament, New Revised Standard Version. Cambridge, UK: Cambridge University Press, 1998.

Attridge, Harold, and George W. MacRae, trans. *The Gospel of Truth*. In *The Nag Hammadi Library in English*, edited by James M. Robinson, 38–51. Leiden: E. J. Brill, 1996.

Augustine. *The Enchiridion: on Faith, Hope and Love*. http://christianbookshelf.org/augustine/the_enchiridion/chapter_56_the_holy_spirit_and.htm.

Barnabas. In *The Apostolic Fathers, Volume II*, edited by Bart D. Ehrman, 12–83. Cambridge: Harvard University Press, 2003.

2 Baruch. In *The Apocrypha and Pseudepigrapha of the Old Testament in English*, edited by R. H. Charles and D. Litt, 2:481–524. Translated by R. H. Charles. Oxford: Oxford University Press, 1913.

Bates, Matthew W. *The Birth of the Trinity: Jesus, God, and Spirit in New Testament and Early Christian Interpretations of the Old Testament*. Oxford: Oxford University Press, 2015.

Bauckham, Richard. *God Crucified: Monotheism and Christology in the New Testament*. Grand Rapids: Eerdmans, 1998.

———. *The Theology of the Book of Revelation*. Cambridge: Cambridge University Press, 1993.

Beale, G. K. *The Temple and the Church's Mission: A Biblical Theology of the Dwelling Place of God*. Downers Grove, IL: InterVarsity, 2004.

Beale, Gregory. "The Final Vision of the Apocalypse and its Implications for a Biblical Theology of the Temple." In *Heaven on Earth*, edited by T. Desmond Alexander and Simon Gathercole, 191–209. Carlisle: Paternoster, 2004.

Bonnington, Mark. "New Temples in Corinth: Paul's Use of Temple Imagery in the Ethics of the Corinthian Correspondence." In *Heaven on Earth*, edited by T. Desmond Alexander and Simon Gathercole, 151–76. Carlisle: Paternoster, 2004.

Booth, William. "Thou Christ of Burning, Cleansing Flame." *The War Cry* (April 14, 1894).

Brenton, L. C. L. *Septuagint with Apocrypha: Greek and English.* Peabody, MA: Hendrickson, 1986.

Bulgakov, Sergius. "The Name of God." In *Icons and the Name of God,* translated by Boris Jakim, 115–66. Grand Rapids: Eerdmans, 2012.

Calvin, John. *Institutes of the Christian Religion.* Translated by Henry Beveridge. Edinburgh: Calvin Translation Society, 1845.

Casey, Robert Pierce, trans. *The Excerpta Ex Theodoto of Clement of Alexandria.* Studies and Documents 1. London: Christophers, 1934.

Colle, Ralph del. "The Triune God." In *The Cambridge Companion to Christian Doctrine,* edited by Colin E. Gunton, 121–40. Cambridge: Cambridge University Press, 1997.

Cyprian. "Epistle 72, To Jubaianus." In *Ante-Nicene Fathers: Volume 5,* edited by Arthur Cleveland Coxe, 379–386. Buffalo, NY: Christian Literature, 1885.

Cyril of Alexandria. *That Christ is One.* In *Five Tomes Against the Nestorians,* translated by P. E. Pusey, 237–319. LFC 47. Oxford: James Parker, 1881.

Didache. In *The Apostolic Fathers, Volume I,* edited by Bart D. Ehrman, 416–43. Cambridge: Harvard University, 2003.

Eastman, B. "Name." In *Dictionary of the Later New Testament & Its Developments,* edited by Ralph P. Martin and Peter H. Davids, 785–87. Downers Grove, IL: InterVarsity, 1997.

Ehrman, Bart D., trans. *The Apostolic Fathers, Volume I.* Cambridge/London: Harvard University Press, 2003.

Ehrman, Bart D., trans. *The Apostolic Fathers, Volume II.* Cambridge/London: Harvard University Press, 2003.

Eusebius. *The History of the Church.* Translated by G.A. Williamson. London: Penguin, 1989.

Forster, Roger. *Trinity: Song and Dance God.* Milton Keynes: Authentic Lifestyle, 2004.

Fossum, Jarl E. "In the Beginning was the Name: Onomanology as the Key to Johannine Christology." In *The Image of the Invisible God. Essays on the Influence of Jewish Mysticism on Early Christology,* 109–34. Freiburg: Universitätsverlag Freiburg, 1995.

———. *The Name of God and the Angel of the Lord.* Tubingen: J. C. B. Mohr, 1985.

Gärtner, Bertil. *The Temple and the Community in Qumran and the New Testament: A Comparative Study in the Temple Symbolism of the Qumran Texts and the New Testament.* Cambridge: Cambridge University Press, 1965.

Gieschen, Charles A. "The Divine Name in Ante-Nicene Christology." *Vigiliae Christianae* 57 (2003) 115–58.

Gignilliat, Mark S. "The Trinity and the Old Testament: Real Presence or Imposition?" In *The Essential Trinity: New Testament foundations and practical relevance,* edited by Brandon C. Crowe and Carl R. Trueman, 175–87. London: IVP, 2016.

Green, Michael. *I Believe in the Holy Spirit.* London: Hodder & Stoughton, 1985.

Hatch, Edwin. "Breathe on me, Breath of God." In *The Congregational Psalmist Hymnal,* edited by Henry Allon et al., 140. London: Hodder & Stoughton, 1886.

Hermas. "The Shepherd." In *The Apostolic Fathers, Volume II,* edited by Bart D. Ehrman, 174–473. Cambridge: Harvard University Press, 2003.

Hurowitz, Victor. Review of The Deuteronomistic History, by Sandra Richter. *Journal of Hebrew Scriptures* 5 (2004–2005). http://www.jhsonline.org/reviews/review157.htm.

Hurtado, Larry W. *At the Origins of Christian Worship*. Carlisle: Paternoster, 1999.
———. *Lord Jesus Christ: Devotion to Jesus in Earliest Christianity*. Grand Rapids: Eerdmanns, 2003.
———. *One God, One Lord: Early Christian Devotion and Ancient Jewish Monotheism*. London: T & T Clark, 1998.
Irenaeus. *Against Heresies*. In *Ante-Nicene Fathers: Volume 1*, edited by Alexander Roberts, et al., 315–567. Buffalo, NY: Christian Literature, 1885.
Jerome. *Dialogue Against the Luciferians*. Nicene and Post-Nicene Fathers: Second Series 6. Buffalo, NY: Christian Literature, 1893.
Johansson, Daniel. "The Trinity and the Gospel of Mark." In *The Essential Trinity: New Testament Foundations and Practical Relevance*, edited by Brandon D. Crowe and Carl R. Trueman, 39–61. London: IVP, 2016.
Johnson, Aubrey R. *The One and the Many in the Israelite Conception of God*. Eugene, OR: Wipf & Stock, 2006.
Justin Martyr. "Dialogue with Trypho." In *Ante-Nicene Fathers: Volume 1*, edited by Alexander Roberts, et al., 194–270. Buffalo, NY: Christian Literature, 1885.
Kenworthy, Scott M. "Debating the Theology of the Name in Post-Soviet Russia: Metropolitan Ilarion Alfeev and Sergei Khoruhii." In *Orthodox Paradoxes: Heterogeneities and Complexities in Contemporary Russian Orthodoxy*, edited by Katya Tolstaya, 250–65. Leiden: Brill, 2014.
Knight, G. A. F. *A Biblical Approach to the Doctrine of The Trinity*. Edinburgh: Oliver & Boyd, 1953.
Köstenberger, Andreas J., and Scott R. Swain. *Father, Son and Spirit: The Trinity in John's Gospel*. Downers Grove, IL: InterVarsity, 2008.
Kunin, Seth. "Judaism." In *Sacred Space*, edited by Jean Holm with John Bowker, 115–48. Themes in Religious Studies. London: Pinter, 1994.
Leithart, Peter J. *A House for My Name*. Moscow, ID: Canon, 2000.
———. "Placing the Name." November 22, 2004. http://www.leithart.com/category/bible-ot-deuteronomy/.
McConville, J. G. "God's 'Name' and God's 'Glory.'" *Tyndale Bulletin* 30 (1979) 149–63.
Mettinger, T. N. D. *The Dethronement of Sabaoth: Studies in the Shem and Kabod Theologies*. Lund: CWK Gleerup, 1982.
———. Review of The Deuteronomistic History, by Sandra Richter. *Journal of Biblical Literature* 122 (2003) 753–55.
Michaels, J. R. *1 Peter*. Word Biblical Commentary. Waco, TX: Word Books, 1988.
Nickelsburg, G. W. E., and J. C. VanderKam, trans. *1 Enoch: A New Translation*. Minneapolis: Fortress, 2004.
O'Collins, Gerald. *The Tripersonal God*. London: Continuum, 2004.
Origen. *Commentary on the Gospel of John*. In *Ante-Nicene Fathers: Volume 9*, edited by Allan Menzies and A. Cleveland Coxe, 297–408. Buffalo, NY: Christian Literature, 1912.
Parke-Taylor, G.H. *Yahweh: The Divine Name in the Bible*. Waterloo, ON: Wilfred Laurier University Press, 1975.
Philo. *On the Special Laws*. www.earlyjewishwritings.com/text/philo/book27.html.
"Psalms of Solomon." http://wesley.nnu.edu/sermons-essays-books/noncanonical-literature/noncanonical-literature-ot-pseudepigrapha/the-psalms-of-solomon/.

Richter, Sandra L. *The Deuteronomistic History and the Name Theology: lĕšakkēn šĕmô šām in the Bible and the Ancient Near East*. BeiheftezurZeitschriftfür die alttestamentliche Wissenschaft 318. Berlin/New York: Walter de Gruyter, 2002.
Rotherham, J. B., trans. *The Emphasized New Testament*. London: H. R. Allenson, 1897.
Salier, Bill. "The Temple in the Gospel According to John." In *Heaven on Earth*, edited by T. Desmond Alexander and Simon Gathercole, 121–34. Carlisle: Paternoster, 2004.
Second Clement. In *The Apostolic Fathers, Volume I*, edited by Bart D. Ehrman, 164–99. Cambridge: Harvard University, 2003.
Selman, M. J. *2 Chronicles: a Commentary*. Tyndale Old Testament Commentaries. Leicester: InterVarsity, 1994.
Seters, John Van. Review of The Deuteronomistic History, by Sandra Richter. *Journal of the American Oriental Society* 123 (2003) 871–72.
Skarsaune, Oskar. *In the Shadow of the Temple*. Downers Grove, IL: InterVarsity, 2002.
Smith, Steve. *The Fate of the Jerusalem Temple in Luke-Acts: An Intertextual Approach to Jesus' Laments Over Jerusalem and Stephen's Speech*. London: T & T Clark, 2017.
Stevenson, Gregory. *Power and Place: Temple and Identity in the Book of Revelation*. BZNW 107. Berlin: de Gruyter, 2001.
Strange, Daniel. "A Little Dwelling on the Divine Presence: Towards a 'Whereness' of the Triune God." In *Heaven on Earth*, edited by T. Desmond Alexander and Simon Gathercole, 211–29. Carlisle: Paternoster, 2004.
Swain, Scott R. "The Mystery of the Trinity." In *The Essential Trinity: New Testament Foundations and Practical Relevance*, edited by Brandon D. Crowe and Carl R. Trueman, 191–98. London: IVP, 2016.
Targum of Chronicles. Translated by J. Stanley McIvor. The Aramaic Bible 19. Edinburgh: T & T Clark, 1994.
Targum of Jeremiah. Translated by Robert Hayward. The Aramaic Bible 12, Edinburgh: T & T Clark, 1987.
Targum Pseudo-Jonathan: Deuteronomy. Translated by Ernest G. Clarke. The Aramaic Bible 5B. Edinburgh: T & T Clark, 1998.
Targum of Psalms. Translated by David M. Stee. The Aramaic Bible 16. London: T & T Clark, 2004.
Tertullian. *On Modesty*. In *Ante-Nicene Fathers: Volume 4*, edited by A. Cleveland Coxe et al., 74–101. Buffalo, NY: Christian Literature, 1885.
Thompson, Alan J. "The Trinity and Luke-Acts." In *The Essential Trinity: New Testament Foundations and Practical Relevance*, edited by Brandon D. Crowe and Carl R. Trueman, 62–82. London: IVP, 2016.
Thurmer, John. *A Detection of the Trinity*. Exeter: Paternoster, 1984.
Turner. Max "Approaching 'personhood' in the New Testament, with special reference to Ephesians." *Evangelical Quarterly* 77 (2005) 211–33.
Uzziel, Jonathan Ben. *The Chaldee Paraphrase on the Prophet Isaiah*. Translated by Rev C. W. H. Pauli. London: London Society's House, 1871.
von Rad, Gerhard. *Old Testament Theology, Volume 1*. Translated by D. M. G. Stalker. San Francisco: Harper, 1962.
———. *Studies in Deuteronomy*. Translated by David Stalker. London: SCM, 1953.
Wainwright, Arthur W. *The Trinity in the New Testament*. London: SPCK, 1962.
Warfield, Benjamin D. "Trinity." In *The International Standard Bible Encyclopedia, Volume 5*, edited by James Orr, 3012–22. Chicago: Howard Severance, 1915.

Wenham, John. *Christ and the Bible*. Guildford: Eagle, 1993.
Wesley, John. *Explanatory Notes upon the New Testament*. London: Epworth, 1950,
Wilson, Ian. *Out of the Midst of the Fire: Divine Presence in Deuteronomy*. Atlanta: Scholars, 1995.
Witherington, Ben, III. *The Acts of the Apostles: a Socio-Political Commentary*. Grand Rapids: Eerdmans, 1998.
Wright, N. T. "New Law, New Temple, New World, Acts 2.1–21; John 15.26–16.15, a sermon at the Eucharist on the Feast of Pentecost, June 8 2003." http://www.westminster-abbey.org/worship/sermons/2003/june/new-law,-new-temple,-new-world.
———. *The New Testament and the People of God*. London: Society for Promoting Christian Knowledge, 1992.
———. "On Earth as in Heaven Acts 16.16–34; John 17.20–end, a sermon at the Eucharist on the Sunday after Ascension Day, York Minster, 20 May 2007." http://www.ntwrightpage.com/sermons/Earth_Heaven.htm.
———. "Spirit of Truth Acts 2.1–21; John 14.8–27, a sermon at the Eucharist in Durham Cathedral on the Feast of Pentecost, 27 May 2007." http://www.ntwrightpage.com/sermons/Pentecost07.htm.

www.ingramcontent.com/pod-product-compliance
Lightning Source LLC
Chambersburg PA
CBHW050843230426
43667CB00012B/2132